MODERN LEGAL STUDIES

Children, Parents

and the State

AUSTRALIA AND NEW ZEALAND
The Law Book Company Ltd.
Sydney : Melbourne : Perth

CANADA AND U.S.A.
The Carswell Company Ltd.
Agincourt, Ontario

INDIA
N. M. Tripathi Private Ltd.
Bombay
and
Eastern Law House Private Ltd.
Calcutta and Delhi
M.P.P. House
Bangalore

ISRAEL
Steimatzky's Agency Ltd.
Jerusalem : Tel Aviv : Haifa

MODERN LEGAL STUDIES

Children, Parents

and the State

by

NDREW BAINHAM, LL.B. (Wales), LL.M.(Cantab.),

Solicitor, Lecturer in Law, University of East Anglia

LONDON
SWEET & MAXWELL
1988

Published in 1988 by
Sweet & Maxwell Limited of
11 New Fetter Lane, London
Laserset by P.B. Computer Typesetting
of Pickering, N. Yorks
Printed in Great Britain by
Butler & Tanner Limited,
Frome, Somerset

British Library Cataloguing in Publication Data

Bainham, Andrew
  Children, parents and the state.—
  (Modern legal studies).
  1. Great Britain. Children. Law
  I. Title II. Series
  344.102'87

ISBN 0-421-36320-7

Preface

This book is about the way in which the respective interests of children, their parents and the state are balanced in the legal system. In recent years the courts have had to determine when a young person under 16 years of age may have access to contraceptive advice and treatment without her parents' knowledge or consent (*Gillick* v. *West Norfolk and Wisbech Area Health Authority*), whether the state is empowered to remove from a mother at birth a baby born with drug withdrawal symptoms (*D (A minor)* v. *Berkshire County Council*) and whether the sterilisation of a 17 year old mentally handicapped girl should be authorised (*Re B. (A minor) (Wardship: Sterilisation)*). These important decisions in the medical arena have focussed public attention on the legal relationship between parents and children and the interest of the state in safeguarding the welfare of children through the agency of local authorities or the courts.

Meanwhile, the public and private aspects of child law have each been the subject of extensive reviews. In 1985 an Interdepartmental Working Party published its *Review of child care Law* which made a host of recommendations for reform of the law in this area. Many of these were accepted by the Government in its White Paper, *The Law on Child Care and Family Services*, published in January 1987. The private law affecting children has been thoroughly investigated by the Law Commission which has published a series of working papers on this subject. At the time of writing, the Commission's final report is eagerly anticipated.

Child law is becoming an increasingly important element in Family Law courses. I believe that the tripartite relationship between children, parents and the state is central to any discussion of the position of children in the legal system. My aim is therefore to present students with a somewhat closer analysis of the nature of this relationship than is to be found in the standard texts on Family

Law. I have concentrated on the legal position of the natural family as one aspect of child law but it has occasionally proved necessary to make reference to the position of substitute carers, particularly when discussing the role of the state.

Many of the issues which have arisen in England have also been encountered in the United States and throughout the text I make reference to American case law. This is not to suggest that comparisons with legal developments in other parts of the world would be any less valuable. However, the constitutional position in the United States is such that the courts there have frequently been required to analyse closely the interaction of the basic rights of parents and children and the legitimate limits of the state's interest in the family. This approach reflects the main theme of this book.

Andrew Bainham
May 1988

Acknowledgements

I owe a special debt of gratitude to two people. My colleague Gareth Miller read and commented on the first draft of the manuscript and gave me his support and encouragement throughout the project. Brenda Hoggett of Manchester University and the Law Commission made many valuable criticisms of the manuscript which led to significant changes. I am, however, solely responsible for any errors or deficiencies which remain.

I should also like to thank my former colleague Clive Lewis, now of Selwyn College, Cambridge, for perusing the page proofs and my colleague Robert Burgess for arranging secretarial facilities. I am grateful to New York University Law School for generously providing me with library facilities while on sabbatical and my colleague Fiona Boyd for sending English materials to me during this period. I was fortunate in having the secretarial services of Helen Cummings and Mary Hansell. I would like to thank them both for their meticulous work on the typescript. I also wish to express my gratitude to the editorial staff of Sweet & Maxwell for all their assistance and to the Board of Modern Legal Studies for allowing me this opportunity of presenting my views. Last but not least, I must not forget the contribution of my wife, Wendy. I would like to thank her for the many sacrifices which she made to enable me to complete this work. I am not sure whether she will appreciate having a book on family conflict dedicated to her! Nonetheless, I dedicate this book to Wendy and to our daughter, Samantha.

I have endeavoured to state the law as at May 1, 1988.

A.B.

Other Books in the Series

Contents

Table of Cases

Table of Statutes

1. Introduction

This book is about the legal relationship between children, their parents and the State. The areas of law chosen for discussion are those which, it is thought, best exemplify this triangular relationship. In this chapter we consider briefly the nature of the respective interests of children, parents and the State. The rest of the book is then devoted to an examination of the interaction of these interests in various contexts.

Chapters 2 and 3 are concerned particularly with balancing the interests of parents and children. Chapter 2 looks at the creation of legal relationships between mothers, fathers and children and what happens to these relationships where parents divorce. Chapter 3 explores the interaction of parents' powers of control with the claims of children to independence. This issue has received new impetus from the landmark decision of the House of Lords in *Gillick* v. *West Norfolk and Wisbech Area Health Authority*.[1] While Chapter 2 is concerned more particularly with conflicts of interest between mothers and fathers, Chapter 3 concentrates on the competing interests of parents and children or, more accurately, young people. In each case we make reference to the public interest in these family conflicts and consider how far it is appropriate for the State to intervene in them.

The next two chapters deal more directly with the State's interest in children. In Chapter 4 we turn to the protective and supportive role of local authorities. We review the circumstances under which the State is permitted to intervene in family life in order to protect the independent interests of children and how far parents are permitted to participate in their children's upbringing where removal from the home environment has proved necessary. In Chapter 5 we analyse the functions of the courts in relation to

---

[1] [1986] 1 A.C. 112.

children and look at two major issues. The first is the relationship between the courts and local authorities as two agencies of the State responsible for safeguarding the public interest in children. This is a much litigated question in the context of the appropriate boundaries between the statutory code for child care and the wardship jurisdiction. The second is the extent of the courts' authority over older children who arguably possess legal capacity to take their own decisions on matters affecting them.

In the remaining chapters we examine the competing interests of children, parents and the State in the key areas of health care (Chapter 6), education (Chapter 7) and financial support (Chapter 8). Finally, in Chapter 9 some concluding observations on the current state of the law are offered.

1. Parents' Interests

During the nineteenth century the authority of fathers was strongly reinforced by the law both in relation to the physical care of their children and over every aspect of their upbringing. In *R* v. *De Manneville*[2] a mother failed in her attempt to recover possession of her baby girl from the father who had forcibly snatched the child from her. The court held that the father alone was entitled to custody in the absence of ill-treatment by him. In *Re Agar-Ellis*[3] the Court of Appeal refused to interfere with a Protestant father's exercise of his so-called "natural rights" to control the religious upbringing of his teenage daughter. He was accordingly allowed to resile from his matrimonial undertaking that the girl should be raised in the Roman Catholic faith. His rights were held to extend to the restriction of contact and correspondence between mother and daughter and a prohibition on the girl attending Roman Catholic places of worship. Her interests were clearly regarded by the court as synonymous with her father's wishes.

During this period, however, the Court of Chancery, exercising its protective jurisdiction over wards, and other courts, developed the principle that they would interfere with a father's authority in extreme cases in the interests of the child's welfare. These cases usually involved conduct which amounted to a serious transgres-

[2] (1804) 5 East 221.
[3] (1883) 24 Ch.D. 317.

sion of prevailing societal mores or which caused physical harm to the child. A good example is *Shelley* v. *Westbrooke*[4] where the poet Shelley was deprived of his daughter's custody in favour of a maternal grandparent because of his "immoral and vicious conduct" in being a professed atheist. Also during this period, there were legislative advances which began to provide opportunities for married women to challenge their husbands' rights to custody. The Custody of Infants Act 1839 permitted the mother to apply for access to her children and custody of those under seven provided that she had not committed adultery. The Custody of Infants Act 1873 removed the adultery bar and extended the age limit to 16. This was further extended to 21 (the age of majority at that time) by the Custody of Infants Act 1886. The 1886 Act also provided the first statutory recognition of the child's welfare as a factor for the courts' consideration along with the conduct and wishes of the parents.

In 1925 the welfare of the child was elevated to its current position of prominence as the "first and paramount consideration" in disputes concerning his[5] "custody or upbringing."[6] At the same time provision was made that in litigated disputes the parents' respective claims should be regarded as equal. Although this had the effect of producing equality of the father and mother before the courts, it did not otherwise disturb the existing balance of familial authority. In the absence of legal proceedings the father continued to hold parental rights to the exclusion of the mother.[7] Remarkably, it was not until 1974 that married mothers became entitled automatically to equal parental rights.[8]

Although since 1925 the child's welfare was theoretically paramount in disputes concerning custody and upbringing, it was not until 1970 that it became firmly established that the court's determination of the child's best interests should override the claims of parents and all other considerations. This judicial failure to give effect to the apparently plain terms of the 1925 legislation

---

[4] (1817) Jac. 266. See also *Symington* v. *Symington* (1875) L.R. 2 S.C. and Div. 415.

[5] Male and female pronouns are used interchangeably to describe children throughout this book. No gender significance is intended unless specifically stated.

[6] s.1 of the Guardianship of Infants Act 1925, now s.1 of the Guardianship of Minors Act 1971.

[7] Where the child was born out of wedlock the mother, as now, had sole parental rights.

[8] When s.1 (1) of the Guardianship Act 1973 was brought into force.

has been explained on the basis that the courts were disposed to interpret this as a sex equality enactment. They did not consider that its purpose was to alter the existing law on the relative weight to be attached to the welfare of children and parental claims.[9] This is not altogether surprising since, as one commentator observes, the 1925 reforms owed their existence more to the pressure of women's organisations for equal rights than to the child protection movement.[10] A particular manifestation of the courts' attitude was their reluctance to interfere with the claims of an "unimpeachable parent" (usually the father) and, conversely, their readiness to punish a wife's matrimonial "misconduct" by refusing to award custody to her.

This attitude, which had been gradually relaxed over some years, was authoritatively disapproved with the advent of divorce reform and the retreat from the doctrine of the matrimonial offence. In *J. v. C.*[11] the House of Lords interpreted the welfare principle to mean that in substance the child's best interests should be the *sole* consideration and should rule upon or determine the course to be followed.[12] There is no better example of the transition brought about by *J. v. C.* than the decision of the Court of Appeal in *Re K.*[13] Here the adulterous wife of an Anglican clergyman was given custody of their two young children since the court felt that their well-being would be best served by this course.

The ascendancy of the child's welfare over parental claims and interests raises important questions about the status of parents under the law. If parents' interests are to be subordinated to those of children before the courts, does this also mean that they may be overridden under the general law where no court is as yet involved? The spotlight has now turned on the extent of authority or control which parents are legally allowed to exert over their children. The legal basis of a parent's authority is sometimes said to be natural guardianship or custody, but more commonly it has been conceptualised in

---

[9] See, for example, *Re Carroll* [1931] 1 K.B. 317. See also J. C. Hall, "The Waning of Parental Rights." [1972B] B C.L.J. 248.

[10] Susan Maidment, *Child Custody and Divorce* (1984), Chap. 5.

[11] [1970] A.C. 668.

[12] *per* Lord MacDermott, pp. 710–711.

[13] [1977] Fam. 179.

the notion of parental rights.[14] The concept is to be found in various pieces of legislation but has never been satisfactorily defined. In recent years its proprietorial connotations have been disapproved and it has become increasingly difficult to reconcile its existence with the predominant emphasis which the law now places on the welfare of children. Opinion has shifted perceptibly towards the idea of children's rights and the correlative duties and responsibilities of parents which this implies. Thus, Dickens has suggested that, the modern function of parental rights is "to permit parents to discharge their duties to their children."[15] This view of the legal relationship between parents and children was shared by the House of Lords in *Gillick* and has led to the suggestion that it is no longer accurate to say that parents have rights at all. A basic question, therefore, which we address later[16] is whether it is necessary to deny altogether the existence of parents' rights in order to promote the rights or welfare of their children.

2. Children's Interests

As noted above, the dominant principle in the modern law affecting children is the welfare principle or best interests doctrine. This poses the question whether the promotion of children's "welfare" is the same as the protection of their "rights". The point is graphically illustrated by one liberationist writer who has drawn a distinction between protecting *children* and protecting their *rights*.[17] The basis of this view appears to be that the welfare principle is antithetical to the idea of children's rights for it supports not the right of children to take their own decisions, but the right of adults whether judges, social workers or other professionals to take decisions on their behalf.

---

[14] The concept of parental rights has been widely discussed. For pre-Gillick assessments see J. M. Eekelaar, "What are Parental Rights?" (1973) 89 L.Q.R. 210; J. C. Hall, *Op. cit.* n.9; M. D. A. Freeman, "What Rights and Duties do Parents Have?" (1980) 144 J.P.N. 380; Susan Maidment, "The Fragmentation of Parental Rights " [1981] C.L.J. 135 and Bernard M. Dickens, "The Modern Function and Limits of Parental Rights" (1981) 97 L.Q.R. 462. For post-Gillick discussions see John Eekelaar, "The Eclipse of Parental Rights" (1986) 102 L.Q.R. 4 and Andrew Bainham, "The Balance of Power in Family Decisions" [1986] C.L.J. 262.

[15] *Op. cit.* n.14, p. 471.

[16] *Post*, Chap. 3.

[17] R. Farson, *Birthrights* (1978) p. 165.

The fallacy in this argument is the assumption that children possess only one type of right which may broadly be equated with self-determination. Any sophisticated theory of children's rights must acknowledge the multi-faceted nature of the concept and embrace aspects of both protectionism and independence for children. Freeman, for example, lists four different species of rights which children may be thought to possess.[18] The first category, which he calls welfare rights, embraces rights of recipience and includes claims to receive such positive benefits as adequate education, housing, health care and economic support. The second category consists of rights of protection. It stresses the need for public intervention to prevent children from being exposed to various forms of harm including abuse or neglect by their parents, economic exploitation and various hazardous activities. The third category is the right to be treated like adults. This demands that adult rights be extended to children on the basis that there is no rational reason for distinguishing between them. The final category may be described as rights of autonomy and calls for greater recognition of the claims of young people to self-determination, their capacity for independent decision-making and freedom from parental control.

Detailed analysis of the alternative theories of children's rights is beyond the scope of the present work, but it is fair to say that most of them recognise that some balance must be struck between liberation and paternalism.[19] In particular, some restrictions on child autonomy are readily justifiable as necessary protections which will enable the child to mature to adulthood and to acquire the capacity for meaningful independence. But equally the autonomy interests of children should be acknowledged by the law. While the welfare principle may be thought to constitute an adequate theoretical base for rights of recipience or protection, the claims of children to a measure of independence in their lives are in danger of being ignored in a legal system which attaches supreme importance to the concept of welfare. This is not to suggest that the best interests criterion is other than an admirable guiding principle for the resolution of individual disputes. What is needed, however, is a sense of appreciation that it cannot *per se*

---

[18] M. D. A. Freeman, *The Rights and the Wrongs of Children* (1983) pp. 40–52.

[19] See, for example, Freeman's theory of "liberal paternalism," *ibid.* pp. 54–60. For other modern theories of children's rights see John Eekelaar, "The Emergence of Children's Rights" (1986) 6 *Oxford Journal of Legal Studies* 161 and Ruth M. Adler, *Taking Juvenile Justice Seriously* (1985).

provide a sufficient foundation on which to construct a theory of children's rights.

3. The Interests of the State

The State's concern for children is exhibited in a wide range of statutes which regulate their relationship with their parents and wider society. The criminal law offers protection from the worst forms of abuse and neglect and complements the statutory code for child care. In addition to the general offences against the person, the Children and Young Persons Act 1933, as amended, contains a range of offences designed to protect children from various forms of harmful behaviour such as exposure to the risk of burning, selling tobacco or intoxicating liquor to them and failing to provide for their safety at entertainments. Other potentially harmful activities are controlled by separate statutes introduced from time to time to meet particular problems, such as the tatooing of minors.[20] Other measures aim to protect children from economic exploitation by, for example, imposing restrictions on child labour,[21] prohibiting payments in connection with adoption[22] and, more recently, proscribing commercial surrogacy arrangements.[23] The State may also seek to provide protection by denying autonomy to the child thereby restricting the child's participation in harmful activities. The obvious example is sexual activity where statute provides that the consent of a girl under 16 is no defence to a charge of unlawful sexual intercourse[24] and the consent of a girl or boy under that age is no defence to a charge of indecent assault.[25]

A central dilemma which faces the State in fulfilling its protective function is that this may conflict with the idea of family privacy or parental autonomy in child-rearing and, in the case of restrictions

[20] Prohibited by the Tatooing of Minors Act 1969.
[21] There are general and specific restrictions. The general restrictions are contained in s.18 of the Children and Young Persons Act 1933. Specific restrictions apply to the employment of children in particular occupations such as mining (The Mines and Quarries Act 1954) and entertainment (ss. 23 and 24 of the Children and Young Persons Act 1933).
[22] s.57 of the Adoption Act 1976.
[23] Surrogacy Arrangements Act 1985.
[24] s.6 of the Sexual Offences Act 1956. The girl herself, however, cannot be prosecuted as a secondary party since the offence exists for her protection (*R.* v. *Tyrell* [1894] 1 Q.B. 710).
[25] s.14 (2) and s.15 (2) of the Sexual Offences Act 1956.

7

on young people, with the notion of self-determination. Both of these ideas are important values in western society, especially in the United States where they are constitutionally protected.

The family autonomy ideology figures strongly in the United States where both federal and state authorities are obliged under the constitution to respect this ideal. The privacy rights of parents to determine upbringing have been recognised by the Supreme Court on many occasions.[26] In *Meyer* v. *Nebraska*[27] the Court interpreted the word "liberty" in the fourteenth amendment to include the rights to marry, establish a home and bring up children. In *Prince* v. *Massachusetts*[28] the parental right to custody was said to create a "private realm of family life which the State cannot enter." The issue of child protection is therefore located within the context of a wider public/private debate. One school of thought regards the family as a private sphere beyond the control of the law. The opposing view is that the family is a social arrangement which can preserve a power structure under which certain dominant members of the family unit, i.e. men, are able to exert control over the subordinate weaker members, i.e. women and children.[29]

Nevertheless, the protective interest of the State is equally well established in American jurisprudence.[30] Because of the public interest in child protection, State interference with the constitutional rights of *children* may be justified by the existence of a "significant State interest." This is a less exacting constitutional limitation than the "compelling State interest" requirement which applies to interference with adult rights. Accordingly, the constitutionality of certain restrictions on the liberties of children may be upheld where similar restraints on adults might be struck down. An illustration is provided by *Ginsberg* v. *New York*[31] where the Supreme Court upheld a criminal statute prohibiting the sale of obscene

---

[26] See, for example, *Wisconsin* v. *Yoder* 406 U.S. 205 (1972).

[27] 262 U.S. 390 (1923).

[28] 321 U.S. 158 (1944).

[29] For a discussion see Katherine O'Donovan, *Sexual Divisions in Law* (1985), Chap. 1.

[30] See the discussion in Susan B. Hershkowitz, "Due Process and the Termination of Parental Rights" 19 Fam.L.Q. 245 (1985).

[31] 390 U.S. 629 (1968).

THE INTERESTS OF THE STATE

materials to minors which it acknowledged would have been unconstitutional if applied to adults.[32]

In England also there is a continuing argument on the permissible level of State intervention in the family. We shall look particularly at the statutory powers and responsibilities of local authorities around which the debate had centred. We shall also examine how far the legislature and the courts in England, in seeking to protect children, are constrained by considerations of family privacy and child autonomy.

---

[32] The Court reasoned that the State may impose laws restricting the liberty of children more severely than that of adults if this will support parents and others who have responsibility for children's welfare in discharging their responsibility. It may also impose such laws to protect children from abuse and from actions which may prevent their growth into "free and independent, well-developed men." See the commentary in Laurence D. Houlgate, *The Child and the State* (1980), p. 35.

2. Mothers, Fathers and Children

1. Introduction

This chapter is concerned with the legal framework under which children's initial relationships with their parents are created and with what happens to those relationships when parents separate or divorce. A central issue is how far it is desirable that *both* parents should continue to be actively involved with their children following their estrangement from each other and how the law may best provide for this involvement. This is an issue which affects a vast and growing number of children. Figures recently released by the Census Bureau in the United States, based on a survey of 57,000 households in that country, reveal that nearly a quarter of all American children now live with one parent and it is estimated that more than half will at some time before reaching adulthood live in single parent households.[1]

The traditional view of the courts has been that children are best left in the physical care of one parent following divorce. Thus, sole custody orders have usually been the option of choice. Support for this approach is found in the work of Goldstein, Freud and Solnit.[2] They allege that children have difficulty relating to two parents who are not in positive contact with one another because such situations engender conflicts of loyalty. The result, they suggest, may be the destruction of the children's beneficial relationships with both parents. Accordingly, they argue that children would benefit more from being allowed to settle down in the home of one parent free from external influences of the other. This theory is used to justify the denial of a legally enforceable right to access.[3]

---

[1] *New York Times*, January 28, 1988.
[2] J. Goldstein, A. Freud and A. J. Solnit, *Beyond the Best Interests of the Child* (1980).
[3] *Ibid.* pp. 116–117.

The weight of expert opinion is now diametrically opposed to this view. Contact with both parents is considered not only beneficial, but "the most critical factor in the child's successful adjustment to divorce."[4] This view is based on the findings of empirical research into families affected by divorce, the most influential of which was a longitudinal study by Wallerstein and Kelly of 60 families over a five year period following separation or divorce.[5] The authors found that least psychological stress was suffered by the children who maintained a good relationship with both parents following divorce. These were usually cases in which the parents had carefully thought out plans for shared child care responsibilities. Conversely, they found that without legal rights to share in decision-making over major aspects of the children's lives, "many non-custodial parents withdrew from their children in grief and frustration" and this resulted in feelings of confusion or rejection in the children.[6] They concluded that it was generally desirable to have arrangements following divorce which enable each parent to be responsible for and genuinely concerned with the well-being of the children.

The concern that both parents be involved with their children after divorce is coupled with a growing awareness of the nurturant abilities of fathers. Since the overwhelming majority of non-custodial parents are fathers, any debate about joint custodial arrangements must raise questions about the level and nature of involvement between men and their children.

Roman and Haddad, while noting that the majority of fathers have not in fact shared parenting responsibilities with the mothers of their children, argue that they are "perfectly equipped to do so." In their view, "they can if they wish do everything that mothers do save give birth and breast feed."[7] Commenting on the respective roles of the sexes, they note that there is, "no intrinsic reason why men cannot be nurturant or women managerial." They

---

[4] Susan Maidment, *Child Custody and Divorce* (1984) p. 279. See also M. Richards, "Behind the Best Interests of the Child. An Examination of the Arguments of Goldstein, Freud and Solnit Concerning Custody and Access at Divorce." [1986] J.S.W.L. 77.

[5] J. Wallerstein and J. Kelly, *Surviving the Break up: How Children and Parents Cope with Divorce* (1980).

[6] *Ibid.* p. 310.

[7] M. Roman and W. Haddad, *The Disposable Parent*: The Case for Joint Custody (1978) p. 89. See also Lee Salk, *My Father, My Son: Intimate Relationships* (1982) and Jerry W. McCant, "The Cultural Contradiction of Fathers as Non Parents" 21 Fam. L.Q. 127 (1987).

argue that it is really a question of motivation and societal support which has not traditionally favoured paternal involvement in nurturing.[8] There is some evidence now that societal attitudes to the child-rearing roles of men and women may be in the process of change.[9]

We shall begin by examining the way in which the law allocates powers and responsibilities between a child's parents and then consider the ways in which these may be redistributed where parents no longer live together. It is still necessary to distinguish between children of married parents and those of unmarried parents since, despite the steady erosion of legal discrimination affecting the latter culminating in the Family Law Reform Act 1987, discrimination remains with regard to the respective children's relationships with their fathers.

2. Children of Married Parents

(A) THE AUTOMATIC POSITION

Section 1(1) of the Guardianship Act 1973 provides that the rights and authority of the father and mother of a child born to married parents shall be equal. It goes on to give each of them a right of independent action by providing that such rights and authority enjoyed by parents shall be exercisable by either without the other. This is arguably qualified, however, by section 85(3) of the Children Act 1975 which states that

> "where two or more persons have a parental right and duty jointly, any one of them may exercise or perform it in any manner without the other or others if the other, or as the case may be, one or more of the others have not signified disapproval of its exercise or performance in that manner."

It is uncertain whether the regime in section 85(3) is intended to apply to the situation of married parents or whether it is confined to persons *in loco parentis* and who possess parental rights. It is a matter of interpretation whether the equal rights and authority arising under section 1(1) are "joint" and therefore governed by

---

[8] *Ibid.*
[9] See Melanie Henwood in, "Inside the Family," Family Policy Studies Centre (1987), Section 2.

section 85(3). The better view is that they are and this will be assumed for the purposes of the following discussion.

The statutory scheme is not without difficulty. First, it appears to impose no duty of consultation over matters of upbringing, the onus apparently resting with the objecting parent to communicate his dissent before action is taken. One parent would therefore apparently be acting lawfully in taking advantage of the temporary absence of the other to make a major decision on a potentially controversial aspect of upbringing. Suppose, for example, that the father suspects, but does not know, that the mother is opposed to the immunisation of babies against whooping cough. While the mother is away he arranges the vaccination of their child. Since the mother has not expressly signified her objection it would appear that the father technically possesses legal authority to arrange the vaccination. The objection to this is that it may be thought that the matter is sufficiently important to call for discussion between the parents before action is taken. Yet the statutory provisions make no distinction between everyday trivial concerns and major strategic decisions affecting the child's future. While no one would presumably disagree that a parent should have independent authority to carry out the tasks involved in daily living with the child and to act alone in emergencies, there may be legitimate objections to unilateral action in the case of important long-term or potentially irreversible decisions. It might be objected that it would be impracticable for the law to require consultation and agreement between parents before action is taken. It must be conceded that such a requirement would be difficult, if not impossible, to enforce. This does not mean, however, that the law should not seek to influence family behaviour by establishing a norm of parental co-operation. The Law Commission is surely correct to assert that it is "an important function of the law to provide a model of behaviour which is generally believed to be desirable."[10]

Secondly, the statutory formula seems to place third parties in an awkward position when dealing with one parent alone. In the above example the doctor or nurse would have proceeded on the assumption that the father possessed legal authority to request the vaccination. If however the mother had *in fact* signified her disagreement then he would have lacked the requisite authority. It

[10] Law Com., Working Paper No. 96 on Custody, para. 4.12.

would then be arguable that the vaccination constituted an assault on the child.

(B) REALLOCATION OF PARENTAL POWERS AND DUTIES

The equal division of parental authority and responsibility may be disturbed by a variety of court orders and, in limited circumstances, by the voluntary agreement of the parents.

While parents may lawfully delegate the temporary exercise of their powers and responsibilities by foster care or childminding, the policy of the law is against allowing private arrangements which transfer the powers and responsibilities themselves. Accordingly, an agreement to surrender parental rights is void at common law.[11] The rule is given statutory expression in section 85(2) of the Children Act 1975 which provides that " ... a person cannot surrender or transfer to another any parental right or duty he has as respects a child."[12] By way of an exception, section 1(2) of the Guardianship Act 1973 (as amended by section 3 of the Family Law Reform Act 1987) permits the father and mother of a child to enter into an agreement regarding the *exercise* of parental rights and duties to take effect while they are living apart. This will not be enforced, however, where the court is of the opinion that to do so would not be for the benefit of the child.

The rule may be subject to further qualifications in future if there is support for the Law Commission's suggestion that in certain circumstances parents might be permitted to share voluntarily their powers and responsibilities by appointing *inter vivos* guardians.[13]

Where parents are in dispute over a particular aspect of upbringing either may apply to the court for an order resolving the issue under section 1(3) of the Guardianship Act 1973. By this procedure the court may provide the solution to a particular issue without otherwise upsetting the equilibrium of parental authority since the court is not empowered to make an order for custody or access.[14] It seems that the procedure is rarely if ever used because, if parents have reached the stage where they are prepared to engage in litigation over their children, they will in practice seek

---

[11] *Vansittart* v. *Vansittart* (1858) 2 De G. & J. 249.
[12] This provision applies equally to all persons possessing parental rights and is not limited to natural parents.
[13] Law Com. No. 91, paras. 4.4–4.31.
[14] s.1(4).

orders for custody or legal custody which will regulate upbringing generally and determine who is to have the care of the children.

Orders dealing with parental disputes may be made under the Guardianship of Minors Act 1971 (where custody or access alone is sought), the Domestic Proceedings and Magistrates' Courts Act 1978 (where one of the parties is also seeking financial support) and the Matrimonial Causes Act 1973 (where a decree of divorce, nullity or judicial separation is sought). The first two statutes empower the court to make orders relating to "legal custody," while the divorce courts, exercising jurisdiction under the Matrimonial Causes Act 1973, continue to apply their own special concept of custody. The precise legal effect of both types of orders is uncertain.

(i) Divorce Court Custody Orders

The obscurity surrounding the legal effects of custody orders has been largely attributable to the different senses in which the term "custody" has been used by the judiciary.[15] In its widest sense it is synonymous with all those legal incidents which attach to natural parenthood including the right to physical possession and control of the child. In its narrowest sense it means no more than to be legally under the physical control of an adult. When used in this sense it is broadly equivalent to the notions of care and control and actual custody.[16] This notion of custody does not include major decision-making powers. In a third intermediate sense custody refers to this "bundle of powers" relating to upbringing, but does not include the right to physical possession and control.

The most common divorce court order provides for sole custody to one parent with reasonable access to the other.[17] Until 1980 the generally accepted view was that such an order had the effect of transferring most, but not all, parental rights to the custodial parent exclusively. These rights were, with one or two exceptions, the powers to control upbringing. Hence, it was thought that the

---

[15] See M. Parry, "The Custody Conundrum" (1981) 11 Fam. Law 213. See also Law Com. No. 96 paras. 4.23–4.26.

[16] The concept of "actual custody" was introduced by s.87 of the Children Act 1975. A person has actual custody of a child where "he has actual possession of his person."

[17] The Law Commission found that in 1985, according to statistics released by the Lord Chancellor's Department, sole custody orders were made in 86 per cent. of cases, being in favour of the wife in 77.4 per cent. and the husband in 9.2 per cent. See "Custody Law in Practice in the Divorce and Domestic Courts," by Priest and Whybrow, supplement to Law Com. No. 96, para. 4.21.

15

non-custodial parent's powers over upbringing would be in suspension during the currency of the custody order. They could, however, be revived in the event of a variation of the order. The non-custodial parent would retain certain rights by reason of his continuing parental status.[18]

However remarks in the Court of Appeal in *Dipper* v. *Dipper* have thrown the issue into confusion.[19] In that case it was suggested that the non-custodial parent does *not* lose his say regarding education and other major matters as a result of the custody order. Cumming-Bruce L.J. said that "the parent is always entitled, whatever his custodial status, to know and be consulted about the future education of his children and any other major matters."[20]

This view is difficult to reconcile with the practice of the divorce courts in making "joint" and "split" custody orders ostensibly to preserve a voice in upbringing for the parent who does not have physical care of the child. Indeed in *Dipper* itself the Court of Appeal, having disapproved the split order made at first instance, went on to approve a joint custody order. It is also difficult to understand why, if *Dipper* is correct, Parliament bothered to create a mechanism whereby the courts might reserve specified rights for the non-custodial parent when making an order for legal custody in favour of the other parent.[21] The reference to the right of consultation is also odd since, as noted above, no such right exists between parents who are cohabiting. The *Dipper* position seems to render virtually indistinguishable the legal effects of a sole custody order, joint custody order and an order for care and control to one parent which otherwise preserves the equality of parental rights.[22] The Law Commission has suggested four possible alternative interpretations of the *Dipper* ruling as it applies to sole custody orders. In essence these are:

---

[18] These rights included appointment of a testamentary guardian, the right to veto or consent to adoption, and the right to object to a change of the child's name. These rights are sometimes referred to as "the residual rights of the natural guardian."

[19] [1981] Fam. 31. The case of *B.* v. *B.* (Parental Rights: Dispute) (1980) 1 F.L.R. 87. has also been thought to cast doubt on the traditional analysis. However, another interpretation of this case is that it merely affirms the right of the non-custodial parent to bring disputes on upbringing back to the court.

[20] *Ibid.* p. 48 *cf.* Ormrod L.J. to the same effect p. 45.

[21] D.P.M.C.A. 1978, s.8(4); G.M.A. 1971, s.11A(1). Discussed by J. C. Hall [1981] C.L.J. 10.

[22] Law Com. No. 96, paras. 2.37–2.38 and 4.23.

1. the custodial parent may exercise responsibility over each aspect of the child's upbringing (subject to exceptions such as change of name and emigration) unless the other parent applies to the court;
2. the custodial parent may do so unless the other parent has signified disapproval. In this eventuality the onus would shift to the custodial parent to bring the dispute before the court;
3. there is a distinction between major and minor issues of upbringing. Major issues are for both parents and fall within 2. above. Minor matters fall within 1. and may be dealt with independently by the custodial parent;
4. whether or not the major issues require joint action, there is in any event a duty of consultation imposed on the custodial parent before action is taken.

Interpretation 1. appears to be the one which most accords with the practice in the divorce courts, but the precise effect of *Dipper* will remain uncertain and clarification in legislation is required. Priest and Whybrow found that the judges whom they interviewed predominantly took the view that a sole custody order does not give the custodial parent the pre-emptive right to take major decisions but that the custodial parent was not under a strict legal duty to consult the non-custodial parent. On the other hand they found that the solicitors interviewed had a different perception of sole custody which they equated with the absolute right to determine the child's upbringing.[23] The only uncontentious point (confirmed by interpretation 1.) is that it is always open to the parent without custody to return to the court for a ruling on a matter of continued concern to him or for variation of the original order.[24]

Another type of order which has been made by the divorce courts vests custody in the intermediate sense of decision-making powers in one parent and gives care and control to the other. "Split orders" were used more often when the matrimonial offence doctrine formed the basis of divorce law. Where, for example, the wife was "guilty" of adultery but was considered the more appropriate parent to look after the child, the court might then, as in *Wakeham* v. *Wakeham*,[25] give care and control to her. But it would leave

---

[23] *op. cit.* n. 17 paras. 5.17–5.26 and see also Priest and Whybrow, "Child Custody in the Divorce Court and the Domestic Court" (1987) 17 Fam. Law 57, 58.
[24] n. 19, *supra*.
[25] [1954] 1 W.L.R. 366.

decisions on upbringing in the hands of her husband as a reward for good behaviour by making a custody order in his favour. These orders are now considered inappropriate in view of the retreat from fault-based divorce and the modern emphasis on irretrievable breakdown of marriage. Additionally, it is now thought wrong that the parent with the daily burden of raising a child should be deprived of the powers comprised in custody.[26] Nevertheless, in theory those orders may still be made and a rare example, in somewhat exceptional circumstances, occurred in *Jane* v. *Jane*.[27] In that case an order was made to enable the husband to consent to a blood transfusion for the child should it prove necessary. The wife was a Jehovah's Witness and had indicated that she would never be willing to provide her consent.

The divorce court may also make an order for joint custody. Traditionally these orders have not been common, but there is evidence that they are on the increase albeit subject to significant regional variation.[28] The orthodox view was that such orders should be confined to cases in which the court considered that a high level of cooperation was likely to continue between the divorcing parents. This view of joint custody, epitomised by *Jussa* v. *Jussa*,[29] may now be replaced by a movement towards an increased use of the order as means of encouraging continuity of responsibility following divorce. Thus, in *Cafell* v. *Cafell*[30] a joint custody order was upheld by the Court of Appeal despite the existence of acrimonious relations between the parents. The court felt that the order could recognise the responsibility and concern of the absent parent and might ease the bitterness between the parties.

The type of joint custody order used in the above cases is thought to have the effect of leaving daily care and control in the hands of one parent while sharing between the parents decision-making powers and responsibilities on significant issues of upbringing. Where the two parties are both parents of a child a similar result may be achieved by an order giving care and control to one party, thus preserving the equality of parental powers other than the claim

[26] See *Williamson* v. *Williamson* [1986] 2 F.L.R. 146.
[27] [1983] 4 F.L.R. 712.
[28] Priest and Whybrow, *op. cit.* n. 17 paras. 5.2–5.6, found that joint custody orders were made in 12.9 per cent. of cases in 1985 but that they were significantly more popular in the South than in the North of England.
[29] [1972] 2 All E.R. 600.
[30] [1984] F.L.R. 169. See also *Hurst* v. *Hurst* [1984] F.L.R. 867.
[31] Law Com. No. 96, para. 2.42.

to physical care to the child.[31] It is again unclear, however, whether parents exercising joint custody are, like cohabiting parents, governed by the regime in section 85(3) of the Children Act 1975. If this section does apply, each parent would have a right of independent action and there would be no duty to consult before action is taken. On the other hand each parent would possess a veto power which would be legally effective if exercised before action is taken.

This scheme has a reasonable chance of practical success where parents are living together, but its suitability to the situation of estranged parents must be doubted. Joint custody, by definition, envisages the absent parent effectively sharing in the upbringing of the child, but this is surely dependent on his being kept informedgof issues affecting the child. If the parent with physical care is able to act independently and is under no legal duty to keep in touch with the other parent, then the efficacy of the order is likely to be substantially impaired. It may be that an order for joint custody does impose a duty of consultation but this is in need of clarification. There would seem to be a case for the enactment of a general provision requiring consultation and joint action between parents, whether living together or not, in relation to important questions affecting the child. This would confine a parent's rights of independent action to everyday concerns and emergencies. This is of course based on the assumption that joint continuing control is desirable following the parents' physical separation or divorce. This question is discussed below.

The English form of joint custody envisages sharing control over upbringing but not sharing the physical care of a child, apart from the limited time during which the parent without care and control exercises access. Another species of joint custody which has acquired a degree of popularity in some countries, notably the United States, results in the child spending substantial periods of time (not necessarily of equal duration) in the care of each parent.[32] There appears to be a nineteenth century English precedent for this type of order. In *Re A and B*[33] the order was that the child should spend part of the year in the care of each parent. However in recent years such orders have been virtually unknown and in *Riley* v. *Riley*[34] the Court of Appeal disapproved in principle

---

[32] See D. J. Miller, "Joint Custody" 13 Fam.L.Q. 345; (1979) Paula M. Raines, "Joint Custody and the Right to Travel: Legal and Psychological Implications" (1986) 24 *Journal of Family Law* 625.

[33] [1897] 1 Ch. 786.

[34] [1986] 2 F.L.R. 429.

of a joint custody order which embraced joint care and control. The original order in that case had provided that the child should live alternate weeks with each of her parents, an arrangement which had lasted for nearly five years with no apparent detriment to the child. The Court of Appeal, stressing the need for a settled home, held that this kind of order was unusual and prima facie wrong. It therefore seems that for the moment orders which contemplate shared care may prove difficult to obtain. On the other hand these orders are commonly made in favour of a parent and step-parent. Here of course the practical situation is quite distinct since the joint custodians will be living together and sharing the physical care of the child in their common home.[35]

The nature of joint custody in America is sometimes misunderstood on this side of the Atlantic. Although a majority of States have now enacted some form of joint custody statute there is considerable variation in the meaning of joint custody from State to State. In so far as a general trend can be detected this is to define joint custody as joint responsibility in matters of health, education and welfare and an increasing number of States distinguish joint legal (decision-making) custody from joint physical (residential) custody.[36] The emphasis is generally on continuing responsibility with the precise arrangements for physical care often being left to the parties. This is closer to the English form of joint custody than is usually acknowledged. Leading advocates of joint custody in the United States also emphasise the importance of continuing joint responsibility rather than any precise mathematical apportionment of physical care. As Schwartz puts it: "Joint Custody requires divorced parents to share the privileges, responsibilities and credit for the care of their children, with each parent having as much contact with each child as is feasible. Parents each continue to parent. They negotiate with each other and work out between themselves the details of shared responsibility."[37]

(ii) Legal custody orders

Legal custody, as defined in section 86 of the Children Act 1975 "means as respects a child so much of the parental rights and

---

[35] The Adoption Act 1976, ss.14(3) and 15(4) expressly encourages joint custody as an alternative to adoption. See the discussion in Law Com. No. 96, para. 2.44.

[36] For a review of custody statutes in the individual States see Jay Folberg, "Joint Custody Law — The Second Wave" (1984) 23 *Journal of Family Law* 1.

[37] Sheila F. G. Schwartz, "Towards a Presumption of Joint Custody" 18 Fam. L.Q. 225 (1984).

duties as relate to the person of the child (including the place and manner in which his time is spent)."

It is a more limited idea than divorce court custody since it encompasses only those rights which relate to the child's person. It is generally agreed that the right to administer the child's property is not included, but there is some uncertainty about which of the other incidents of the parent/child relationship may be said to be personal and which non-personal. It is likely that most other powers over upbringing are included in legal custody subject to the express exception that a custodian may not, by virtue of possessing legal custody, effect or arrange for the child's emigration unless he is also the parent or guardian. But in general terms an order for legal custody appears to be similar in its effect to a sole custody order in the divorce court. In particular it does not affect the basic incidents of natural parenthood. The person with legal custody should accordingly acquire exclusive powers over upbringing unless the non-custodial parent brings an issue of upbringing back before the court.[38]

The differences between divorce court orders and orders for legal custody are more apparent where the court wishes to preserve for the parents a measure of joint control. When making an order for legal custody it may order that the parent without legal custody shall retain all or some of the parental rights and duties (other than the right to actual custody) jointly with the custodial parent.[39] In essence this means that the court is precluded from making the now discredited split order and may not *in terms* make a joint custody order.[40] It may, however, produce substantially the same effect as a joint custody order in relation to all or some aspects of upbringing by making an express reservation of parental rights. This mechanism has the advantage that the court may distinguish between areas of concern which it desires to leave under joint control and other matters which it wishes to make the exclusive preserve of the parent with actual care.[41] The statutory formula does not however provide for shared physical care. Where an order for legal custody is made the court is

---

[38] It is not certain whether *Dipper* v. *Dipper* applies to orders outside the divorce court. If it does, it is possible that the parent without legal custody would retain some say in upbringing, depending on which interpretation of *Dipper* is adopted.

[39] D.P.M.C.A. 1978, s.8(4); G.M.A. 1971, s.11A(1).

[40] See *Douglas* v. *Douglas* (1986) March 25, C.A.T. No. 387.

[41] Priest and Whybrow found evidence that this type of order is rarely used in practice. *Op. cit.* n. 23, p. 62 and n. 17, paras. 5.41–5.45.

not empowered to reserve the right of actual custody to the non-custodial parent. It has been suggested that the court may be able to achieve the result of shared care by limiting its order to actual custody, thus overcoming the prohibition on sharing which applies where a legal custody order is made.[42] The issue remains in doubt however and the statutory scheme operating in the Magistrates' Court appears ill-designed for giving effect to a policy favouring the active participation in the care of a child by both parents following their separation.

(iii) Access

Access or the right to maintain physical contact with a child is included in the concept of parental rights, in divorce court custody, and in legal custody where that concept applies.[43] Since access is included in these concepts, it is arguable in strict theory that a non-custodial parent loses his right to access in the absence of an order specifically providing for it. But it is unlikely that custody orders are intended to remove what is regarded as a fundamental incident of the relationship between a parent and his child. In *M. v. M. (Child: Access)*[44] Wrangham J. expressed the view that access should be regarded as the right of the *child*. Despite this emphasis on the child's claims there is also plenty of authority supporting the proposition that courts will not deprive a *parent* of access unless its exercise would be likely to result in positive harm to the child.[45] Perhaps therefore the better view is that access should be seen as a mutual right of parent and child.

Courts considering orders for custody or legal custody may make access orders whether or not they make any other order.[46] Sole custody orders are usually accompanied by orders for reasonable access which may be defined by the court in default of agreement. A parent while exercising access will have the same

[42] Law Com. No. 96, para. 2.48.
[43] C.A. 1975, s.85(1); M.C.A. 1973, s.52(1) and C.A. 1975, s.86 respectively.
[44] [1973] 2 All E.R. 81.
[45] See *S. v. S. and P.* [1962] 2 All E.R. 1. For examples of refusal of access, applying the harm criterion, see *Rashid* v. *Rashid* (1979) 9 Fam. Law 118 (breaches of access orders and removal of the child from the country without authorisation) and *Wright* v. *Wright* (1981) 2 F.L.R. 276 (religious indoctrination). This principle does not apparently apply in the *public* sphere where the child is in care. See *Re K.D. (A Minor)* (Ward; Termination of Access) [1988] 1 All E.R. 577. discussed below, Chap. 9.
[46] The statutory provisions are discusssed in Law Com. No. 96, para. 2.55.

legal duties as anyone with actual care, but will not have legal powers over upbringing going beyond this.

The enforcement of access is problematic. In many reported cases the custodial parent has been obstructive and in some instances this has spilled over into indoctrination of the children against the absent parent. In such cases the courts have not been willing to allow the custodial parent's lack of cooperation to deprive the child of potentially beneficial contact with the other parent, and a certain amount of distress on the part of the child may be accepted as an unfortunate but inevitable accompaniment to access.[47] The courts have been reluctant to impose a penal order on a recalcitrant parent and prefer instead to think in terms of putting something more workable in place of the existing order.[48] This might involve a change of custody,[49] and in an extreme case, in which neither parent is prepared to co-operate, a care order might be made.[50] However in cases where the children themselves have an implaccable opposition to seeing the non-custodial parent the courts have been forced to accept the futility of seeking to enforce access and to recognise that insistence on compliance with the order could harm the children. A fortiori the threat of physical harm to a child would be a reason for refusing access.[51]

The reality is that many access orders prove in practice to be unenforceable. This is not to say that they are valueless. Access orders may be viewed as an important affirmation of the public interest in that they give notice to divorcing parents that society expects them to continue to co-operate for the well-being of their children.

(C) THE POLICY OF THE LAW

The sole custody paradigm reflects an assumption that when parents separate it is better for their child to be under the exclusive

---

[47] Re E. (A minor: Access) [1987] 1 F.L.R. 368.
[48] See Thomason v. Thomason [1985] F.L.R. 214, P. v. W. [1984] 1 All E.R. 866 and Tilmouth v. Tilmouth [1985] F.L.R. 239.
[49] Williams v. Williams [1985] F.L.R. 509.
[50] R. v. G. (Surrey County Council Intervening) [1984] Fam. 100.
[51] For refusal of access based on the child's opposition see Corkett v. Corkett [1985] F.L.R. 708. For refusal based on the threat of physical harm, namely sexual abuse, see S. v. S. (Child Abuse: Access) [1988] 1 F.L.R. 213. The two decisions should be contrasted on the issue of whether refusal of access to one child necessitates refusal of access to other children in the family.

care and control of one of them and that the role of the other parent in the child's life will at best be a subsidiary one. The degree of involvement which is envisaged for the parent without custody varies considerably under the different orders made by the courts. If an access order is not sought he may be left to drop out of the child's life by default.[52] Where an access order is made this still has the effect of relegating the parent to the status of a visiting relative and does not provide for continued parenting in any realistic sense.

It is now increasingly accepted that the legal system should endeavour to create the conditions which maximise the amount of contact between the child and *both* parents following divorce. As we have noted, the principal claim is that children who maintain meaningful relationships with both parents following divorce are better adjusted psychologically. A number of other benefits are thought to result from the continued participation in upbringing by the absent parent, including greater co-operation over financial support and a reduction in the incidence of re-litigation of custody issues.[53]

While there appears to be a large measure of support for this general policy direction opinion is divided on what are the most appropriate legal mechanisms for giving effect to it. The English joint custody model has been attacked, particularly by feminist writers, who argue that it reinforces role stereotypes by allowing men (who represent the bulk of non-custodial parents) to continue to exert control over their ex-wives via the children without having to shoulder the burden of daily care.[54] Without wishing to detract from the validity of this criticism, it is equally arguable that it is the prevalence of sole custody orders in favour of mothers and the apparent maternal preference on the part of some of the judiciary which most contributes to the myth that child-rearing is a function properly confined to women.[55] In the United States some courts

---

[52] He is not, for example, required to attend the court appointment to discuss the arrangements for the future care of the children. See G. Davis., A. MacCleod and M. Murch, "Undefended Divorce: Should Section 41 of the Matrimonial Causes Act 1973 be repealed?" (1983) 46 M.L.R. 121.

[53] Raines, *op. cit.* n. 32, p. 629.

[54] See, for example, Bottomley, "Resolving Family Disputes: a critical view" in M. D. A. Freeman (ed.), *The State, the Law and the Family* (1984) p. 298.

[55] There are many examples of judicial opinion that children, especially young children, are better off with their mothers. See, *e.g. Greer* v. *Greer* (1974) 4 Fam. Law 187 and more recently, *Allington* v. *Allington* [1985] F.L.R. 586 *cf.* the remarks of Bingham L.J. in *A.* v. *A.* (Custody Appeal: Role of Appellate Court) [1988] 1 F.L.R. 193.

even went so far as to treat the preference for mothers in the case of younger children as a legal presumption. This practice has now been declared unconstitutional by the Supreme Court of Alabama in *Ex p. Devine.*[56] The "tender years doctrine" continues, however, to be a relevant factor in custody disputes and may operate as a "tie-breaker" where all other things are considered equal. It is true that the vast majority of sole custody arrangements are entered into by agreement and that the courts' orders often merely give effect to the wishes of the parties. However, the conclusion to be drawn from this may be that many divorcing parents, both men and women, are content to accept the existence of the role stereotypes to which feminists raise objection.

Roman and Haddad in their critique of the feminist position note that, "it is a central tenet of feminism that fathers ought to be more involved with home and child care and mothers less so." But they refer to the apparent inconsistency of the feminist position regarding intact and divorcing families respectively. Feminist theory, they argue, is, "largely restricted to intact families. There is near complete disregard for the father of the divorced family and the need for his continuing participation in the life of his children."[57]

The objective must surely be to find a legal solution which aids the breakdown of these sexist roles by encouraging men and women to accept the continuing parental responsibility of men. This is where the English joint custody model is deficient since it fails to provide adequately for divorcing parents to share in the physical care of their children.

Shared care is an important feature of joint custody in other countries, and in some jurisdictions there is a legislative presumption in favour of joint custody including joint physical custody.[58] The California Civil Code, for example, contains such a presumption in order to give effect to an official state policy designed

> "to assure minor children of frequent and continuing contact with both parents after the parents have separated or dissolved the marriage, and to encourage parents to share the rights and responsibilities of child-rearing in order to give effect to this policy."[59]

---

[56] 398 So. 2d 686 (1981). See also *Pusey* v. *Pusey* 728 P. 2d 117 (1986) (Utah).
[57] *Op. cit.* n. 7, p. 151.
[58] See the discussion in Law Com. No. 96, para. 4.44.
[59] CAL. CIV. CODE s.4600(a) (West Supp. 1986). For a good review of the position in other jurisdictions in the United States see Raines, *op. cit.* n. 32, pp. 626–627.

The main proposals which have emerged in England seek to achieve the same objectives but without the use of joint custody orders as such.

In her book *Child Custody and Divorce*, Susan Maidment urges the enactment of a legal presumption that the equality of parental rights which existed during marriage should be preserved following divorce. This should be accompanied by a further presumption in favour of access or parental contact arrangements which should be a mandatory consideration whether or not there is an application for access.[60] That being the case the courts could confine their orders to residence orders which allocate the child's physical care between the parents.[61] Maidment recognises that there will be cases where co-parenting would be damaging in view of the parents' unwillingness to co-operate and suggests that the courts should retain the power to remove parental rights in the interests of the child, "but only where serious attempts have been made to create a spousal relationship where equal parental rights can operate."[62]

The Law Commission also provisionally favours the establishment of a new scheme which would preserve the parental status of both parties following divorce or separation.[63] Under this, both parents would, prima facie, retain equal legal parental powers and responsibilities including the power of independent action, but these would only be *exercisable* during the time that the child is in the physical care of the parent concerned since "the exercise of most parental responsibilities cannot be separated from the care of the child."[64]

It is central to the Commission's position that it is inaccurate to view the concepts of custody, care and control and access as "differently-sized bundles of powers and responsibilities in a descending hierarchy of importance."[65] Powers and responsibilities "run with the child" and are imposed to the full extent on the person with the care of the child. The Commission thus rejects the validity of the distinction between major and routine matters of upbringing. It proposes that *all* decisions affecting the child, of whatever level of gravity, should be exercised by the parent with

---

[60] *Loc. cit.* n. 4.
[61] *Ibid.* p. 280.
[62] *Ibid.* p. 281.
[63] Law Com. No. 96, paras. 4.51–4.57.
[64] *Ibid.* para. 7.17.
[65] *Ibid.* para. 4.51.

actual care at the relevant time, subject only to those issues specially singled out by statute or governed by court order.[66] Thus, again under this scheme, the courts would be primarily concerned with the allocation of the child's time between the two parents by means of care and control orders. The Commission therefore sees the division of legal powers and responsibilities between parents as temporal rather than qualitative.[67] Its position seems to amount to a rejection of the *Dipper* philosophy since it favours exclusive control in the parent with physical care at the relevant time.

This is an extremely important issue since it is generally envisaged under joint custody arrangements elsewhere that the parents will confer and engage in joint decision-making on major questions. The distinction between what is major and what is minor is undoubtedly elusive, but the view that qualitative distinctions cannot usefully be made is surely questionable. The Commission gives the example of a child who spends a weekend on an access visit with his father (and also the father's new wife if he has one). It is said that the father (and wife)

> "will have full responsibility for and power to decide what the child eats, when he goes to bed, whether and where he goes to church, what he does with his time, to summon medical attention in the event of an accident or illness, and so on."[68]

All of this may be readily accepted since the actions in question are daily operational concerns, or in the case of the accident or illness, an emergency. But it is suggested that sensible qualitative distinctions may be drawn between the decision whether the child is to attend church on a particular Sunday, and the decision whether that child is to be raised as a practising Christian at all, in a different faith or as an atheist. Equally, it is one thing to recognise the independent power of a parent with actual care to determine whether a child's high temperature justifies a visit from the doctor, and quite another to allow the same parent to decide unilaterally that an abortion should be performed on the child or that she should act as donor in a transplant operation. Yet under

---

[66] *Ibid.*, paras. 4.54–4.57. Matters which the Commission suggests might need to be governed by express individual provision restricting or qualifying a parent's power of independent action include emigration, change of name, consent to adoption and marriage, education, religious upbringing and serious medical treatment.

[67] *Ibid.* para. 4.51.

[68] *Ibid.*

the Commission's proposals these matters would, prima facie, be determined solely by the parent with care at any given time and without any general provision requiring consultation with the other parent, unless specifically provided for by court order. This might conceivably make the outcome of major strategic or irreversible decisions affecting the child a matter of chance rather than rational deliberation between the two parents. It is fair to say that the Commission does envisage the reservation of joint control in some cases under the terms of a court order. However this might not be done in many cases and where express provision is not made a parent would lose all control over the child during the time that the child was not physically with him.

The view taken here is that legislation should embody a general provision requiring consultation and mutual consent between parents, whether living together or not, in relation to fundamental questions affecting the child. It might be necessary to spell out in the legislation examples of issues which would require joint action but it is doubtful whether any such list could be exhaustive. An individual parent's rights of independent action would, under this regime, be confined to everyday routine matters and emergencies. This scheme would continue to apply unless and until a court orders in the interests of the child that one parent should have exclusive control over a particular matter. It is thought that the absence of a legal duty to notify and consult the other parent would dilute considerably the likely success of any arrangement for joint custody or time-sharing.

The Commission does not favour the enactment of a statutory presumption providing for joint custody or time-sharing largely on account of the practical difficulties which it feels would arise in England, since it is said that this society is not generally geared to joint child care.[69] Other objections to orders for joint physical custody were thought to be the stresses which might be caused to parents and children where one parent is reluctant to agree to that type of arrangement and the disruption which it might cause in the lives of children who might constantly have to divide their time between two homes. The Commission prefers a case by case approach in which the judges would enjoy a broad discretion to determine the appropriate level of involve-

[69] *Ibid.* paras. 4.45–4.46.

ment with the child of both parents following divorce.[70] The practical problems involved in shared care should not be under-estimated. It is submitted however that it would be a mistake to assume that, because an equal division of care is impracticable in many cases, we should abandon attempts to *maximise* contact in those cases. The orientation which is argued for here is not a presumption of absolute equality of time-sharing, but rather a requirement that *in every case* a concerted effort should be made to involve both parents to the fullest extent possible following divorce. The precise arrangement would undoubtedly vary signi-ficantly from case to case depending on the practical limitations facing particular parents. Experience in the United States suggests however that these practical difficulties may be exaggerated and that even such expedients as telephone contact may be valuable in maintaining a child's connection with a parent. In America the principle of shared care is widely accepted and attention is now turned on the means whereby this principle may be given best effect in practice.[71] In England also it appears that supervision orders may be made with a view to assisting in the implementation of a joint custodial arrangement.[72]

The Law Commission's suggested new scheme would undoubtedly create a conceptual and procedural basis for the active continuing participation of both parents in child-rearing and would, at the same time, overcome the objections to the severance of legal from physical custody. But any encouragement towards joint custodial arrangements or equal time-sharing would be implied rather than express.[73] Thus, it seems that it would be open to the courts to perpetuate the current preference for sole custody by allocating care and control to one parent either exclusively or almost exclusively.

The Commission's Supplement to Paper No. 96 clearly reveals the exclusive nature of current custodial dispositions and the significance of gender represented by the overwhelming majority

---

[70] The Commission's view should be contrasted with that of the Booth Committee whose report was strongly in favour of joint custody and which expressed the hope that such orders would be made "in the vast majority of cases." See *Report of the Matrimonial Causes Procedure Committee* H.M.S.O. (1985), para. 2.27.
[71] For a valuable discussion see Ken Magid and Parker Oborn, "Children of Divorce: A Need for Guidelines" 20 Fam.L.Q. 331 Law Com. No. 96.
[72] Priest and Whybrow, *op. cit.* n. 17 para. 7.21.
[73] *Ibid.* para. 4.53(*b*).

of custody orders in favour of mothers.[74] It also reveals, from a sample of 3,000 cases drawn from 10 courts across the country, that in about 90 per cent. of joint custody cases the orders did not envisage the parents performing equal child care duties but rather that the children would live mainly with their mothers. It may therefore be argued, as one commentator has done, that what is required is a custody regime which establishes "a norm that post-divorce co-operation, at least in the restricted area of child care, is to be desired and expected."[75]

The crux of the problem seems to be the widely held perception in society that child-rearing is the exclusive function of women and, in order to combat this, the legal system will need to be much more assertive than hitherto in affirming the equal parental role and responsibility of men. The active promotion of this end requires the legislature to lay down a guiding principle which directs the judges to think in terms of joint custody or relatively equal time-sharing, and which places the onus squarely on those wishing to deprive one parent of active involvement to demonstrate why this would be necessary in the interests of the child.[76] While there are undoubtedly some cases of parental unfitness it is difficult to disagree with Maidment that under the existing system legal responsibility is being removed from one parent "for no other reason than that his marriage is dissolved."[77]

Ultimately, the success of any scheme will be judged not on the basis of its conceptual clarity but on whether it delivers in terms of improving the quality of post-divorce arrangements in a substantial number of cases. One view is that whatever type of orders are made their significance is largely symbolic since they are all virtually unenforceable without the co-operation of the parents.[78] But whether or not it is possible to force people to continue to act as parents it is important for the legislation to counter the suggestion that post-divorce arrangements for children can ever be *purely* a matter for private arrangement and irrelevant to the public interest.

A legal policy which supports joint parenting following divorce has potentially far-reaching implications for the private ordering of

---

[74] Priest and Whybrow, *loc cit.* n. 17.

[75] Richards *Op. cit.* n. 4, p. 88.

[76] As to the variation in attitudes towards joint custody among the judiciary see Priest and Whybrow *op. cit.* n. 23, pp. 58–59.

[77] *Op. cit.* n. 4, p. 267.

[78] Michael King, "Playing the Symbols—Custody and the Law Commission" (1987) 17 Fam. Law 186.

custodial arrangements.[79] It is likely that the existing imbalance of custody orders favouring mothers arises much more from the voluntary agreements of parents than it does from any judicial bias in favour of women.[80] But the adoption of the above policy orientation might suggest that there should be some restraints on the ability of a parent to opt-out of his responsibilities by agreement. The Law Commission seems to feel that in general private arrangements should be upheld subject to the court's power to refuse to enforce those which it considers are not for the benefit of the child, the reasoning being that the parental role can be encouraged but never imposed.[81] On the other hand, the issue has been presented by Maidment as one of children's rights so that "the child's right to be protected against the damage caused by losing one parent should thus be seen as creating a correlative duty or responsibility on each parent to continue his role as parent to his child."[82]

Presented in this way the issue is the familiar one of balancing parental claims to autonomy with the independent claims of children. This is well illustrated by parental requests for leave to remove the child from the jurisdiction for the purposes of family emigration. Traditionally, the English courts have looked favourably on genuine decisions of one parent to emigrate with her reconstituted family despite the drastic implications of the move for the relationship between the child and the other parent.[83]

It has been suggested however that courts in the United States have often upheld the parental right to travel at the expense of continuing with joint custodial arrangements which benefit children. In doing so they have, according to Raines, too often "focused on the parents' perceived advantages in the move while claiming to have analysed the move in the context of the child's best interest."[84] Moreover, she refers to studies of joint and sole

---

[79] For a general discussion of private ordering on divorce see Mnookin and Kornhauser, "Bargaining in the Shadow of the Law: The Case of Divorce" 88 Yale L.J. 950 (1979).

[80] See the discussion in J. Eekelaar, *Family Law and Social Policy* 2nd Ed. (1984) pp. 79–80.

[81] Law Com. No. 96, para. 4.59.

[82] *Loc. cit.* n. 4.

[83] See, for example, *Poel* v. *Poel* [1970] 1 W.L.R. 1469, *Chamberlain* v. *De La Mare* (1983) 4 F.L.R. 434, *Lonslow* v. *Hennig (formerly Lonslow)* [1986] 2 F.L.R. 378, *Belton* v. *Belton* (1987) 2 F.L.R. 343 and *Re F. (A Minor) The Independent*, November 12, (1987).

[84] Raines, *op. cit.* n. 32 p. 656.

custody fathers which concluded that fathers with joint custody had greater self-esteem than those who were limited to visitation rights.[85] She concludes on the evidence of psychological research "that such moves should seldom be granted since the psychological detriment to the children and the remaining parent caused by such a move is rarely justified."

It may therefore be that the courts in both countries will in future need to take a significantly more restrictive attitude to such applications since the effect of allowing a parent to leave the country with the child is tantamount to a *de facto* sole custody order.

While it is self-evident that parents cannot be forced to continue to discharge their child-rearing responsibilities, there is arguably a better chance that they will do so in a system which embodies a legal presumption of joint parenting on divorce.

3. Children of Unmarried Parents

(A) THE AUTOMATIC POSITION

At common law a child born out of wedlock was *filius nullius* (nobody's child) and his relationship with both his father and mother was not legally recognised. In due course the mother became solely entitled to custody. In contrast to the equal legal authority now enjoyed by married parents, it remains the case that in relation to a child of unmarried parents the mother has the parental rights and duties exclusively.[86] Until recently, the child of such a union suffered the imposition of status discrimination and was labelled "illegitimate." This terminology has now been removed by the Family Law Reform Act 1987 which enacts the general principle that references in all future legislation

"to any relationship between two persons shall, unless the contrary intention appears, be construed without regard to whether or not the father and mother of either of them, or the father and mother of any persons through whom the relationship is deduced, have or had been married to each other at any time."[87]

---

[85] Ibid. p. 644.
[86] Children Act 1975, s.85(7); Guardianship Act 1973, s.1(7).
[87] s.1(1).

The Act removes many of the remaining vestiges of discrimination affecting children born out of wedlock. In particular all children will now have equal rights of inheritance irrespective of whether their parents were or were not married to each other.[88] All children are now placed in an equal position with regard to financial support from their father or mother under the Guardianship of Minors Act 1971. The much criticised affiliation proceedings, which were previously the only means whereby anyone might seek financial support from the natural father for a child born out of wedlock, are abolished.[89] Nevertheless important legal distinctions remain in relation to the acquisition of citizenship and the child's relationship with his father.

(i) Establishing paternity

The initial difficulty facing an unmarried father is to establish in law that he is in fact the father of the child. This presents no problem for the married man since he has the benefit of a legal presumption that a child born to a married woman is the child of her husband.[90] No such presumption applies to unmarried couples even where they are in a stable cohabitation. It is therefore necessary to adduce evidence of paternity which has normally been provided by blood tests or birth registration.

The traditional form of blood test has suffered from the limitation that it can only exclude a particular man from paternity and cannot conclusively identify him as the father. This is not to underestimate its value since the exclusion of one or more men may lead to the inevitable conclusion that some other man is the father.[91] This limitation has been overcome with the advent of the "D.N.A. genetic finger-printing" test, although this is not yet widely in use. The technique enables positive identification of the origin of very small samples of body fluid or tissue with almost total certainty.[92]

---

[88] s.18.

[89] ss.12 and 17.

[90] This presumption may be rebutted under s.26 of the Family Law Reform Act 1969 by evidence that it is more probable than not that the husband is not the father. As to the standard of proof in paternity cases see *W*. v. *K*. *(Proof of Paternity)* [1987] 151 J.P. 156.

[91] For a discussion of the value of such tests see S. M. Cretney, *Elements of Family Law* (1987) at pp. 237–238 and "Bromley's Family Law," 7th Ed. (1987) pp. 247–251.

[92] See A. Bradney, "Blood Tests, Paternity and the Double Helix" (1986) 16 Fam. Law 378. See also L. J. Connor, "DNA Testing: The Answer to a Maiden's Prayer" (1988) 152 J.P. 152.

The courts had an early opportunity to comment on the value of the procedure in *Re J. (A minor) (Wardship)*.[93] Here the mother placed her three-day-old baby in voluntary care. Because of her mental condition the local authority seriously doubted her ability to care for the child. The alleged father indicated his willingness to raise the child himself but only if it was proved to his satisfaction that he was in fact the father. The issue for Sheldon J. in wardship proceedings was whether the mother should be restrained from leaving for South Africa before the D.N.A. test could be carried out. He held that, since the test could establish paternity as a virtual certainty, it was in the interests of the child and the father that it should be carried out. Accordingly, he granted an injunction under section 37 of the Supreme Court Act 1981 preventing the mother from leaving the jurisdiction until it had been carried out. The case may be viewed as establishing the principle that a mother should be obliged to co-operate with the court in paternity proceedings. The co-operation of alleged fathers may also be enforced by the courts' power to draw adverse inferences from their failure to submit to testing and by regarding such failure as corroborative evidence of paternity.[94]

It is doubtful whether, at present, the D.N.A. test may be ordered other than in wardship proceedings since the powers derived from the Family Law Reform Act 1969 appear to be limited to conventional blood tests. However, when the Family Law Reform Act 1987 is implemented, the courts will be empowered to direct "scientific tests" in any civil proceedings in which the parentage of any person falls to be determined.[95] This power should extend to D.N.A.

In cases in which the mother refuses to acknowledge paternity it will be necessary for the father to initiate legal proceedings himself in order to establish his connection with his child. There is no legal procedure whereby he may unilaterally acknowledge or register his paternity. Neither may he commence legal proceedings for the sole purpose of establishing paternity. Although the 1987 Act introduces a procedure for obtaining a declaration of parentage this is available only to the child himself.[96] In order to bring the issue before the court the father will need to commence proceedings for custody or access to seek a parental rights order.

The other method of providing evidence of paternity is by birth

---

[93] [1988] 1 F.L.R. 65.
[94] *Turner* v. *Blunden* [1986] Fam. 120 and *McVeigh* v. *Beattie* (1988) 132 S.J. 125.
[95] s.23.
[96] s.22.

registration. Entry of the man's name on the births register is prima facie evidence of paternity.[97] An entry of the father's name may be made only in the following circumstances:

1. At the joint request of the mother and father;
2. At the request of the mother alone on production of a declaration by her stating the man to be the father and a statutory declaration by him acknowledging his paternity;
3. At the request of the father alone on production of equivalent declarations; or
4. At the request of either the mother or father on production of a certified copy of a "relevant order" and, where the child has attained 16, the written consent of the child.[98]

The net result is that the father cannot register his paternity without either the cooperation of the mother or an order of the court. Relevant orders for these purposes are orders which give him parental rights or which require him to make financial provision for the child.

The conclusion to be drawn from these provisions is that, quite apart from the question of parental powers, the law will not recognise the relationship between father and child *at all* unless either the mother consents or a court has made a finding of paternity. In view of the psychological benefits to children of paternal contributions to their upbringing it is arguable that, following the example of some Scandinavian countries, a system of compulsory disclosure of paternity should be introduced.

In Sweden, for example, a mandatory paternity action is commenced in all cases in which the father does not voluntarily acknowledge his paternity. It is understood that this results in the identification of fathers in approximately 95% of all non-marital births. Moreover, the encouragement of voluntary acknowledgement is so effective under this system that litigation is only required in roughly 20% of cases.

It seems that the Scandinavian legislation was motivated primarily by financial considerations and the State's interest in recouping from unmarried fathers part of the costs of child support. While this may of itself be a good enough reason for compulsory disclosure of paternity, the child's interest in knowing the identity of his father

[97] s.34 Births and Deaths Registration Act 1953.
[98] 1953 Act, s.10 as amended by s.24 Family Law Reform Act 1987.

and the opportunity of establishing a relationship with him is an even better reason. It is difficult to see whose interests are served by the current system of voluntary disclosure apart from those mothers who wish to exclude fathers from any participation in the lives of their children and those fathers who are concerned to evade their financial and other responsibilities to their children. The public interest, it is suggested, would be best served by compulsory disclosure.

(ii) The legal status of unmarried fathers

The father's position has been judicially likened to that of a "beached whale,"[99] an expression conveying his relative impotence with regard to effective legal action to establish his relationship with his child. He has no automatic right to contribute to the care of the child or to be consulted on decisions relating to upbringing. *A fortiori*, he has no right to physical possession of the child. This lack of an automatic legal nexus between father and child has important repercussions. The father is accordingly excluded from the definition of "parent" for the purposes of the Children and Young Persons Act 1969, the Child Care Act 1980, the Children Act 1975 and the Adoption Act 1976, the effect of which is to withhold from him the procedural and substantive rights available to married fathers under this legislation. Thus, he has no *locus standi* in 1969 Act proceedings, at present no right to apply for access where his child is in care under the amended section 12 of the 1980 Act and his consent is not required for adoption or freeing for adoption. Under the Family Law Reform Act 1987 he will be entitled to be regarded as either the "parent" or "guardian" of the child for the purposes of the above Acts only where he has a court order in his favour giving him parental rights or some form of custody.[1] It is intended that he will be brought within the access provisions of the 1980 Act when the relevant provision of the Family Law Reform Act 1987 is brought into force.[2] The original proposal of the Law Commission that the father's consent to adoption should be required where he had an access order in his favour was dropped in the Commission's "Second Report on Illegitimacy."[3]

---

[99] Per Waite J. in *R.* v. *Oxford Justices, ex. p. D.* [1984] 3 All E.R.

[1] ss.7 and 8. In relation to care procedures he must have been awarded "actual custody."

[2] By virtue of s.2 (1). It appears that there was an error in the draftsmanship of the relevant part of the 1987 Act. This is expected to be rectified when the reformed child care legislation appears or by means of a separate means of a separate amending provision. See *The Times*, March 15, 1988.

[3] Law Com. Report No. 157 (1986), para. 3.4.

(B) REALLOCATION OF PARENTAL POWERS AND DUTIES

Until the 1987 Act the only statutory procedure available to an unmarried father was to seek legal custody or access under the Guardianship of Minors Act 1971.[4] This procedure, although invoked by many fathers, was deficient in two respects. First, as we have noted, legal custody is a more limited notion than full parental rights so that a father who obtained an order in his favour would not thereby acquire full parental status. Secondly, since it is not possible to make an order for joint legal custody, this procedure could not be invoked by a cohabiting unmarried couple who wished to share parental responsibility.

The 1987 Act meets these objections by creating a new procedure whereby the father may apply to the court for a "parental rights order."[5] By this process he may (if successful) obtain *all* the rights of natural parenthood and he will share these with the mother. The court does not have power under this procedure to remove all the authority of the mother nor is it able to confer on the father authority in relation to individual aspects of upbringing.[6] Once equal parental status has been acquired, however, disputes between the two parents may be resolved in the normal way under the Guardianship legislation where it is possible to award legal custody to one parent while preserving a say in upbringing for the other.

Despite the existence of these legal procedures, the absence of an *automatic* legal relationship of parenthood may still leave the father in a vulnerable position. This is especially the case when considering his standing *vis-à-vis* social welfare agencies. In *Re M. and H. (Minors)*[7] the unmarried parents of two children had lived together in Cardiff until 1980. Thereafter they separated and both remarried other people. In 1982 the mother placed the children in voluntary care and indicated that she did not want them back. In 1983 the council passed a resolution assuming her parental rights. The father returned to Cardiff in 1985 from the Yemen (his country of origin) and indicated his desire to take over the care of the children. The council assessed the suitability of the father and his new wife and arranged for them to have access on nine

[4] ss.9 and 14.
[5] s.4.
[6] See Law Com. Report No. 157, paras. 3.1–3.2.
[7] [1987] 3 W.L.R. 759 At the time of writing an appeal to the House of Lords is pending. *cf. Re L. (A minor)* [1985] J.S.W.L. 50.

occasions at a Roman Catholic children's home. They concluded that the visits had been neither harmonious nor successful and in January 1986 they refused the father further access. He applied to the County Court under the 1971 Act and succeeded in obtaining an order for access. The issue for the Court of Appeal was whether the judge had had jurisdiction to hear the father's application.

Glidewell L.J. noted that the father was not a "parent" within the meaning of section 87(1) of the Child Care Act 1980 and therefore lacked the right to receive notice of the resolution assuming parental rights or to object to it. But his right to apply for custody or access was not removed by the fact that the child was in care.[8] However, applying the principle in *A.* v. *Liverpool City Council*[9] the court was obliged to refuse to exercise its jurisdiction since it had no power to challenge the merits of the local authority's decisions relating to a child in its care.

If these facts were to recur after the implementation of the 1987 Act the father would be able to challenge the decision to terminate his access.[10] This reform follows a recommendation in the Review of Child Care Law.[11] It is interesting to note however that the Review, while proposing the enactment of a legal presumption of reasonable access to children in care for married parents and an unmarried mother, would not extend this to an unmarried father unless he is already entitled to access under a court order.[12]

The broad effect of the 1987 reforms will be that unless an unmarried father has previously been awarded actual custody he will not be in a position to contest the initial decision to take his child into care. Once the child is in care he will effectively lose his right to apply for custody, will have no presumption of access in his

---

[8] This had been held previously in *R.* v. *Oxford Justices ex p. H.* [1975] Q.B. 1 and *R.* v. *Oxford Justices ex. p. D. supra*, n. 99.

[9] [1982] A.C. 363. See also *Re D. (A minor) (1987) The Times*, October 16, where Latey J. suggested that Magistrates' clerks should do all in their power to discourage such applications in view of the jurisdictional difficulties. See also *Re P. (Minors) (Access) P.* v. *P. (Gateshead MBC Intervening)* (1988) *The Times*, February 19, where the Court of Appeal applied the same principles to the situation of a child who had entered care under s.2(2)(*b*) of the Guardianship Act 1973. It seems likely that the restrictions apply to all children in care by whatever route. *Quaere* whether they apply to those in voluntary care. The better view is that they do applying the wardship analogy (see *W.* v. *Nottinghamshire C.C.* [1986] 1 F.L.R. 565.)

[10] *Supra*, n. 2.

[11] Para. 21.18.

[12] Para. 21.17.

favour and will be limited to challenging access decisions which would have the effect of terminating completely his contact with the child. He will have no right to apply for discharge of the care order since, without a custody order in his favour, he will not be a "parent" for the purposes of care proceedings. The overall effect of applying *A*. v. *Liverpool City Council* in this context is arguably a denial of natural justice to unmarried fathers. They have no realisic way of seeking to regain control over a child in care.

It is, however, recommended in the Review of Child Care Law that unmarried fathers should have the right to apply for discharge of care orders. But the reasoning behind this recommendation was that this would avoid multiple applications to different courts since fathers had a right to apply for custody outside care proceedings.[13] Notwithstanding the effective removal of this right by the decision in *Re M. and H. (Minors)*, it is to be hoped that this recommendation will be effected when the child care legislation is reformed.

(c) FURTHER REFORM—THE CASE FOR AUTOMATIC PARENTAL RIGHTS

There is universal agreement that children of non-marital relationships should not be penalised by the imposition of legal disadvantages not suffered by the children of marital unions. Both the English and Scottish Law Commissions in their respective reports on illegitimacy[14] accepted as a general policy objective that "to the greatest extent possible, the legal position of a child born to unmarried parents should be the same as that of one born to married parents."[15]

The English Commission in its first report thought that the term "illegitimate" should be replaced with "non-marital" since the former expression had pejorative connotations, but it was felt necessary to continue to distinguish for certain purposes between the two groups of children.[16] The Scottish Commission thought that any distinguishing term would be unnecessary and would "rapidly take on old connotations,"[17] and therefore felt that labels

[13] Para. 20.4.
[14] Law Com. No. 118 (1982) (first report) and No. 157 (1986) (second report); Scot. Law Com. No. 82 (1984).
[15] Law Com. No. 157, para. 1.1.
[16] Law Com. No. 118, para. 4.51.
[17] Scot. Law Com. No. 82, para. 9.2.

should be avoided. This approach later commended itself to the English Commission.[18] At the same time it reaffirmed its view that a distinction should continue to be drawn between the respective legal positions of married and unmarried parents. In the case of the latter "the mother alone should have parental rights and duties although the father should be able to acquire these by legal process."[19]

As we have seen, the automatic extension of parental rights and duties on proof of paternity to an unmarried father, once favoured by the English Commission,[20] has now been rejected. It seems that the Commission resiled from its original view largely on account of representations by the National Council for One Parent Families and others to the effect that automatic parental rights could subject mothers to interference and harassment from unmeritorious fathers. In particular it was feared that the risk of interference might operate on the mother as a disincentive to disclosure of paternity. Other objections were expressed during the Commission's consultation process. It was said that automatic rights for the father might produce stress and insecurity where the mother had married a third party. It was pointed out that the vast majority of the countries which had sought to abolish the discrimination against those born outside marriage had not conferred automatic rights. Finally it was suggested that to do so might cause practical problems where the child was in the care of a local authority.[21] The Commission rejected the proposal that an unmarried couple should be able to share parental rights by some formal act other than marriage (and without having to go to court) being influenced by "the widely felt anxiety lest the institution of marriage be further eroded by blurring the legal distinction between marriage and other relationships."[22]

This may be criticised on several grounds. First, the entirety of the reforms which seek to equalise the legal position of marital and

---

[18] Law Com. No. 157, paras. 2,3.
[19] No. 118 para. 7.26; No. 157 para. 1.1.
[20] Law Com.W.P. No. 74 (1979).
[21] Law Com. No. 118 para. 4.50. Eekelaar has criticised this evidence on the basis that it is representative of the position of the members of one organisation which should not be regarded as a microcosm of society, and he suggests that such cases may represent a small proportion of the total of illegitimate births. See John Eekelaar, "Second Thoughts on Illegitimacy Reform" (1985) 15 Fam. Law 261, 262.
[22] Law Com. No. 118, para. 4.8.

non-marital children may be thought to debase the institution of marriage, but may nevertheless be considered justified in order to satisfy the legitimate claims of the two groups of children to equality before the law. Secondly, the denial of an equal parental status to fathers may pressure couples into marriage as a device for achieving this equality. This may itself be thought to detract from the voluntary nature of marriage.[23] Thirdly, if it is accepted that a relationship with both parents is central to the welfare of children, the refusal to give full legal recognition to the natural ties with one parent seems to amount to a policy which attaches more importance to the institution of marriage than to the psychological needs of children.

A number of commentators have argued that it ought to be possible in certain instances for parental rights to be shared without requiring an application to the courts. Eekelaar favours a compromise between automatically vesting rights in the father and requiring him to go to court. This would be to allow sharing only where the two parents enter into a formal agreement for this arrangement, possibly registrable with the registrar of births. This device, he argues, "would at one stroke bring parental rights to unmarried, cohabiting, parents and exclude the obviously unmeritorious individuals."[24]

The same concern to exclude the latter is shared by Ingleby who is also unhappy about the creation of parental status on the basis of genetic parentage alone. He would however countenance it where there is evidence of cohabitation or financial support, and also where there is joint acknowledgment. The Law Commission is also now considering a reform which would allow an unmarried mother to share parental responsibilities with another individual, such as the father of her child, by appointing him an *inter vivos* guardian.[25] This was thought less objectionable than the suggestion that parental rights should flow automatically from registration of paternity, since it would preserve the mother's freedom of choice in determining whether she wished to share upbringing with the father. The Commission also had in mind the resource implications of requiring all fathers to apply to the courts.

The requirement of commencing legal proceedings undoubtedly represents a hurdle which many fathers will not feel able to

---

[23] See the discussion by Ingleby [1984] J.S.W.L. 170, pp. 172–174.
[24] *Op. cit.* n. 21, p. 261.
[25] Law Com. No. 91, paras. 4.20–4.24.

surmount, and to preserve it means that the absence of a legal relationship between the majority of unmarried fathers and their children is considered acceptable or at least that it is a matter about which we can afford to be complacent. A policy of placing obstacles in the way of the creation of *initial* paternal relationships is, it is suggested, irreconcilable with the policy of fostering the *continuation* of such relationships in the case of divorcing parents. When viewed in juxtaposition, the incongruity of the two approaches is striking.

The above proposals would go only part of the way towards meeting these objections since they would all make the acquisition of legal parenthood for fathers dependent on something more than the genetic parentage which suffices for mothers. Joint acknowledgment or appointment of the father as guardian may additionally be criticised for allowing the mother to determine the level of involvement between father and child. This assumes that the interests of the child are coincidental with those of the mother. But the fact that *she* may wish to exclude the father from the life of the child is far from conclusive that this would be in the *child's* best interests. If psychological research indicates that children need two parents, this surely holds good whether or not those parents are married. In the context of divorce it has been seen that the opposition of a custodial mother to paternal visits is not considered a legitimate reason for refusing access. It is also arguable that, if the matter is seen in terms of children's rights, there is a case for requiring the mother to disclose the name of the man whom she knows or believes to be the father. In this way the creation of the initial relationship between father and child might be facilitated or at least not obstructed.

Ultimately, the critical question relates to the onus of commencing proceedings, since automatic legal rights for the father would shift the onus on to the mother if she wished (for whatever reason) to exclude him from involvement in raising the child. Notwithstanding the understandable objections expressed in the Law Commission's consultation process this would seem to be a more sensible and just approach. The essence of this approach would be positive thinking about the potential contribution which could be made by the father in the child's life, as opposed to the negative and pessimistic view that a father who wishes to be involved is likely to be bent on causing disruption and interference in the life of the mother.

Eekelaar has rightly criticised the negative posture of the Law Commission in "operating a stereotyped image of the unmarried father as a social deviant."[26]

It is also suggested that the practical results of this reform would be beneficial in the majority of cases in so far as these can be predicted at all. First, automatic rights would give legal recognition to the *de facto* sharing of responsibility which exists in the many cases (albeit still the minority) where parents are cohabiting and would relieve them of the inconvenience of taking formal steps to achieve this. Secondly, there would probably be a significant number of cases where the father has no wish to be involved with either the mother or the child. In these cases the mother would exercise her rights free from interference and the possession of parental powers by the father would be academic. There might conceivably be a difficulty if the mother desired to place the child for adoption since the father's consent would have to be obtained or dispensed with in these circumstances. However, his lack of interest in the child would be unlikely to result in his opposition to adoption. Thirdly, there would be cases in which the father might wish to be involved with the child (possibly encouraged by legal recognition of his parental status), but the two parents might not wish to live together. In some of these cases the mother might welcome some support from the father in addition to financial support. This itself might be more forthcoming if the father perceived that he had a realistic part to play in upbringing.

It must however be conceded that there would be cases in which the mother would not welcome any connection with the father. Some of these instances would involve undesirable individuals who should be excluded from contact with the child but, applying the divorce analogy, cases of genuine unfitness would be uncommon. Why then should the onus not be on the mother to demonstrate this unfitness to a court in the minority of cases in which the father represents a genuine threat to the welfare of the child? The positive benefits which would be likely to accrue in the majority of cases may be thought to justify some inconvenience to the mother in a few atypical situations. There is of course the problem of the rapist, which has been put forward by some as a justification for withholding parental status from fathers. The obvious way around this difficulty would be to create a specific statutory exception excluding convicted rapists from parental status.

[26] *Op. cit.* n. 21, p. 262.

Is the denial of parental status to unmarried fathers a matter which affects the legal status of their children? The intention behind the Family Law Reform Act 1987 is that by removing statutory labels from the children themselves, any necessary distinctions between them based on marriage may be drawn by distinguishing between *fathers* rather than children. Thus, according to the Scottish Law Commission, following these reforms "it would be a matter for argument whether it was any longer justifiable to refer to a legal status of illegitimacy." But the Commission concedes: "Whether minor differences in the rules applying to different classes of persons justify the ascription of a distinct status is a matter for commentators rather than legislators."[27]

The view taken here is that it is not correct to present the parental rights issue as one which only affects the legal position of parents. Defining the issue as one of fathers' rights has the effect of marginalising it. But exclusive rights for the mother *does* result in a discriminatory status being imposed upon the children since it continues to be necessary to distinguish between two groups of children *viz.* those enjoying by operation of law a full legal relationship with *both* parents, and those denied any realistic legal nexus with their fathers. Moreover, it is suggested that it would be quite wrong to describe the denial of the legal status of parenthood as a minor matter. It is something which is fundamental to both father and child whose legal positions are inextricably linked. It results in a discriminatory status for both of them.

This idea of mutuality seems to find support in the judgment of the European Court of Human Rights in *Johnston and Others* v. *Ireland*.[28] In that case the Court held, *inter alia*, that the laws of the Irish Republic violated Article 8 of the European Convention[29] in failing to provide an appropriate legal regime reflecting the natural family ties between an illegitimate girl and her parents. This amounted to a failure to respect the family life not just of the girl but of necessity that of each of her parents. In so deciding the Court was influenced

---

[27] Scot. Law Com. No. 82, para. 9.3. Cf. Law Com. No. 118, para. 4,45.
[28] December 18, 1986, Series A, No. 112.
[29] Article 8(1) of the European Convention for the Protection of Human Rights and Fundamental freedoms provides, "Everyone has the right to respect for his private and family life, his home and his correspondence."

by its previous judgment in the *Marckx* case,[30] where it stated that "respect" for family life, understood as including the ties between near relatives, implied an obligation on the state to act in a manner calculated to allow those ties to develop normally. Whether English law is now in conformity with the Convention is arguable. Undoubtedly it is more liberal than was Belgian law at the time of the *Marckx* case and, unlike Irish law at the time of the *Johnston* case, it clearly does provide the means whereby an unmarried father might eliminate or reduce the differences between his legal position and that of a married father, *i.e.* by applying for a parental rights order or legal custody. On the other hand the court in the *Marckx* case held that Belgian law violated the Convention in failing to acknowledge an unmarried mother's maternity from the moment of birth and in requiring her to recognise her child or to take legal proceedings for this purpose. This was a failure to respect family life under Article 8. It also violated Article 14[31] since the interest of an illegitimate child in having the maternal bond was no less than that of a legitimate child. It may therefore be that in due course English law will be required to give effect to an automatic *paternal* bond.[32]

[30] *Marckx* v. *Belgium*, 18 Y.B. 248, Eur. Court H.R., Series A, No. 31. For a useful discussion of the implications of the case for English law see Maidment, "The Marckx Case," (1979) 9 Fam. Law 228.

[31] Article 14 provides, "The enjoyment of the rights and freedoms set forth in this convention shall be secured without discrimination on any ground such as sex, race, colour, language, religion, political or other opinion, natural or social origin, association with a national minority, property, birth or other status."

[32] On October 15, 1986 the European Commission declared admissible complaints of an unmarried father concerning his procedural and substantive rights where his child was taken into care at the behest of the mother. It may be that this will provide the European Court with an opportunity of ruling on the automatic legal standing of unmarried fathers under English law, see Application No. 11468/85.

3. Parental Control and the Independence of Children

1. Introduction

This chapter is concerned with the nature of parents' legal authority and how this relates to the legal capacities of children and young people.

We noted in Chapter 1 that the modern emphasis is on the welfare of children and the duties of parents to secure this. At the same time there remains strong support for the idea that parents should enjoy a large measure of freedom in determining how to raise their children. This parental autonomy ideology has been robustly defended in certain academic works.[1] It also received a powerful, if short-lived, judicial boost from the decision of the Court of Appeal in the *Gillick* case.[2] The Court decided unanimously that parents possessed, prima facie, the right and duty to control completely their children.[3] The *Gillick* litigation showed quite clearly that the debate is not a purely semantic one about whether the parental position should be characterised in terms of "rights" or "duties." Whatever language is adopted by the courts and the legislature there remain fundamental questions about the nature and extent of parents' powers, the capacity of minors for independent decision-making and the determination of who is to have the final say where the interests of parents and mature adolescents are in conflict with one another.

It should be noted at the outset that a distinction needs to be drawn between the legal position of parents and children in relation to each other and their respective legal relationships with

[1] The most influential work has probably been J. Goldstein, A. Freud and A. J. Solnit, *Before the Best Interests of the Child* (1980).
[2] [1986] 1 A.C. 112.
[3] See particularly Parker L.J. *ibid.* p. 124.

third parties. This chapter is concerned primarily with the former issue but, inevitably, some discussion of the latter question is required since we are often concerned with the child's activities outside the home. This was so in the *Gillick* case itself where the issues revolved around the relationship of children and parents, not just *vis à vis* each other, but also with the medical profession. We begin by considering the legal basis of parents' powers over their children. We then examine the extent to which the law recognises the legal capacity of minors to take their own decisions. Finally, we consider how these competing claims are balanced in the legal system.

2. Parental Powers

(A) THE NATURE AND EXTENT OF PARENTAL AUTHORITY

The principal difficulty in seeking to establish the perimeters of parental authority is that the legal concept of parental rights has never been properly defined. Section 1(1) of the Guardianship Act 1973 simply provides that "a mother shall have the same rights and authority as the law allows to a father." This reference to the general law is repeated in the definition of parental rights and duties in section 85(1) of the Children Act 1975 where the expression is said to include "all the rights and duties which by law the mother and father have in relation to a legitimate child and his property." It is therefore necessary to extract from the general law those rights and duties which have been recognised to attach to parenthood. We must then seek to establish the extent or duration of authority in relation to each of them. A number of commentators have attempted to enumerate the legal effects of the relationship between parent and child.[4] Most of the so-called "rights" relate to control over various spheres of upbringing and are more appropriately described as "powers". They include all those areas of responsibility with which we might expect parents to be concerned, including physical care and control, secular and religious education, medical treatment, discipline and selection of the child's name.

---

[4] See, for example, M. D. A. Freeman, "What Rights and Duties do Parents have?" (1980) 144 J.P. 380 and Susan Maidment, "The Fragmentation of Parental Rights" [1981] C.L.J. 135.

47

It is important to appreciate at the outset that when the judiciary and sometimes the legislature have made reference to "parental rights" they have usually been referring to these parental powers of control over upbringing. The Law Lords in *Gillick* were using the expression in this sense. This accords with Dickens' definition of a parental right as, "a parental discretion to act regarding a child in a way others have a correlative duty to permit or a duty to forbear from preventing."[5] These discretions are "privileges" or "liberties" in the Hohfeldian sense.[6] In layman's language they amount to legal powers to take action and to authorise others to take action, in relation to a child. They should be contrasted with rights in the sense of legal claims against third parties which are enforceable in the courts. Those who assert that parents have no rights are really saying that they lack this second species of rights and not that they lack rights in the first sense. The argument over rights is therefore about whether it is an appropriate choice of language to describe parental "powers" as "rights."

Before *Gillick* there was little authority on the extent of parental powers since the courts had rarely been called upon to consider the issue. They had normally been involved with specific disputes relating to individual children which had been determined on the basis of the courts' view of their best interests. They had not been required to consider what the technical position was on the limits of parents' powers since they were able to override them and substitute their own decision on the matters in issue. What made the *Gillick* case so special was that it did not involve directly the welfare of particular children, but was rather concerned with the general relationship in law between health practitioners, children and parents. It therefore provided the House of Lords with an ideal opportunity for laying down guidelines to govern the automatic relationship between them.

A Health Notice issued by the Department of Health and Social Security[7] advised that, in exceptional circumstances, a doctor might lawfully provide advice or treatment on contraceptives to a girl under 16 without prior parental consultation or consent, provided that he acted in good faith to protect her against the harmful effects of sexual intercourse. Mrs. Gillick objected to the Notice and sought assurances from her Health Authority that no

[5] Bernard M. Dickens, "The Modern Function and Limits of Parental Rights" (1981) 97 L.Q.R. 462.

[6] W. N. Hohfeld, *Fundamental Legal Conceptions* (1919).

[7] H.N. (80) 46.

minor daughter of hers would receive such advice or treatment without her permission. Having failed to obtain this she sought, *inter alia*, a declaration that such action would be unlawful since it would infringe her parental rights.

Mrs. Gillick lost at first instance before Woolf J., won in the Court of Appeal and eventually lost by a majority of three to two in the House of Lords. The majority speeches now constitute the definitive guidance on the legal limits of parents' authority. Lord Templeman was in broad agreement with the majority on the parental rights issue but dissented on the separate issue of a girl's capacity to consent to contraceptive advice or treatment which, in his view, she lacked because of the public policy restrictions on sexual intercourse with girls under 16. These public policy considerations were evidenced by the existence, *inter alia*, of the offence in section 6 of the Sexual Offences Act 1956. The speeches are susceptible to differing interpretations. The majority rejected the idea of *absolute* parental control over children which had found favour with the Court of Appeal. Lord Fraser, specifically rejecting *Re Agar-Ellis*, said that parental rights existed for the benefit of the child and not for the benefit of the parent. Their existence was, in his view, justified only in so far as they enabled a parent to discharge his duties towards his child. He agreed with the approach of Lord Denning M.R. in *Hewer* v. *Bryant*[8] that the parent's right of control arising from custody was "a dwindling right which the courts will hesitate to enforce against the wishes of the child and the more so the older he is." Lord Scarman said that the common law had never regarded parental rights as sovereign and beyond review or control. He agreed that they derived from duty and existed only so long as they were needed for the child's protection. Thus, while it was clear that there existed a parental right to authorise medical treatment, the question arose as to the extent and duration of that right. In his opinion the parent's right "yields to the child's right to make his own decisions when he reaches a sufficient understanding and intelligence to be capable of making up his own mind on the matter requiring decision."[9]

It is therefore apparent from this decision that parental authority is qualified rather than absolute and that the law imposes limitations on it quite irrespective of whether or not a dispute reaches the courts. It is envisaged that a doctor might, in certain

[8] [1970] 1 Q.B. 357 p. 369.
[9] n. 2, p. 186.

circumstances, decide to ignore a parent's protests and could be acting lawfully in doing so, without having to obtain the prior authorisation of a court.

The more difficult issue is to decide precisely how the law limits parental control. It was accepted that there would be certain exceptional situations in which parental authority could be overridden. These included parental neglect or abandonment of the child, circumstances in which a parent could not be found, and where emergency action was required.[10] But following *Gillick* it is not clear whether the result of the decision is that the child's legal capacity operates as a restraint on the *exercise* of parental powers or whether it has the effect of *terminating* them altogether. The difficulty is compounded by the different reasoning adopted by Lord Fraser and Lord Scarman and the fact that Lord Bridge simply agreed with both of them on the parental rights issue. Lord Scarman appeared to suggest that parental powers would be extinguished but Lord Fraser did not apparently share this view. As we have seen, Lord Fraser approved Lord Denning's opinion that parental powers *diminished* as the child gradually matured into independence. On this view they would remain in existence until the child attains majority.

A crucial preliminary question must be whether it is possible to draw general conclusions about the nature of parental powers from a decision in one area of activity. Is the concept of parental rights to be viewed as a unitary one or must regard be had to the subject-matter of the activity which a parent is seeking to control? We shall see that in the case of the legal capacities of minors it is vital to distinguish between different areas of activity. Only the issue of contraceptive advice and treatment was directly before the court in *Gillick*, but this did not prevent Lord Scarman from expressing his reasoning at a broad level of generality. He would apparently apply the mature minor test generally in the law except where Parliament has intervened directly by fixing a statutory age.[11] Lord Fraser also, while confining most of his judgement to the immediate contraception issue, did approve of Lord Denning's general remarks about the nature of parental rights in *Hewer* v. *Bryant* and the decision of the House of Lords in *R.* v. *D.* relating to a parent's right of physical control. It seems unlikely that Lord Fraser regarded the contraception question as a special case. The

[10] See Lord Fraser, *ibid.* p. 165 and Lord Scarman, p. 189.
[11] *Ibid.* p. 186.

better view would therefore seem to be that the principles which emerge from *Gillick can* be extrapolated to other areas of activity, subject to the important qualification that they cannot be applied where statute directly governs the matters in issue.

It is clear that Lord Fraser was of the view that the child's capacity for decision-making *per se* would not bring about an automatic termination of parental powers over medical treatment. In order to proceed without parental consent the doctor would, in his judgment, need to be satisfied as to five matters *viz.*

> "(1) that the girl will understand his advice;
> (2) that he cannot persuade her to inform her parents or allow him to do so;
> (3) that she is very likely to begin or to continue having sexual intercourse with or without contraceptive treatment;
> (4) that unless she receives advice or treatment her physical or mental health or both are likely to suffer; and
> (5) that her best interests require him to act without consent."[12]

There is substantial scope for parental involvement under Lord Fraser's formulation, not least with the requirement that the doctor should always seek to persuade the girl to allow this. Moreover, despite the language used in places by Lord Scarman it is submitted that he also had in mind restrictions on the *exercise* of parents' powers. He expressed himself to be in agreement with Lord Fraser's speech and he accepted as a general proposition that "parental rights clearly do exist, *and they do not wholly disappear until the age of majority*."[13] Further, the tenor of his judgment is one of approval of the content of the D.H.S.S. circular which had emphasised that in the normal case it would be expected that parents would be involved. Only in exceptional cases would the doctor be justified in exercising his clinical judgment to proceed without their knowledge and consent.[14]

The implication of Lord Fraser's guidelines is that (subject to the exceptional situations mentioned earlier) a parent's authority will remain intact unless *all* of the conditions are met. Perhaps the most significant of these is the last. Parents' powers, according to

---

[12] n. 2, p. 174.
[13] *Ibid.*, pp. 183–184. Emphasis added.
[14] *Ibid.*, pp. 189–190.

this criterion, survive unless the child's best interests demand that they are overridden. This could be interpreted as a reiteration of the familiar welfare principle but with the significant modification that the assessment of the child's best interests (upon which depends the lawfulness of the parents' proposals) would be made by third parties dealing with the child and/or the parents and not by the courts. In the case of contraceptive advice this would be the medical profession. Perhaps it is this feature of *Gillick* which most represents a change from the orthodox view of parental rights, put forward by the Law Commission in 1982. This was that

> ". . . under our law, unless and until a court order is obtained, a person with parental rights is legally empowered to take action in respect of a child in exercise of those rights. It is true that if appropriate procedures are initiated he or she may be restrained from exercising those rights if it is not in the child's interests that he or she should do so: but unless and until such action is taken the person with parental rights would be legally entitled to act."[15]

This analysis accepts the welfare limitation on parental rights but envisages a court action in order to activate it. *Gillick* now suggests that third parties (in this case the medical profession) may themselves invoke the limitation and act as arbiters of the best interests of children in their dealings with them.

If this is what the House of Lords intended the implications are far-reaching.

It is interesting to speculate, for example, on whether other third parties such as school authorities, religious leaders, etc., would be legally entitled to ignore parental instructions regarding their children because they happened to disagree with the parents' views of their best interests. The prospect that such officials might be legally entitled to refuse to do things which are requested by parents is hardly worthy of comment. But *Gillick* now also suggests that third parties may take positive action in relation to a child in contravention of the express wishes of a parent. They may arguably do so where they judge that the child is sufficiently mature to disagree with his parents on the matter in question and where they take the view that the child's view of his interests is the correct one.

[15] Law Com Report No. 118, para. 4.19.

Take the example of religious instruction and church member-ship. Suppose that X, a Protestant child aged 14, wishes to convert to Roman Catholicism and to undergo the necessary training. In situation 1, X's parents support his decision and seek to enrol him at the local Roman Catholic Church. Having discussed the matter with X, the priest takes the view that it would be in his best interests to remain a Protestant. Clearly, there is no legal means of requiring the church authorities to admit X to the Catholic communion in accordance with his parents' wishes. In situation 2, X's parents object to his proposed change of religion but the priest believes him to be mature enough to take his own decision and that it would be in his best interests to become a Catholic. The *Gillick* case suggests that the church would be legally entitled to accept X.

In each of the above situations the parents and the priest have arrived at opposite conclusions as to X's interests in accordance with their own subjective judgments. But there can be no objective evaluation of what X's best interests were unless and until the matter is brought before a court for an *ex post facto* adjudication. What if the court then finds that X's best interests were not to join the Roman Catholic Church after being raised for most of his life as a Protestant and that, in any event, X was immature at the relevant time and unable to appreciate the implications of the change. In these circumstances, applying *Gillick*, the priest apparently acted unlawfully by infringing the parental right to determine X's religion. Since X had no capacity to decide for himself, parental rights remained intact.

What remedy would be available to the aggrieved parents in this situation? If it is asserted that parents have rights then the question of the enforcement of those rights must be relevant. The *Gillick* ruling provides no answer to this question. Is the House of Lords perhaps suggesting that a tort of interference with parental rights is known to the law? It seems unlikely, especially since parents no longer have the right to sue for loss of a child's services caused by the actions of third parties. This action would seem to have been grounded in the concept of interference with parental rights, but was abolished by the Ad-ministration of Justice Act 1982.[16] The absence of an appropriate remedy supports the view that it may be inaccurate to say that parents have legal rights in the more usual sense.

---

[16] s.2(b). For a detailed discussion of the scope of the tort see, *Bromley's Family Law* (6th Ed.) (1981), pp. 329–332.

Does *Gillick* mean that parents' powers are unqualified where the child is young or immature and lacking capacity to engage in self-help? It would be surprising if the law were to impose limits on parents' authority over resourceful adolescents and at the same time uphold unrestrained authoritarianism in relation to comparatively defenceless children. Yet the *Gillick* ruling would seem to suggest that where the test of maturity is not satisfied parental control is maintained. It should be remembered that the implication of this is that a parent could *withhold* consent to medical treatment just as easily as he could *give* it. It was of course accepted in *Gillick* that the courts would have power to override parents' powers, but this would only be a safeguard to the small minority of children who are made the subject of legal proceedings. Fortunately there is judicial support for the view that the law imposes automatic restraints on the exercise of parents' powers despite the incapacity of their children. This has arisen in the context of the parental right to physical possession which includes the power to control a child's movements.

In *R.* v. *D.*[17] the child was a ward of court and in the care of the mother. The father broke into her flat, accompanied by two armed men, and removed the child from the country by force. The House of Lords held in these circumstances that the father could be guilty of the common law offence of kidnapping his own minor child. [18] The critical factor was held to be the absence of the child's consent and significance was also attached to the absence of a lawful excuse, which could have been provided by the authorisation of the custodial parent.

It might be argued that the determining factor here was the wardship of the child. Since care and control was vested in the mother, she alone had a legal right to possession of the child to the exclusion of the father. Some support for this view is derived from the reservation expressed by Lord Bridge that it was preferable for the court not to answer the question of whether a parent might be convicted of common law kidnapping with an unqualified affirmative. In his view the preferred

---

[17] [1984] A.C. 778.
[18] The facts arising in this case could equally have given rise to proceedings for contempt of court since the child was a ward. They would now be likely to amount to an offence under s.1 of the Child Abduction Act 1984.

answer would have been that it was possible when a parent acts in contravention of a court order restricting his parental rights, thereby leaving open the question of whether it was possible in other circumstances.[19]

The other four Law Lords were not prepared to accept this qualification. They preferred to base their decision squarely on the presence or absence of the child's consent. Lord Brandon said that he saw "no good reason why, in relation to the kidnapping of a child, it should not in all cases be the absence of the child's consent which is material, whatever its age may be."[20]

The reference to the child's lack of consent is interesting since, at the time of the abduction, the child was only five years old and, therefore, arguably lacked the mental capacity either to give or withhold consent. The court's reasoning was based on the imputation that if the child *had* been able to provide a valid consent, this would not have been forthcoming. The difficulty with this is that there must be some principle which distinguishes those acts to which an immature child can be presumed to have consented and those to which the child may be presumed to have objected.

Take, for example, the situation of a father who wishes to take his toddler for a walk. The toddler objects! Is the father legally entitled to take the child with him by force? The answer to this question must surely be "Yes." But what is it (leaving aside the court order) which distinguishes this hypothetical situation from the factual situation in *R. v D?* It is submitted that the matter turns on the reasonableness of the purported exercise of parental control. In the hypothetical example, the father's behaviour was routine and reasonable. The father in *R. v. D.* acted wholly unreasonably.

This principle that parental powers must be exercised reasonably has long been applied in relation to the so-called right of discipline which admits of only moderate and reasonable corporal punishment.[21] Moreover, it has recently been applied by the Court of Appeal in the context of the parental right of control.

---

[19] n. 17, p. 797.

[20] *Ibid.* p. 806.

[21] *R. v. Hopley* (1860) 2 F. & F. 202. It may be that with the abolition of corporal punishment in state schools brought about by the Education (No. 2) Act 1986 there will be demands for the complete removal of the parental right to inflict corporal punishment. This is already the position in certain Scandinavian countries. It should also be noted that the European Commission has found that parental rights over minors in relation to placement in a hospital psychiatric ward are not unlimited. See *Jon Neilsen* v. *Denmark* (Application No. 10929/84) discussed at 29 *Childright* 14 and 39 *Childright* 3.

In *R. v. Rahman*[22] a teenage girl, currently preporting for her "O" level examinations, initially came to England with her parents when she was two years old. Her mother returned to Bangladesh and her father placed her with foster parents with the assistance of the local authority. Under this arrangement parental rights remained vested in the father. One day while the girl was walking to school she was accosted by her father. He bundled her into a car against her will on the pretext that he wished her to visit her ailing grandmother in Bangladesh. A struggle ensued which culminated in her rescue by the police.

The father's conviction for the common law offence of false imprisonment was upheld. It was argued on his behalf that the case was distinguishable from *R. v. D.* in two respects. First, there had been no infringement of the rights of the other parent and secondly, there had been no contravention of a court order. Lord Lane C.J. rejected these contentions taking the view that unlawfulness could arise, other than by breach of a court order, where the detention was "for such a period or in such circumstances as to take it out of the realm of reasonable parental discipline." At the same time he reaffirmed the basic right of control enjoyed by parents and indicated that "the sort of restriction imposed upon children is usually well within the bounds of reasonable parental discipline and is therefore not unlawful." This case suggests that the legality of parental actions may be evaluated partly by considering the presence or absence of the child's consent and partly by the application of a general test of reasonableness.

The above decisions, taken together, show quite clearly that parents' powers are not limited solely by a positive assertion of autonomy by a child. They support the proposition that *all* parental powers must be exercised reasonably and in accordance with the best interests of the child. Failure to comply with these requirements may lead to *ex post facto* adjudications by the courts that a parent has exceeded his lawful authority. Not only may this be a tortious assault on the child but, it may also constitute a criminal offence. The courts' role in such cases differs from their traditional function in children cases. Normally where they act to protect a child, applying the welfare principle, they do not call into question the legality of expressed parental preferences. They simply supersede them because they disagree with them. The distinction may appear subtle at first sight, but is nevertheless

---

[22] (1985) 81 Cr.App.R. 349.

critical. The result of these cases appears to be that parents' powers are *automatically* qualified or restricted by operation of law, both by the child's relative claim to autonomy, by the reasonableness of their exercise and by the child's best interests. This is a formula which invests third parties with considerable responsibility. Just as they may have regard to the child's level of understanding in deciding whether they must abide by the wishes of parents so, it may be argued, must they have regard to the reasonableness of what parents propose. If they come to the conclusion that the parents are falling short of these standards, it is arguable that they may be entitled to ignore them and deal directly with the child. It may be that the tests of reasonableness and acting in the child's best interests are two ways of expressing the same limitation on parental rights since, as Lord Hailsham once noted in the context of consent to adoption, a reasonable parent pays regard to the welfare of his or her child.[23]

Is there a case for saying that under *Gillick* the child's acquisition of legal capacity brings about a complete termination of parental rights over the matter in issue? This more radical assessment of the majority speeches is mooted by Eekelaar.[24] He adopts a literal interpretation of Lord Scarman's speech and suggests that the additional criteria listed by Lord Fraser might have been intended by him to be matters pertaining to professional discipline only and not legal requirements. On this view, where the child acquires capacity, parental rights in the relevant spheres of activity would be extinguished before the child attains majority. However, for the reasons given above, it is suggested that the correct interpretation is that the parents' powers endure until majority, albeit in qualified form.

(B) RIGHTS OR DUTIES—IS TERMINOLOGY IMPORTANT?

The shift in emphasis which has resulted in a conceptualisation of the parental position in terms of duties or responsibilities rather than rights has been taken up by the Law Commission in its Working Paper on Custody. The Commission suggests that "parenthood" should become the primary legal status. It describes its essential features and the Commission's preferred choice of terminology as follows:

[23] *Re W. (An Infant)* [1971] A.C. 682, 699.
[24] John Eekelaar, "The Eclipse of Parental Rights" (1986) 102 L.Q.R. 4 and "The Emergence of Children's Rights" (1986) 6 *Oxford Journal of Legal Studies* 161, 177–182.

"Parenthood would entail a primary claim and a primary responsibility to bring up the child. It would not, however, entail parental 'rights' as such. The House of Lords in *Gillick* v. *West Norfolk and Wisbech Area Health Authority* has held that the powers which parents have to control or make decisions for their children are simply the necessary concomitant of their parental duties. This confirms our view that 'to talk of parental "rights" is not only inaccurate as a matter of juristic analysis but also a misleading use of ordinary language.' We suggest therefore that the expression should no longer be used in legislation."[25]

The obvious question at this juncture is whether the use of particular expressions, in legislation or by the judiciary, has any substantive significance or whether alternative terminology is used simply to convey the same basic power structure within the family. Is there any meaningful distinction between parental "rights," "powers", or "authority" on the one hand and "duties" or "responsibilities" on the other? It is certainly possible to describe all parents' actions as a discharge of their duties or responsibilities, but to do so might obscure real distinctions between their *power* to act in relation to the child and their positive *duty* to take certain action. Parents are placed under cast-iron legal duties in certain areas but, at the same time, they enjoy considerable discretion concerning matters of upbringing. Dickens' definition of parental rights captures this distinction particularly well. He contrasts parental discretions with duties *stricto sensu* which may be thought to give rise to a correlative claim on the part of the child that certain action will or will not be taken. These strict legal obligations include the provision of suitable education and adequate food, clothing and medical care.[26] These basic duties are designed to ensure *minimum* standards of treatment for all children and to prevent harm. This leaves open, as Dickens observes, "a parental discretion to employ control over children for purposes not violating children's interests, but equally not advancing their welfare or best interests."[27]

Education is a prime example. Parents are deprived of their discretion not to educate their child at all. They are however allowed

---

[25] Law Com. Working Paper No. 96 para. 7.16. See also Report No. 118, para. 4.18 and Working Paper No. 91, para. 1.11.

[26] Education Act 1944, s.36 and Children and Young Persons Act 1933, s.1, respectively.

[27] *Op. cit.* n. 5, p. 464.

some latitude in deciding how to discharge this basic duty. Indeed the principle of parental choice in education is recognised in legislation.[28] So far as religious education is concerned there is no legal duty placed on parents to ensure this. Their discretion is wholly unfettered by the law. They have a free choice between the many different religions on offer in western society or they may opt to raise the child as an atheist.

Is Dickens still correct, in the light of *Gillick*, to argue that the parental discretion to control children may be lawfully exercised in a manner which is not calculated to advance their welfare or best interests? As a matter of legal theory it would seem that the law now requires parents to act in accordance with the best interests of their children. This is, however, so inherently vague a standard of behaviour that it is right to distinguish it from the strict legal obligations imposed on parents in relation to the child's basic needs. Perhaps the true point of distinction is in the question of enforcement. Where parents fail to comply with their statutory duties, there are public agencies charged with the responsibility of securing compliance or taking other action to protect the child. The local education authority may set in motion school attendance procedures where parents are failing in their legal duty to ensure the child's regular attendance at school. The local authority may institute care procedures where the child is being abused or neglected. No such public body exists to superintend parental actions to ensure that they are in the best interests of a child. This would not only be completely impracticable but it would also constitute a decisive shift in favour of increased State intervention in the family.[29]

The proposed abandonment of rights terminology is motivated by a desire to get away from proprietorial ideas about the parent-child relation and to that extent is to be welcomed. At the same time it is to be hoped that the disappearance of the language of rights in the family context will not deflect attention from the construction of a theory of *children's* rights. As we noted in Chapter 1, protection of the *welfare* of children is not necessarily the same or as satisfactory as respect for their *rights*.

It is also thought that there *is* some place for the language of rights in the context of family relations. Parents as individual

[28] Post, Chap. 7.
[29] Post, Chap. 4.

citizens clearly do have fundamental rights as against the State. Under the European Convention for the Protection of Human Rights and Fundamental Freedoms, to which the United Kingdom is a signatory, everyone has, *inter alia*, "the right to respect for his private and family life, his home and his correspondence."[30] Parents may invoke the Convention where the State has taken action which they allege is an unwarranted interference with their independence in child-rearing which, *inter alia*, this article protects. Parents' rights are also protected by the United States constitution. The American experience shows quite clearly that these fundamental protections are not solely concerned with parents' rights *vis à vis* the State. Both parents and children have fundamental rights under the constitution and these may come into conflict with one another. Constitutional litigation in the United States has sometimes been concerned, therefore, with balancing the rights of parents and children.[31] At this fundamental level at least it seems that it is necessary to recognise the co-existence of the rights of both parents and children and to concentrate on the legal mechanisms for reconciling them when they conflict.

An alternative approach to the whole question of the choice of terminology would be to view it as fundamentally unimportant. The argument would be that the label which the law attaches to parental authority is not nearly as important as the substantive question of its extent and duration. Suppose, for example, that the law gives parents a discretion to determine where a child under 16 is to live. Suppose also that A, a child of 15, wishes to leave home. It is certainly arguable that it will not matter one iota to A whether the parental restriction is justified legally as an exercise of his parents' rights, powers or discretion or a discharge of their duty or responsibility to provide him with accommodation. Either way he will not be entitled in law to leave home and it is this which is his sole concern. There is some attraction in this approach. Parental control will in reality remain in the modern law, albeit subject to the important qualifications articulated in *Gillick*. Its description as a discharge of responsibilities will not bring about any change of substance in the balance of power within the family.

Nevertheless, if the change in legislative terminology does come about, we may at least hope that it will have a symbolic and

[30] Art. 8(1).
[31] Post, Chap. 9.

educative effect on the way in which society perceives the parental role. Some might argue that this is reason enough for the proposed changes.

3. The Legal Capacities of Children and Young People

(A) THE GENERAL LAW

Section 1 of the Family Law Reform Act 1969 reduced the age of majority from 21 to 18 following the recommendations of the Latey Report.[32] Young people below this age are denied legal capacity to perform a variety of acts. The rationale for these disabilities is that they lack the requisite maturity and understanding and should therefore be protected from their own improvidence. The law does not however draw a clear line for all legal capacities at 18 but allows minors of various ages a measure of independence in relation to specific matters. It is therefore necessary to have regard to the particular sphere of activity in order to establish whether a minor is authorised to behave independently.

It should be noted at the outset that the question of legal independence for young people may be sub-divided into two quite distinct issues. The first is their legal position in society at large and in particular their capacity to enter into various transactions with third parties. The second is their position *vis-à-vis* their parents. This dichotomy may be illustrated by the law governing the marriage of people aged 16 or 17. Those in this age group are permitted under the civil law to marry, but only with parental consent.[33] Here the law recognises the essential capacity of the 16 year old to contract a valid marriage but denies this capacity where a parent objects. Thus the minor is liberated from the public restrictions on marriages but not from the legal control inherent in the parent-child relationship. The legal rules governing consent to medical treatment among the same age group provide an interesting contrast. Section 8(1) of the Family Law Reform Act 1969 provides:

---

[32] Report of the Committee on the Age of Majority (1967) cmnd. 3342.

[33] Marriage Act 1949, s.3; Family Law Reform Act 1969, s.2. Interestingly, contravention of the consent requirement will not invalidate a marriage. Marriage Act 1949, s.48(1)(*b*).

"The consent of a minor who has attained the age of six-teen years to any surgical, medical or dental treatment ... shall be as effective as it would be if he were of full age; and where a minor has by virtue of this section given an effective consent to any treatment *it shall not be necessary to obtain any consent for it from his parent or guardian.*"[34]

The intention of Parliament here appears to have been to confer complete legal independence on the relevant age group *both* in their dealings with the medical profession *and* in the context of their family relations with their parents. It follows from these examples that it may be necessary to consider in relation to other age-related rules whether it was Parliament's intention to free the child, not only from his basic disabilities under the civil law, but also from parental control. This may be no easy matter since the statutes will usually fail to deal expressly with the parent-child relation in the way that the above two statutes did.

It is not intended to attempt an exhaustive account of the position of children under the civil law, nor to provide a cata-logue of the statutes dealing with their capacities or responsibilities.[35] Some examples may be given by way of illus-tration. At the age of five a child may be given intoxicating liquor in private;[36] at 10 he may be convicted of a criminal offence provided he has a "mischievous discretion";[37] at 12 he may buy pets;[38] at 13 he may engage in limited gainful employ-ment subject to restrictions mainly relating to school hours;[39] at 14 he may possess an air weapon and at 15 a shotgun;[40] at 17 he may hold a licence to drive any motor vehicle except a heavy goods vehicle.[41] On attaining majority he acquires capacity for almost all legal acts including marrying without consent, making a will, changing his name by deed poll, entering into all types of contracts, owning land and commencing legal proceedings in his

---

[34] Emphasis added.
[35] Useful discussions may be found in M. D. A. Freeman, "Coming of Age?" [1977] L.A.G. Bull. 137; "At what age can I?" (1984) 10 *Childright* 11 and John Vickers, "The Legal Steps to Adulthood" (1987) 151 J.P. 281.
[36] Children and Young Persons Act 1933, s.5.
[37] Children and Young Persons Act 1933, s.50.
[38] Pet Animals Act 1951, s.3.
[39] Children and Young Persons Act 1933, s.18.
[40] Firearms Act 1968, s.22.
[41] Road Traffic Act 1972, ss.4 and 96.

own right. A limited number of incapacities remain until 21, notably consent to homosexual acts in private.[42]

The age of 16, which was not mentioned in the above list, is something of a watershed. In some respects young people at 16 and 17 exist in a legal "Twilight Zone" between minority and adulthood. The law equates their position with that of adults in a number of important respects. We have already noted that this is so regarding medical treatment. Sixteen is also the age at which compulsory education ceases, the child becomes eligible to enter the employment market, to claim certain social security benefits in his own right and to marry (albeit with parental consent). The important question of the age at which a child is allowed to determine where he will live and to leave his parents' home is now shrouded in uncertainty. At common law this depended on the so-called "age of discretion" which was fixed, in the interests of certainty and uniformity at 14 for a boy and 16 for a girl. The question used to arise in the context of habeas corpus proceedings where the age of discretion would determine whether the court would order a child to be returned to his parents. In the leading authority of *R. v. Howes*[43] Cockburn C.J. unequivocally endorsed the fixed-age approach to capacity in these words: "We repudiate utterly, as most dangerous, the notion that any intellectual precocity in an individual female child can hasten the period which appears to have been fixed by statute for the arrival of the age of discretion."[44]

This approach was strongly disapproved by the House of Lords in *Gillick* which, as we have seen, preferred to adopt a test of maturity and understanding as a general determinant of capacity. The issue of the right to leave home was not, of course, directly before the Court but it is likely that *Gillick* principles now apply in this area in the absence of express statutory provision. There is however an argument that the matter is *impliedly* governed by statute. This is because care proceedings may be taken in relation to a child up to the age of 17 where he is, *inter alia*, in moral danger or beyond the control of his parent.[45] Wardship proceedings might be instituted for a similar purpose up to the age of 18. Either of these two ages might therefore be seen as the age at which

---

[42] Sexual Offences Act 1967, s.1.

[43] (1860) 3 E. & E. 332.

[44] *Ibid.* pp. 336–337.

[45] s.1(2)(*d*) and (*e*) of the Children and Young Persons Act 1969.

Parliament intended young people to be free from their parents' physical control. It is understood that in practice the police tend to use the age of 17 based on the existence of the statutory care provisions. We return to the issue of "official" control over older teenagers in Chapter 5.

Some important disabilities do remain at 16. In particular a young person of this age, in common with younger children, generally lacks contractual capacity and is protected against liability by the principle of "qualified unenforceability." The effect of this is that he may sue, but may not be sued, on contracts entered into by him. By way of exception he is bound by contracts for "necessaries" i.e. goods suitable to his station in life and actual requirements and contracts of employment provided that, taken as a whole, they are beneficial to him. Certain other limited categories of contract are binding on the child unless repudiated by him either during minority or within a short time of attaining majority.

The Law Commission initially considered simplifying the law by the adoption of a general rule that minors of 16 and over would be fully liable on *all* contracts while those under that age would be completely immune from liability.[46] Its final report however recommended only limited reforms which have now been implemented by the Minors' Contracts Act 1987.[47] These include provision that minors' contracts should be capable of being ratified on majority and that in certain circumstances the supplier of goods to a minor should be entitled, in the event of non-payment, to recover them or the proceeds of sale representing them.

One approach to the position of those over 16 might be to recognise that, since they already have a substantial measure of legal capacity, they should be invested with a general capacity to perform *all* acts under the civil law. This solution has been provisionally put forward, subject to exceptions, by the Scottish Law Commission.[48] The drawback with this approach is that responsibility is a necessary concomitant of independence. Thus, the more freedom enjoyed by young people under the law, the more responsibility would be likely to be demanded of them.

[46] Law Com. Working Paper No. 81 on "Minors' Contracts" (1982) Part XII.
[47] Law Com. Report No. 134 on "Minors' Contracts" (1984). For an assessment of the 1987 Act see Jessica Holroyd "The Minors' Contracts Act 1987" (1987) 84 L.S.Gaz 2266.
[48] Scot. Law Com. Consultative Memorandum No. 65 on "Legal Capacity and Responsibility of Minors and Pupils" (1985).

There might, for example, be legitimate concern about making credit facilities generally available to young people for fear that they might behave irresponsibly and get into debt, although the greater fear might be that they would be exposed to exploitation by unscrupulous lenders.

To what extent does the law recognise the legal capacities of those *under* 16? This was another important aspect of the *Gillick* case.

(B) THE IMPACT OF THE GILLICK DECISION

We have seen that section 8(1) of the Family Law Reform Act 1969 gives those over 16 the right to consent to all forms of medical treatment. The question which the House of Lords had to determine was whether it was the intention of Parliament to withhold legal capacity from children below the statutory age. Prima facie it might have appeared that this was the purpose of drawing a clear line at 16 but this would have been to ignore section 8(3) which provides:

> "Nothing in this section shall be construed as making ineffective any consent which would have been effective if this section had not been enacted."

The majority took the view that subsection (1) had been enacted merely for the avoidance of doubt concerning the position of those over 16. It was therefore necessary to go on to consider whether at common law a minor under that age could in any circumstances provide a valid consent. It was held that, in the absence of an express statutory provision to the contrary, a child did not, by virtue of age alone, lack the necessary capacity. Lord Scarman said that the child acquires this capacity "where he reaches a sufficient understanding and intelligence to be capable of making up his own mind on the matter requiring decision." He went on to warn: "If the law should impose upon the process of 'growing-up' fixed limits where nature knows only a continuous process, the price would be artificiality and a lack of realism in an area where the law must be sensitive to human development and social change."[49] Lord Fraser agreed with the application of the maturity test to determine capacity but, as we have seen, did not take the view that satisfaction of this was enough *per se* to enable the girl to act

[49] n. 2, p. 186.

independently of her parents. The majority decision therefore rejects a rigid demarcation of capacities according to age and favours the adoption of the "mature minor rule" as the most significant determinant of capacity.

The crucial issue again is how far the *Gillick* reasoning may be lifted from the narrow context of contraception and applied generally to the capacities of young people under the civil law. In looking at this question the most important consideration would appear to be the presence or absence of legislation expressly governing the situation. It was the absence of such a provision relating to medical treatment which enabled the House of Lords to look to the common law and to apply the test of maturity. Section 8 of the Family Law Reform Act 1969 is unusual in that it prescribes a statutory age but preserves the validity of consents at common law. This two-tier approach is untypical in that where a statutory age is specified this will normally be conclusive of capacity. Otherwise there would be little point in having a statutory age. Clearly it would be absurd to imagine that Parliament has intended that precocious children under 16 should be permitted to opt out of the compulsory education system, marry or take up full-time employment. *Gillick* does not provide a legal basis for circumventing most age-related provisions. It can only be applied where statute is silent or in those rare cases where the fixed-age is not intended by Parliament to be conclusive of capacity.

Whether the mature minor rule can be applied universally to govern the relations between parent and child is a more difficult issue. The problematic situation will be where the child *does* have legal capacity to perform an action and the parent wishes to prevent this. If Parliament has recognised the legal capacities of young people of specified ages to take certain action irrespective of their level of maturity, it is not clear why parents and third parties should be legally empowered, by collusion, to restrict this independence on the somewhat dubious basis that a particular child is immature. Imagine the position of a 14 year old who wishes to take up part-time employment in a "Saturday job." Her parents do not wish her to take it for whatever reason and instruct the potential employer not to engage their daughter. Under the legislation applying to child employment the girl would not be prevented in law from taking the job.[50] But the legislation does not deal with the child's position in the family. It is probably the case

[50] s.18 of the Children and Young Persons Act 1933.

that Parliament did not consider at all the relationship between the child's capacity to take employment and the generalised parental power of control. It is not therefore clear whether the legislature was concerned simply to regulate the child's position *vis à vis* third parties (i.e. employers) or whether it also intended to affect the common law governing the child's relationship with his parents in relation to the matter of employment. It seems likely that Parliament's objective in setting a statutory age was to produce consistency and certainty in the rule governing the relations between children and wider society. Perhaps, therefore, the better view is that *Gillick* cannot be applied here since it was the intention of Parliament that *all* children should be allowed to take up limited employment. As a matter of policy, this interpretation would also assist third parties in their dealings with children, since they would not be obliged in law to take steps to ascertain the parental attitude in individual cases. It may therefore be that *Gillick* can never govern family relations where it is clear that parliament has invested the child with full legal capacity.

(C) EMANCIPATION

Where the law gives to adolescents a significant amount of independence, as it does in the case of those over 16, it is questionable how far it should provide at all for the continuance of parental control until majority. A young person over 16 might be thought to have a legitimate grievance if his parents are authorised to prevent him from doing things which the law allows him to do. Moreover it is not simply the young person who might wish to establish an independent legal status. The parents themselves might wish to be relieved from their legal responsibilities where their child has a separate *de facto* existence and no longer forms part of their family unit in any realistic sense.

The doctrine of emancipation has never formed part of English law but has long existed in the United States and has undergone something of a revival during the last 20 years.[51] A form of emancipation also exists in France.[52] Emancipation may be defined broadly as a legal procedure whereby parent and child are

---

[51] See Katz, Schroeder and Sidman, "Emancipating Our Children—Coming of Legal Age in America" 7 Fam.L.Q. 211 (1973); Cady, "Emancipation of Minors" 12 Conn.L.R. 62 (1979) and Dana F. Castle. "Early Emancipation Statutes: Should they Protect Parents as Well as Children?" 20 Fam.L.Q. 343 (1986).
[52] Discussed by the Scottish Law Commission, *op. cit.* n. 48, paras. 4.15–4.17.

mutually released from some or all of the legal incidents attaching to their relationship. In effect it is a process for obtaining a "divorce" from one another. As a by-product of this process the child may also be released from some, if not all, of his legal disabilities. In America it exists in two forms which have come to be known as "Judicial Emancipation" and "Statutory Emancipation." The former is taken to refer to a finding at common law that a child is emancipated. The latter is a statutory procedure whereby a petition may be presented to a court by a child that he be emancipated by order of the court.

The common law version or judicial emancipation requires renunciation of legal duties by a parent and cannot arise on the child's initiative alone. A finding that the child is emancipated is however to some extent dependent on the intent and conduct of the child. Factors such as leaving home and being self-supporting may be considered crucial in arriving at this conclusion. It is nonetheless established that the child himself may not unilaterally obtain a change in legal status through this process. Hence judicial emancipation has been described as a right of the *parent* rather than the child, although a more balanced view is that the "so-called parental right to effect an emancipation might be described more accurately as the right of negation; by refusing to consent the parent can prevent a finding of emancipation."[53] This form of emancipation usually arises in the context of civil actions, the success or failure of which turn on the existence of the parent-child relation. The emancipation question then represents a preliminary hurdle which has to be overcome. It is doubtful whether these principles would be appropriate in the less litigious environment of English society.

Statutory emancipation has greater potential. A large number of American states have now enacted emancipation statutes but these are by no means uniform in content or purpose.[54] The statutes enacted before 1970 were largely concerned with the limited purpose of removing the protections of minority which inhibited the child's ability to engage in business transactions.[55] An increase in the number of statutes since 1970 has been accompanied by a shift in emphasis whereby emancipation is now seen as a device for

[53] Castle, *op. cit.* n. 51, p. 358.
[54] Extracts of the emancipation statutes in California and Connecticut are set out in W. Wadlington, C. H. Whitebread and S. M. Davis, "Children in the Legal System" (1983), Chap. I.
[55] Castle, *loc. cit.* n. 53.

resolving family conflict by the legal termination of the parent-child relation.[56] Used in this way it may represent an alternative to public procedures for the removal of children from their parents where they are abused or neglected or where they are beyond parental control.

There is considerable variation in the preconditions for presenting emancipation petitions and in the effects of decrees. The basic procedure is that minors of a specified age (which varies between states) may present a petition to the court. If the decree is granted the petitioner will typically acquire all the rights and responsibilities of adulthood subject to any conditions which the court sees fit to impose. An emancipated minor may thus enter into all types of contract, consent to all forms of medical treatment, buy and sell land, decide where to live and work or the manner of his education, dispose of his property by will, etc. Essential conditions of emancipation are usually that the child should be living separate and apart from his parents and should have achieved financial self-sufficiency. In the light of these conditions the procedure may be seen as a process for bringing the formal legal position into line with the *de facto* situation.

In England there is no procedure approximating to emancipation. Where the age of capacity is lowered by statute for certain purposes this is of course a form of partial emancipation. But there exists no general legal procedure for the removal of the wider incapacities affecting minors or to bring about an early termination of the parent-child relation. The closest that English courts have come to this is their refusal to *enforce* parents' powers against the wishes of an older child. Thus in *Krishnan* v. *Sutton L.B.C.*[57] the court refused to order a local authority to return to her father a 17 year old girl in their voluntary care. She did not wish to return to him and the court decided that as she was old enough to decide these matters for herself it would not interfere. This is not the same as emancipation however since the court's order did not bring about any change in the legal status of parent and child *vis-à-vis* each other. In the context of that case emancipation would not, in any event, have been appropriate given that the girl was in care and was not living independently.

---

[56] *Ibid.* pp. 360–363.
[57] [1969] 3 All E.R. 1367.

4. Parents' Powers and Children's Liberties— A Question of Balance

The *Gillick* case illustrates that parents' powers and children's liberties may coexist and that it is the task of the law to establish mechanisms for balancing these competing interests. Before this position is reached there is the preliminary issue of whether a child has capacity *at all* under the civil law with respect to the matter being considered. If the child does not, the further question of how to balance the child's autonomy interest and parents' powers does not arise. If the child *does* have capacity under the civil law, this second issue must be addressed.

(A) CIVIL LAW CAPACITY—AGE OR MATURITY?

If it is considered desirable that persons under the age of majority should be accorded a limited amount of capacity under the civil law this could in theory be achieved either by the fixed-age technique, or by widespread application of the mature minor rule or by a combination of these techniques i.e. the fixed-age could be chosen for some areas with the mature minor rule applying to others. This is the approach in England but it appears to have arisen haphazardly over the years. For the sake of simplicity and coherence there is much to be said for adopting one technique to the exclusion of the other. There are advantages and disadvantages with each of them.

The fixed-age technique offers certainty and consistent treatment of young people in the relevant age bracket. This is surely an important practical consideration for third parties who will wish to know whether they are authorised to deal directly with children of different ages. This "across the board" equality according to age may also be seen as more egalitarian, a characteristic which some would regard as an essential prerequisite of children's rights.[58] But the existing age-related rules may be criticised as arbitrary and incoherent. Such rules should be kept under regular review and should be formulated in accordance with informed assessments of the cognitive development of children. Another criticism of the age-related approach is that its rigidity fails to take into account the different intellectual capacities and rates of development of individual children. The very justification for imposing legal

---

[58] *Post*, Chap. 9.

disabilities on children is that they lack sufficient understanding to perform certain acts in the law. If therefore it can be demonstrated that a *particular* child *does* exhibit sufficient maturity to enable him to exercise an informed choice, there may be no good reason for the law to deny him this opportunity.

Conversely, the mature minor rule admits of greater flexibility in distinguishing between levels of intellectual and emotional attainment in children. The application of the maturity test may, however, prove difficult in practice. Lord Scarman emphasised in *Gillick* that there are many components to legal capacity in the case of contraception. It was not sufficient, he said, that the girl should understand the nature of the choice proferred to her. She would also be required to possess sufficient maturity to enable her to understand the moral and family questions involved, the long-term problems associated with the emotional impact of pregnancy and its termination, and the health risks of sexual intercourse at her age.[59] Perhaps the principal criticism of the mature minor rule is that it suffers from the standard defect of indeterminate concepts in that it is dependent on the individualistic and possibly idiosyncratic evaluations of adult decision-makers. In short there would be nothing to prevent a finding that a child is immature wherever the decision-maker happens to disagree with the child's preferences.[60] This could be a recipe for unequal treatment of individual children in materially identical situations and might therefore be a serious threat to the advancement of children's rights. Even more fundamentally, it clearly cannot work in relation to those spheres such as education and child employment where the state wishes to establish a policy of universal application.

On balance therefore there is a strong case for the adoption of a rational system of age-related rules to govern the child's relations in wider society. In so far as *Gillick* suggests that these relations might be governed by the mature minor rule it is to be treated with caution. This aspect of the majority ruling should be confined to the particular sphere of medical treatment where the age-related rule is unusual in not

[59] n. 2, p. 189.
[60] See John Eekelaar, "The Emergence of Children's Rights" (1986) 6 *Oxford Journal of Legal Studies* 161, 181.

operating as a conclusive determinant of capacity. Later it will be suggested that a much better solution to the contraception question would be an unequivocal statutory rule conferring capacity on *all* children regardless of age.[61]

(B) THE CHILD IN THE FAMILY UNIT

It will now be assumed that the civil law has recognised the capacity of a child to act in a particular matter either under statute or because he has satisfied the maturity test. The question at this stage is whether this autonomy should be removed by the opposition of a parent. In the context of a functioning family it may well be that the mature minor approach is the best one to adopt since it provides a flexible mechanism for balancing family interests.

The *Gillick* decision rejects the notion that parental powers are absolute but it does not favour absolute autonomy for adolescents either. The speeches of both Lord Fraser and Lord Scarman support a participatory model of decision-making which entails an attempt by the doctor *in every case* to persuade the girl to allow her parents to be consulted. It is impossible to interpret this as support for the provision of contraceptives on demand which full autonomy would imply. The correct interpretation, it is suggested, is that the majority are according to parents *and* children qualified or relative autonomy. In the case of parents this implies that the doctor must have regard to their interests in being consulted. In the case of the girl it implies the right of self-help which enables her to seek professional advice and to participate in the decision-making process to an extent commensurate with her emotional and intellectual maturity. The test of maturity seems particularly well adapted to govern these relative interests.

As we have seen however, there is an argument that where the child has capacity under statute it is also Parliament's intention that these matters should be taken completely outside the control of parents. In the final analysis this must be a question of statutory interpretation and it is obvious, having regard to the different effects of the statutes governing marriage and medical treatment respectively, that the results of this exercise may differ.

Whatever may be the position under various statutes the more general issue of policy is whether the law should uphold parental

---

[61] *Post*, Chap. 6.

control over older teenagers. It may be that there is a case for introducing into England an emancipation procedure to enable older teenagers to obtain a judicial release from the parent-child relationship and to acquire sufficient legal capacities to maintain effectively a separate existence away from their parents' home. Where this is already the *de facto* position the purpose would be to give formal legal recognition that the young person is no longer a subordinate member of a family unit which has ceased to function. Foster and Freed in their celebrated Bill of Rights for children proposed that the child should have a right to emancipation from the parent-child relationship "when that relationship has broken down and the child has left home due to abuse, neglect, serious family conflict, or other sufficient cause and his best interests would be served by the termination of parental authority."[62] It might be argued that there would be no purpose in a formal decree of emancipation where the child is already *in fact* independent from his parents. This would be to assume, however, that the process is *solely* concerned with the relationship between parent and child. As we have observed, emancipation can also have important legal consequences for the child and for third parties. Thus the emancipated minor may deal with the latter as an adult. He would also be beyond the scope of the child care procedures. The decree would not therefore be superfluous in these circumstances.

An alternative method of liberating children over 16 would be to reduce further the age of majority thereby granting them adult status at a stroke. It is suggested however that this would be manifestly undesirable in view of the large numbers of teenagers who remain as members of their parents' family unit. To confer complete legal autonomy on them would be artificial since it would not reflect the factual dependence which exists in most cases.

The argument against emancipation is based on this factual dependency. The process should not be seen as entirely advantageous to children since it will not only liberate them from their parents' control but will also terminate their parents' financial and other obligations towards them.

It is also for this reason that some emancipation statutes allow parents to petition. It is fair to observe however that parental control and parental financial obligations need not *necessarily* go hand in hand. In English law a parent's duty to maintain remains in full force throughout the child's minority while, as we have

---

[62] Foster and Freed, "A Bill of Rights for Children" 6 Fam.L.Q. 343 at 347 (1972).

seen, parental control gradually diminishes as the child approaches adulthood. Nevertheless, the express purpose of formal emancipation is to achieve a complete severance of the child's legal position from his parents before he attains the statutory age of majority. In these circumstances there might be legitimate objections to the preservation of parental support obligations. In short, the view might be taken that the child should not be permitted "to have his cake and eat it." Hence emancipation may have serious legal consequences for children who, having left the family home, are unable to achieve economic self-sufficiency outside it. These consequences were until recently ameliorated in England by the existence of the independent right of children who had attained 16 and were no longer in "relevant education" to claim income support (formerly supplementary benefit).[63] The parental claim to child benefit correspondingly ceased in these circumstances.

These concerns were exhibited in the United States by a reluctance on the part of judges to find that parental support rights had been terminated. They often found as a result that the conditions for emancipation were not made out or they resorted to the concept of partial emancipation.[64]

Whatever legal techniques are utilised, the true value of *Gillick* has been the way in which it was highlighted the independent interests of parents and children and the need for the law to find a means of accommodating their potentially conflicting claims.

---

[63] s. 20(3) of the Social Security Act 1986. The problem of economic self-sufficiency for 16 and 17 year olds living outside the family home will now, however, be exacerbated by the removal of this independent entitlement, albeit subject to exceptions, by s. 4 of the Social Security Act 1988.

[64] See Katz, Schroeder and Sidman *op. cit.* n. 51, pp. 225–227.

4. Local Authorities and the Family

1. Introduction

In this chapter and the next we discuss the State's interest in children and consider how this interrelates with the interests of parents in determining their own child-rearing practices and the independent interests of children and young people.

The protective role of the state towards children is reflected in a long history of legislative measures. Some of this legislation was genuinely motivated by a concern for child protection, while some of it is more satisfactorily explained as a mechanism for the social control of children who were perceived as threats to the civil order. Hence the child care legislation was originally designed primarily to control delinquents and was not the product of a welfarist drive to protect children from abuse or neglect.[1] This feature has given rise to a blurring of the distinction between these two categories of children which is perpetuated in the modern statutory code and child care procedures.[2] Thus it has been remarked that "legislation and procedures designed primarily for one purpose are being used for a wholly different purpose."[3]

There is a continuing debate on the permissible level of state intervention in the family. One view is that in recent years there has been an escalation in intervention by local

---

[1] The historical development of legislation affecting children is traced in J. M. Eekelaar and T. Murray, "Childhood as a Social Problem: A Survey of the History of Legal Regulation" (1984) 11 J.L.S. 207.

[2] The statutory code is now principally constituted by the Children and Young Persons Act 1969 and the Child Care Act 1980.

[3] John Eekelaar, Robert Dingwall and Topsy Murray, "Victims or Threats? Children in Care Proceedings" [1982] J.S.W.L. 68.

authorities which calls for the imposition of greater legal controls over their social services departments.[4] This school of thought has been challenged by Dingwall, Eekelaar and Murray who argue that it is unsupported by empirical evidence.[5] The authors conducted a study of child care practice in three local authority areas. They concluded that child care agencies operate within a framework of cultural limitations embodied in what they call the "rule of optimism." When coupled with structural restraints in agency organisation, they argue that the result is that agency staff will prefer the least coercive form of intervention in the family which it is possible to follow in the circumstances.[6] This implies that wherever possible the observed conduct of parents will be interpreted in a way which is least discrediting. Put crudely, they will get the benefit of the doubt.

According to this thesis only the worst cases of abuse and neglect are likely to result in the removal of the child from the family and it is denied that there has been a dramatic upsurge in welfare intervention.

This academic disagreement is mirrored in ambivalent public attitudes which seem to lurch between support for parents' rights and condemnation of "agency failure" whenever a well publicised child homicide occurs. A comparatively recent example was the death of Jasmine Beckford.[7] Conversely, a public furore was created in June 1987 by the alleged wrongful diagnosis of child sexual abuse by Cleveland Social Services which had led to large scale compulsory removal of children into care.[8]

[4] Several predominantly anti-interventionist collections of essays have been published. See for example H. Geach and E. Szwed (eds), *Providing Civil Justice for Children* (1983). A. Morris, H. Giller, E. Szwed and H. Geach, *Justice for Children* (1980) and L. Taylor, R. Lacey and D. Bracken, *In Whose Best Interests?* (1980).

[5] R. Dingwall, J. M. Eekelaar and T. Murray, "*The Protection of Children: State Intervention and Family Life*" (1983). See also Robert Dingwall and John Eekelaar, "Rethinking Child Protection" in M. D. A. Freeman (ed.), *The State, the Law and the Family* (1984), p. 93.

[6] *Ibid.*, pp. 218–219.

[7] See "A Child in Trust," the report of the Panel of Inquiry into the circumstances surrounding the death of Jasmine Beckford (1985). For a critique of the Report see Robert Dingwall, "The Jasmine Beckford Affair" (1986) 49 M.L.R. 489.

[8] A Committee of Inquiry was set up to look into the Cleveland affair. Its report is still awaited at the time of writing. On the problems associated with the diagnosis of sexual abuse see Sean Enright, "Refuting Allegations of Child Sexual Abuse" (1987) 131 N.L.J. 633, 672.

Despite this apparent conflict between family autonomy and child protection they are not necessarily incongruous ideas since public involvement in the family of a *supportive* nature may be the best means of assisting both parents and children in a difficult family situation. This notion of family support envisages a partnership between parents and the state in the process of raising children. In 1985 an Interdepartmental Working Party published its "Review of Child Care Law" (hereafter "the Review") which made a host of recommendations for the improvement of the law in this area. Its proposals were substantially (though not entirely) accepted by the Government in a White Paper entitled "The Law on Child Care and Family Services" (hereafter "The White Paper") published in January 1987.[9] Many of the suggested changes are designed to emphasise the partnership between parents and local authorities and to improve the public image of care by providing for greater involvement of parents in decisions affecting children in care. Such a partnership necessarily involves a power-sharing arrangement between parents and authorities. Under existing law the precise distribution of power between them is uncertain and it is one of the aims of the reforms that the mutual rights and responsibilities of parents and local authorities should be clearly defined by statute.

2. Compulsory Intervention in the Family

The task for the law in formulating grounds for state intervention is to strike a balance which offers to children protection from the risk of positive harm, but which does not represent a threat to the security of families by allowing the removal of children simply because they are not receiving optimum care. It would be unduly indulgent to protection agencies to invest them with power to remove children from parents on the sole basis that some other person could do better than them in raising their children.

The principal legislation governing the removal of abused and neglected children into care is the Children and Young Persons Act 1969 (hereafter the 1969 Act) which also governs procedures relating to delinquents. Under the 1969 Act the local authority may seek an order of the juvenile court committing a child to its care. It is important to distinguish it at the outset from the

[9] Cm. 62.

voluntary care system under the Child Care Act 1980 (hereafter the 1980 Act) whereby a child may be *received* into care in various specified circumstances but never taken into care against the wishes of a parent (unmarried fathers excepted). Parental rights may, however, be removed compulsorily where a child originally entered voluntary care. This is achieved by the authority passing a resolution under section 3 of the 1980 Act. It should be emphasised that this is a purely administrative procedure within the local authority and that no judicial inquiry or court order is initially required. Where a resolution is passed the authority must give written notice to the parent on whose account it was passed. This is so even where the parent may have consented to the resolution.[10] If the parent then objects within one month of service of the notice, the resolution will lapse unless the authority brings the matter before the juvenile court within one month of service of the parent's counter-notice.[11] On hearing the complaint, the juvenile court may order the continuation of the resolution where it is satisfied that the grounds relied on by the authority existed at the time of passing the resolution, that *a* ground (not necessarily the same ground as that originally relied on by the authority[12]) exists at the date of the hearing, and that it would be in the interests of the child to do so.[13]

Considerable controversy surrounds the framing of the grounds for compulsory action. At one extreme the anti-interventionists argue that it should take place only in very narrowly defined circumstances. The arch-exponents of this view are the influential American writers, Goldstein, Freud and Solnit.[14] They would limit state powers to situations in which parents voluntarily place their children in public care, the death or disappearance of parents, conviction of a serious sexual offence against the child, serious bodily injury inflicted against the child and failure to provide medical treatment, but only where the child would face death as a result. The narrowness and rigidity of these grounds have been criticised by Freeman who contends that Goldstein et al, in their anxiety to preserve the family as a private sphere, "have erred in

---

[10] This change was brought about by Sched. 2, para. 46 of the Health and Social Services and Social Security Adjudications Act 1983 following complaints that some parents were unwittingly "signing away" their rights.

[11] s.3(2)–(5) of the Child Care Act 1980.

[12] *W. v. Nottinghamshire County Council* [1982] Fam. 53.

[13] s.3(6).

[14] *Before the Best Interests of the Child* (1980).

drawing the line too close to the parents' interests and too far from the children's."[15]

At the other end of the spectrum, protectionists argue that the State should enjoy a flexible power to take over the care of a child wherever this can be demonstrated to be in the best interests of the child. In fact this is already the basis on which the child may be placed in care under the inherent jurisdiction of the wardship court.[16] This approach may be criticised both for its indeterminacy and because the adoption of the welfare principle as the normal ground for care would represent a decisive shift in the balance between family privacy and state interference.[17] These considerations lie at the heart of the jurisdictional issues which arise from the relationship between the *parens patriae* function of the Crown and the statutory code for child care.[18]

The existing grounds for compulsory action lie between these two extremes. Under section 1 of the 1969 Act a specific precondition must be satisfied, coupled with a general requirement that in every case the child is in need of care and control which he is unlikely to receive unless the order is made. Finally, the court has a discretion to determine whether or not it should make an order. In exercising its discretion it is required by section 44(1) of the Children and Young Persons Act 1933 to have regard to the welfare of the child. In other words, the court is not obliged to make an order where a primary condition and the care and control test are both satisfied. It will need to satisfy itself that the making of a care order would be the right solution to the child's predicament.[19] The primary conditions are significantly wider than those advocated by Goldstein et al, but much more restrictive than would be the position under a broad welfare criterion. They are that:

(a) the child's proper development is being avoidably prevented or neglected or his health is being avoidably impaired or neglected or he is being ill-treated; or

---

[15] M. D. A. Freeman, "Freedom and the Welfare State: Child-Rearing, Parental Autonomy and State Intervention" [1983] J.S.W.L. 70, 91.

[16] The best modern example is the Court of Appeal decision in *Re C.B. (A Minor)* [1981] 1 All E.R. 16.

[17] See Eekelaar et al, *op. cit.* n. 3, p. 69.

[18] *Post*, Chap. 5.

[19] Alternative orders which the court might make in appropriate circumstances are an order that the child's parent or guardian enter into a recognisance to take proper care of him and exercise proper control over him, a supervision order or a hospital or guardianship order within the meaning of the Mental Health Act 1983. (s.1(3) of the 1969 Act).

(b) it is probable that condition (a) will be satisfied having regard to the fact that the court or another court has found that it is or was satisfied in the case of another child or young person who is or was a member of the household to which he belongs;

(bb) it is probable that condition (a) will be satisfied having regard to the fact that a person who has been convicted of an offence under Schedule 1 of the Children and Young Persons Act 1933 (essentially violent or sexual offences against children) is, or may become, a member of the same household as the child or young person; or

(c) he is exposed to moral danger;

(d) he is beyond the control of his parent or guardian; or

(e) he is of compulsory school age and is not receiving efficient full-time education suitable to his age, ability and aptitude and to any special educational needs he may have; or

(f) he is guilty of an offence, excluding homicide.

The grounds for passing a resolution under section 3 of the 1980 Act are:

(a) that the child's parents are dead and he has no guardian or custodian; or

(b) that a parent of his —

(i) has abandoned him, or

(ii) suffers from some permanent disability rendering him incapable of caring for the child, or

(iii) suffers from a mental disorder within the meaning of the Mental Health Act 1983, which renders him unfit to have the care of the child, or

(iv) is of such habits or modes of life as to be unfit to have the care of the child, or

(v) has so consistently failed without reasonable cause to discharge the obligations of a parent as to be unfit to have the care of the child; or

(c) that a resolution under (b) is in force in relation to one parent of the child who is, or is likely to become, a member of the household comprising the child and his other parent; or

(d) that throughout the three years preceding the passing of the resolution the child has been in the care of a local authority under section 2 of the 1980 Act, or partly in the care of a local authority and partly in the care of a voluntary organisation.

The grounds bear some resemblance to the 1969 Act conditions but are by no means identical. In particular the 1980 Act grounds generally focus on the *parents'* behaviour or condition whereas the 1969 Act conditions are more child-centred. As noted in the Review, one consequence of this is that where a resolution is passed on ground (b) this has the effect of removing only the rights of the incapable or unfit parent although the rights of the other parent might then be removed on ground (c).[20] The local authority must believe that one or more of the conditions is satisfied.

Various criticisms may be levelled at individual grounds. The three year ground can be criticised for offending against the "voluntary principle" in that it allows a voluntary arrangement to slip into compulsion simply by the effluxion of time.[21] The "moral danger" condition under the 1969 Act and the "habits and modes of life" condition under the 1980 Act may be thought to allow subjective value judgments to intrude. They raise moral questions which are difficult to apply in a pluralistic society where there is no absolute consensus on what is an acceptable family environment for children.[22] The condition of "being beyond the control of his parent or guardian" is open to the general objections which can be made to "status offences." The main criticism is a civil liberties argument that the child should not be penalised for non-criminal misbehaviour. But a more general objection to the grounds for compulsory action is based on their technicality which has resulted in a significant increase in the use of wardship by local authorities in an effort to circumvent the restrictions of the statutory code.[23]

Perhaps the most problematic of these technicalities is that, subject to the special conditions relating to previous abuse or neglect of a child in the same household or the presence in that household of a child offender, a care order may not be made *solely* on the strength of a risk of harm to the child at some future time.[24] The other conditions must be satisfied at the time when proceedings are commenced. This has caused particular difficulty in

[20] Para. 15.5.
[21] See, *e.g. W.* v. *Nottinghamshire County Council* n. 12.
[22] See, *e.g. Alhaji Mohammed* v. *Knott* [1969] 1 Q.B. 1.
[23] *Post*, Chap. 5.
[24] *Essex County Council* v. *T.L.R. and K.B.R.* (1978) 143 J.P. 309.

relation to newly born babies who will not realistically be in the care of their parents until they leave hospital. But if social services are concerned that such a child is "at risk" they may not wish to allow him to leave with the parents. How can they establish the necessary evidence of *present* abuse or neglect? The matter came before the House of Lords in *D. (A minor)* v. *Berkshire County Council.*[25] 1w,03,06,18   The local authority relied here on section 1(2)(a) of the 196! Act. The mother was a registered drug addict who, against medical advice, persisted in using drugs excessively (both orally and intravenously) while pregnant. She did so realising that she might cause harm to her unborn child. At birth the baby was found to be suffering from drug withdrawal symptoms which necessitated intensive care in hospital for two months. The only adverse behaviour alleged against the mother was the abuse of her own bodily health during pregnancy which directly affected the foetus and was manifested at birth.

Hollings J. decided that this conduct was insufficient since the 1969 Act contemplated some action towards a living child and the mother's care had not yet been tested.[26] The House of Lords disagreed. It was held that the statutory expression "is being" envisaged a continuing situation which involved consideration of the past, present and future development of the child. In embarking on this inquiry it was open to the court to have regard to events which occurred while the child was *in utero*. Lord Brandon thought that a liberal construction should be placed on the statute since it was designed for the protection of children who might be only a few weeks or a few days old. Lord Goff laid stress on the need to establish a continuum of neglect impairing the child's health. In his view it would not be sufficient for the child to be born with defects arising from maternal neglect during pregnancy unless the court was satisfied that this was likely to continue after birth.

For this reason it is felt that the speculation that expectant mothers who smoke, drink or fail to attend ante-natal clinics during pregnancy will thereby risk losing their children through care procedures, is unnecessarily alarmist. These activities only affect the health of the *unborn* child since this is inextricably linked

---

[25] [1987] 1 All E.R. 20 (D.C.); 27 (C.A.) and 33 (H.L.). For an assessment of the case see Andrew Bainham, "Protecting the Unborn—New Rights in Gestation?" (1987) 50 M.L.R. 361.

[26] "Child" is defined by s.70 of the 1969 Act as "a person under the age of fourteen."

to the mother's health during pregnancy. They do not affect the health of the *living* child who has an existence independent from the mother. Only where a parent is continuing to disregard the welfare of the living child will care proceedings be appropriate.[27] Indeed it is only in these circumstances that it will be possible to satisfy the care and control test which was not in issue in the *Berkshire* case.

This case is a classic illustration of the way in which the technical conditions of the statutory code could stand in the way of the protection of a child. Only by straining language and coming close to investing the foetus with the legal status of a "child" could the desired result be achieved.

On a more general level the present grounds are defective in their lack of uniformity or coherence. This is compounded by the fact that children may also be committed to care in wardship, divorce and certain other family proceedings on yet another basis.[28] In these proceedings the ground for the care order is that there are "exceptional circumstances making it impracticable or undesirable" for the child to be under the care of a parent or other individual.[29]

The White Paper accepts the recommendations in the Review that the resolution procedure should be abolished. Despite embracing a judicial procedure for challenging a resolution once made, the administrative nature of the procedure has been widely condemned as offending against the rules of natural justice.[30] The general principle is accepted that the transfer to local authorities of parents' powers and responsibilities should only be effected by a full court hearing following due legal processes.[31] It is also proposed that all existing grounds for compulsory action should be subsumed in a single composite ground which would apply in all proceedings in which the compulsory transfer of parental rights is

---

[27] In this case the mother and father continued to be drug-addicted following the birth of the child and the court must have felt that the magistrates were justified in thinking that the parents were unfit to safeguard the child's future health. By analogy a mother who, following the birth, is persistently drunk might be found unfit to have the care of her child.

[28] For a full account see Law Com. Working Paper No. 100, "Care, Supervision and Interim Orders in Custody Proceedings" (1987), Part II.

[29] For an example of a care order in divorce proceedings see *R. v. G. (Surrey County Council Intervening)* [1984] Fam. 100.

[30] See particularly M. Adcock, R. White and O. Rowlands, *The Administrative Parent* (1983).

[31] White Paper, para. 5.

sought apart from wardship.[32] This would assimilate the grounds in care and family proceedings.

A broad welfare test was rejected in that it would lead to widely varying and subjective interpretations and would not offer a sufficient degree of statutory protection against unwarranted state intervention in family life. The preferred ground concentrates on the risk of harm to the child coupled with a requirement that the making of a care order would be justified applying a broad welfare test. The freestanding conditions such as those relating to moral danger, truancy and parental unfitness would disappear although situations which they might have covered may also satisfy the new ground. Three elements will in future have to be proved. These are:

(a) evidence of harm or likely harm to the child; and that
(b) this is attributable to the absence of a reasonable standard of parental care or the child being beyond parental control; and
(c) that the order proposed is the most effective means available to the court of safeguarding the child's welfare.[33]

The reference to "likely harm" is designed to overcome the restriction on orders in cases of apprehended harm. It will be possible for a care order to be made where there is a risk of future harm and it is anticipated that this will lead to a reduction in the use of wardship by local authorities. This will also be important where a parent wishes to resume the care of a child in voluntary care. The local authority may be able to forestall this by commencing proceedings for the transfer of parental rights founded on the risk of harm to the child. This may prove to be an invaluable safeguard given the proposal that a parent should no longer be obliged to give 28 days' notice of his intention to remove a child who has been in voluntary care for six months or more.[34] The return home of children in care is an area in which there is great public concern, heightened by the Jasmine Beckford inquiry, which culminated in the enactment of the Children and Young Persons (Amendment) Act 1986. As yet unimplemented, this provides,

[32] para. 59.
[33] *Ibid.*
[34] para. 22.

inter alia, for regulations to be made requiring consultation and medical and other supervision in such cases.

The 1986 Act and the White Paper proposals taken together are further evidence of the continuing tension between child protection and respect for family independence. Ultimately all that the legislation can seek to do is to achieve a reasonable balance between them. This quest for the right balance is evident in the new ground. In particular, when applying the harm criterion, it is envisaged that the court will be required to balance the chance of the harm occurring against the magnitude of that harm if it does occur.[35]

3. State Support for the Family

So far we have been considering the state's role in restraining behaviour which may be harmful to children. But the state also has a positive and supportive function in relation to families which is reflected most obviously in the provision of health, welfare and housing benefits, much of which is directed specifically at families with children. One of the main themes of the Review was the need to present the care option as a family service provided by the local authority. This approach was accepted in the White Paper which adopts as one of its guiding principles that "services to families in need of help should be arranged in a voluntary partnership with the parents."[36]

In theory the existing child care legislation gives precedence to family support and preventive work with families in difficulty. The leading provision is section 1 of the 1980 Act which provides:

> "It shall be the duty of every local authority to make available such advice, guidance and assistance as may promote the welfare of children by diminishing the need to receive children into or keep them in care under this Act or to bring children before a juvenile court; and any provision made by a local authority under this subsection may, if the local authority think fit, include provision for giving assistance in kind, or in exceptional circumstances, in cash."

[35] para. 60.
[36] para. 5.

The section clearly suggests that a child should remain in his natural family wherever possible and this is reinforced by section 2(3) which provides that, where a child has had to go into care, the authority is under a duty to endeavour to secure that the child's care is taken over by a parent, guardian, relative or friend in so far as this is consistent with his welfare.

The Review was concerned about the way in which the existing preventive duty is framed in the legislation. Its statutory form was criticised in that it "centres on the negative aim of keeping children out of care and court, laying insufficient stress on the value of positive family support, and gives the impression of care as a last resort."[37] Accordingly, the White Paper provides that authorities should no longer be under a statutory duty to diminish the need to receive children into care. Instead the legislation should underline the positive aim of providing support to the family and reducing the risk of long-term family breakdown.[38] To this end it is proposed that authorities should have a broad "umbrella" power to provide services to promote the care and upbringing of children. Their preventive duties should remain only in relation to *compulsory* care.[39] The duty to diminish the need for this would continue on a generalised level emphasising that the provision of services to that end should be on a scale "appropriate to the needs of the area."

The duty to receive children into care is contained in section 2 of the 1980 Act. Of the 68,000 children in care on March 31, 1985, 31,000 had entered care by this route.[40] An authority has a *duty* to receive a child into care where he has no parent or guardian or has been abandoned or where his parent or guardian is unable to take care of him either temporarily or permanently. In every case the intervention of the council must be necessary in the interests of the child's welfare.

The Review recommended that voluntary care be replaced by a new concept of "shared care" which would be complemented by a family service for short-term assistance to be known as "respite care."[41] The respite care model already

[37] Review, para. 5.10.
[38] White Paper, para. 22.
[39] para. 18.
[40] para. 1.
[41] Review, Chaps. 6 and 7.

exists in relation to handicapped children[42] and the Review proposed its extension to all children who might need it. It is an arrangement which is designed to provide a short break for parents who, perhaps because of illness or some other temporary difficulty, require assistance with the care of a child. Under this regime the primary responsibility for the child would remain with the parents who would delegate day-to-day care to the person actually looking after the child. Such cases are at present dealt with by means of a voluntary reception into care but this was felt to be associated with an erosion of parental rights and responsibilities which was inappropriate in cases of temporary need. The local authority's functions would have been limited to providing a range of placements, referring parents to them and making appropriate arrangements for supervision of the placement.[43] Respite care would have lasted for a maximum continuous period of one month or a cumulative total of three months in any 12. If the child remained away from home after this period care would have continued under the shared model.[44]

The distinctive legal characteristic of this form of care would have been that it would have involved no transfer of parental powers and duties to the local authority apart from the statutory duties regarding placement. The substitute care-givers would have acquired no parental powers going beyond those necessary to enable them to discharge the duties which attach to actual custody of a child.

The new concept of shared care would have been based on the existing voluntary care scheme but was intended to embrace statutory clarification of the mutual rights and responsibilities of parents and authorities, to provide for greater participation by parents whenever possible and to promote a positive image of care as a family service.[45]

The White Paper however favours the retention of the voluntary care system subject to reforms which would emphasise the voluntary partnership between parents and local authorities. It was accepted that their mutual rights and responsibilities would need to be spelled out in legislation. But the Government did not think the distinction between respite care and shared care to be

[42] Under Sched. 8 of the National Health Service Act 1977 and s.21 of the National Assistance Act 1948.
[43] Review, para. 6.3.
[44] paras. 6.5–6.6.
[45] para. 3.10.

"readily sustainable in practice" and concluded that "it would not be helpful to make this distinction in law."[46]

It may be that the distinction between respite care and voluntary or shared care is in any case more illusory than real. The main point of distinction appears to be that some formal powers would pass to the authority under the latter but not under the former arrangement where the authority's powers would be wholly dependent on parental delegation. But the reformed voluntary care scheme will also depend to a very large extent on parents' co-operation with local authorities which in practice may be difficult to distinguish from a delegation of parental functions.

4. Voluntary Partnership or Balance of Power?

The idea of a voluntary partnership between parents and local authorities raises questions about the allocation of their mutual rights and responsibilities towards the child. Are parents entitled to be consulted on the child's placement and kept informed of any proposed changes in this respect? Is the authority entitled to change the child's religion or decide major medical issues affecting him? How far is the child himself entitled to be involved in decisions affecting him? What opportunity do parents and children have to challenge decisions of the local authority with which they disagree? The partnership ideal is one of harmonious co-operation but the care process is fraught with potential for conflict. Where such a conflict arises it is important that the legal system should recognise and accommodate the various competing interests before major decisions are taken. Moreover the existence of the voluntary partnership begs the question whether children themselves are to be admitted to this partnership.

(A) THE LEGAL EFFECTS OF THE CARE PROCESS

(i) Parents and the local authority

The White Paper identifies a lack of clarity in the mutual rights and responsibilities of parents and local authorities as perhaps the most striking defect in the present law.[47] Just as the criteria for admission to care differ according to the route whereby the child

[46] White Paper, para. 26.
[47] para. 7.

enters care, so also the legal effects of care depend on which procedure is chosen.[48]

The theoretical basis of reception into care under the 1980 Act is the "voluntary principle." Under this procedure the authority does not acquire a parental status since the bulk of parental rights do not pass to it but remain vested in the parent or guardian. But inevitably certain powers associated with parenthood must be transferred if the authority is to be able to discharge its duties toward the child. It will of course have the same basic duties to cater for the child's material needs which are imposed upon any person having the actual care of a child.[49] Additionally, certain express duties are imposed by the Act which include the provision of accommodation and maintenance[50] and the general duty, in reaching decisions relating to the child, to give "first considera-tion" to his welfare.[51] The authority is also obliged to review the case of each child in care every six months.[52] These statutory duties also apply to children in compulsory care under the 1969 Act.

The flavour of voluntary care is therefore that the local authority acquires duties rather than rights. The legislation is silent on whether the wider custodial powers of parents to decide matters of upbringing are to be exercisable by the authority either solely or jointly with the parents. There is no express provision, for example, determining whether it is obliged to consult the parents regarding placements or the provision of medical treatment. In practice authorities obtain the written consent of parents authoris-ing them to arrange medical and dental treatment for the child while in care.

The voluntary principle might be thought to imply that the child should be immediately returned on a parental request. After all, many children enter this form of care not because of parents' unfitness or shortcomings but because of some temporary family difficulty such as illness. Section 2(3) of the 1980 Act seemed to confirm this view by providing that a local authority is not

---

[48] For an illuminating discussion of the legal effect of the different routes into care see Susan Maidment, "The Fragmentation of Parental Rights and Children in Care" [1981] J.S.W.L. 21.

[49] These include the provision of adequate food, clothing, medical aid and lodging. See s.1(2) Children and Young Persons Act 1933.

[50] s.21.

[51] s.18.

[52] s.20.

authorised "to keep a child in their care under this section if any parent or guardian desires to take over the care of the child." But section 2(2) requires the authority "to keep the child in their care so long as the welfare of the child appears to them to require it." Further, where the child has been in care for more than six months a parent must give 28 days' notice to the authority of his intention to resume care and control and it is a criminal offence to remove the child in contravention of this requirement.[53] In *London Borough of Lewisham* v. *Lewisham Juvenile Court Justices*[54] the House of Lords decided that a child remains in care under section 2 despite a parent's 28 days' notice provided that the child has not been physically removed or delivered up to the local authority. The House also decided that the effect of section 2(2) and section 2(3) was that the local authority was not under a mandatory duty to return the child on demand and that in essence it had 28 days' breathing space in which to decide whether to take further action to secure a firm legal basis for keeping the child in care. The current options are either to pass a resolution assuming parental rights under section 3 or, if the authority is concerned that a ground may not exist, to seek care and control in wardship proceedings. But the authority has no residual discretion to keep the child in care following a parental request for return unless it takes one of these legal steps. Where the child has been in care for less than six months the authority's position is more precarious since the notice provision does not apply. Prima facie, a parent is entitled to remove the child summarily. Even here, however, the authority will be entitled, applying *Lewisham*, to retain the child for just long enough to enable it to pass a resolution or ward the child, assuming that the parent has not already suceeded in regaining physical care of the child.

This position will change when the reforms in the White Paper are implemented. The notice requirement was thought to be inconsistent with the concept of the voluntary partnership and will be abolished. This may give rise to some concern that the child will be inadequately protected but it will remain the case that a local authority considering the return of a child will need to be satisfied that this is consistent with his welfare. Thus, the authority will still be entitled to retain care at least long enough to enable it to seek an emergency protection order. This can then be followed by an

[53] s.13.
[54] [1980] A.C. 273.

application for a care order.[55] The White Paper also deals with one of the major criticisms of the voluntary system. This is that because the respective powers and duties of authorities and parents are unclear there can be "a blurring of the very real distinction between the position of parents of children in care under a voluntary arrangement and those whose children are committed to care following a court order transferring parental powers and responsibilities to the local authority."[56] It is proposed that parents will retain all their powers and responsibilities except those which are expressly delegated by them to the authority to enable it to look after the child. It is envisaged that matters such as the initial placement, schooling and access and any subsequent changes to these arrangements will be settled by mutual agreement tailored to the individual circumstances of the family.[57] The local authority will be placed under specific statutory responsibilities, in addition to those flowing from actual custody, which will apply to *all* children in their care.[58]

The legal effects of the two compulsory procedures are broadly similar. Where a care order is made by the juvenile court the local authority has the same powers and duties as the child's parent or guardian would have apart from the order.[59] Similarly, a section 3 resolution vests in the authority "the parental rights and duties with respect to that child." In each case statute provides that the council may not change the religion of the child[60] and that the parent's right to refuse or consent to adoption is preserved.[61] Equally the parental duty to maintain is preserved.[62] Part III of the 1980 Act, which governs the treatment of children in care, applies equally to both situations. The main difference between the effects of the two procedures is that a resolution transfers to the council only those rights and duties held by the parent on whose account the resolution was passed. Where parental rights were held jointly with another person (in most cases the other natural parent) the rights and duties will, as a result of the resolution,

---

[55] paras. 22–23.
[56] para. 27.
[57] para. 23.
[58] para. 27.
[59] Child Care Act 1980, s.10(2).
[60] s.4(3); s.10(3).
[61] s.3(10).
[62] s.4(2).

"be vested in the local authority jointly with that other person."[63] Apart from these specific provisions there is no general definition of the respective powers of local authorities and parents. In particular it is uncertain whether the authority may consent to the marriage of a child in its care or whether it may administer his property.

The legal effects of a care order in family proceedings are even less clear. Under the relevant provisions the authority is required to receive the child into its care as if under section 2 of the Child Care Act 1980 with the important difference that it is obliged to keep the child in care despite parental requests for his return. Part III of the 1980 Act (which governs the treatment of children in care) also applies. Beyond this the authority acquires no parental rights and in certain instances there is some doubt about the precise distribution of power between the authority and the court which committed the child to its care. This is because, where the order was made by the High Court or a divorce county court, the court retains the right to give directions to the authority. We explore this later when we consider the relationship between the *parens patriae* function of the Crown and the statutory powers and responsibilities of local authorities.[64]

One of the main objectives of the Review and White Paper is to harmonise the effects of care orders made in care and family proceedings.[65] Any differences between the effects of a resolution and those of a care order will disappear with the abolition of the resolution procedure. It is intended under the reformed legislation that parental powers and responsibilities will formally pass to the local authority. It is recognised however that the child may often return home while in care and that in many cases it will continue to be important to involve the parents in decisions affecting the child. To this end authorities will be required to inform and consult parents on major decisions such as where a child is to live and on access arrangements.[66]

(ii) Children and the local authority

So far we have been examining the position of the local authority *vis-à-vis* the parents under various care procedures. We

---

[63] s.3(1).
[64] *Post*, Chap. 5.
[65] White Paper, para. 36.
[66] para. 35.

must now consider briefly how far the authority is required by law to take account of the wishes of children in its care. Under section 18 of the 1980 Act local authorities are required, in reaching any decision relating to a child in their care, to ascertain so far as is practicable the wishes and feelings of the child regarding the decision and give due consideration to them having regard to his age and understanding. Failing to comply with these requirements may lead to judicial review of the council's decision. There have, for example, been some successful challenges to the proposed closure of children's homes where the respective authorities have failed to give first consideration to the interests of individual children who would be affected by the closures.[67] There is evidence to suggest however that in practice the wishes of children in care are not accommodated as fully as they might be and that this is one of the chief complaints of the children themselves. Research by the National Children's Bureau among a group of young people in care revealed dissatisfaction with the opportunities for consultation over decisions affecting them and calls for the right to know about the development of plans for their future.[68]

The requirement of section 18 and the practice of authorities must now be reassessed in the light of *Gillick*. This decision, on the interpretation adopted in Chapter 3 supports the right of a mature child to participate in all decisions affecting him, the implications of which he is able to understand. In theory this is what section 18 already requires, but it may be that *Gillick* will give rise to a climate in which there may be greater willingness to challenge the decisions of local authorities which, it can be shown, were taken without appropriate consultation with the child in question. The difficulties associated with the test of maturity resurface in this context. There is ample scope for disagreement on the *weight* to be attached to a child's views and the evaluation of maturity is dependent on subjective assessments, in this case by social workers.

The more radical interpretation of *Gillick* supports the right of young people with the requisite capacity to take independent decisions. On this analysis it might be argued that the local authority is *obliged* to comply with the mature child's wishes. It might be contended that the authority cannot enjoy a degree of

---

[67] See *Liddle* v. *Sunderland B.C.* (1983) 13 Fam.Law 250; *R.* v. *Solihull M.B.C. ex. p. C.* [1984] F.L.R. 363 and *R.* v. *Avon C.C. ex. p. K* [1986] 1 F.L.R. 443.

[68] R. Page and G. A. Clark, "Who Cares?" National Children's Bureau (1977).

control over the child exceeding that of the natural parents. Hence, just as the natural parents' rights are displaced by the rights of the mature child, so also should be the rights of the institutional parent. Whether this is a necessary deduction is an issue which also arises in relation to the courts' authority over young people and we shall return to it in that context.[69]

Clearly there is no scope for the application of *Gillick* principles where the statutory code itself governs the matter in issue. We have seen that the local authority is, for example, under a statutory duty to provide the child with accommodation and maintenance under section 21 of the 1980 Act. That section goes on to give the authority a discretion in discharging that duty by allowing it to board the child with foster parents, place him in a community home or a voluntary home or make such other arrangements as seem appropriate to it. It would be contrary to the intention of the legislature to *require* the authority to follow the wishes of a child in relation to these alternatives even where that child is of a sufficient age and maturity (under the *Gillick* formulation) to make an informed choice between them. More generally, it would seem that local authorities who considered themselves *bound* to follow the wishes of mature children as a consistent policy might be held to have fettered their discretion to perform their statutory duty under section 18 to give first consideration to the child's welfare. This is not the same thing as giving first consideration to their preferences.

The position of a young person in care who has attained the statutory age of capacity for certain activities is more problematic. Here there *is* a case for saying that the child's views should prevail over those of the local authority where they conflict. The policy argument for allowing such a child to decide independently is based on discrimination. It may be thought discriminatory that full autonomy as regards a particular issue should be denied to children in care when it is allowed to all those who are not in care.

The Review however seemed to take the position that a certain amount of discrimination is justifiable. Its reasoning was that, because of the supposed greater vulnerability of children who are in care, local authorities needed to assume greater responsibility over them than their parents would otherwise have. Accordingly, children of 16 or 17, who at common law were thought to be able

[69] *Post*, Chap. 5.

to determine such matters as where they should live regardless of the views of their parents, should not have the final say as against the local authority. Their rights, it was thought, should be limited to receiving information about the opportunities for leaving care and of challenging certain decisions.[70]

The White Paper accepts as a guiding principle the desirability of involving as far as appropriate the child in decisions about the services provided for him.[71] It also accepts, where a child is older, his part in the making of voluntary agreements and arrangements for his care. Where a 16 or 17 year old is capable of making his own agreement with the authority, both sides should be able to withdraw from such an arrangement.[72] The views of children under that age would continue to be taken into account in accordance with the general duty under section 18, which would be preserved.

Possibly the single reform which would do most to accommodate the wishes of children in care would be the creation of a legal right to attend and be represented at case conferences.

(B) CHALLENGING DECISIONS

The courts' involvement in the care process was until recent years largely confined to disputes over whether the child should initially enter care or should be discharged from care once there. The statutory code did not provide for the use of the courts in order to challenge decisions of local authorities affecting a child in their care.

The leading criticism of care proceedings is that they are based on a quasi-criminal model arguably appropriate in dealing with delinquents, but completely inappropriate in relation to abused and neglected children for whom care proceedings are principally used. The use of this model has given rise to a number of significant procedural defects, the net result of which is that there has been a failure to accommodate properly the contributions of interested parties in the proceedings. The most striking of these defects is that parents are not accorded party status, the child being the sole respondent. Parents' rights of participation are restricted to meeting allegations against them by calling evidence

[70] Review, para. 3.13.
[71] White Paper, para. 9.
[72] para. 25.

95

and by cross-examining witnesses.[73] They are however allowed to represent the child unless the proceedings were brought at the parents' request on the basis that the child is beyond their control, the child objects[74] or a separate representation order has been made by the court (discussed below).

Other interested parties such as grandparents, other relatives and foster parents have no right to appear in the proceedings. Appeal is to the unlikely venue of the Crown Court and is the child's alone. This means that a parent may not appeal in his own right against the making of a care order and the local authority may not appeal against a refusal to make the order.

Various piecemeal improvements have been made to care proceedings which have served to provide a better separation and accommodation of the competing interests. Most importantly the Children Act 1975 made provision for "separation orders" to be made where the court considered that there existed a conflict of interest between parent and child.[75] The effect of the order is that the parent is not to be treated as representing the child. Where it is made the court has a discretion to arrange separate representation of the child by the appointment of a guardian *ad litem*. This reform was not however accompanied by any improvement in the standing of parents although it is now possible for them to obtain legal aid where a separate representation order has been made.[76] In some respects it weakened their position since they could no longer lodge an appeal on the child's behalf where the child's guardian *ad litem* refused to do so. Having no right of appeal themselves they are deprived by the separation order of *any* appeal right.[77] The Children and Young Persons (Amendment) Act 1986, as yet unimplemented, overcomes these problems by requiring that parents be made parties to the proceedings where the court decides that there is a conflict of interest between them.

---

[73] Rule 14B(1) of the Magistrates' Courts (Children and Young Persons) Rules 1970.

[74] Rule 17.

[75] Children and Young Persons Act 1969, s.32A, inserted by Children Act 1975, s.64.

[76] s.28(6A) of the Legal Aid Act 1974, introduced by s.65 of the Children Act 1975.

[77] *A.R.* v. *Avon C.C.* [1985] Fam. 150. They are also in a weak position on an application for discharge of a care order where the child's guardian *ad litem* wishes to withdraw the application. See *R.* v. *Wandsworth West Juvenile Court* [1984] F.L.R. 713, discussed by W. F. Miles, "Discharging Care Orders—Parents' Procedural Problems" (1987) 84 L.S.Gaz. 2353.

and their child. It also makes provision for the participation of grandparents, but not other parties.[78]

The White Paper offers more comprehensive reforms in the shape of wider rights of participation in care proceedings and enhanced rights of appeal. In future it is intended that anyone whose legal position could be affected by the proceedings will be accorded party status.[79] Others may be allowed to take part in the proceedings as the court directs.[80] The court will also be placed under a duty to appoint a guardian *ad litem* in *all* cases except where it appears unnecessary to do so in order to safeguard the child' interests.[81] Appeal rights will be conferred on all parties to the original proceedings and appeal will lie to the Family Division of the High Court.

The failure of the 1969 Act to provide judicial control over local authority decision-making has given rise to a host of largely unsuccessful attempts by parents and others to challenge such decisions in wardship.[82] The call for greater accountability of local authorities has however elicited a response from Parliament and legislation now provides a measure of judicial control in the sensitive areas of the use of secure accommodation for children in care[83] and access decisions.[84]

The access question is of monumental significance to natural parents. Their chances of eventually resuming the care of their child are likely to be slender unless they can preserve a healthy amount of regular contact with him. It therefore comes as no surprise that most of the challenges to local authorities' decisions have related to the termination or restriction of access.

It has never been doubted that where the local authority has acquired parental rights by court order or resolution it has the power to determine access, i.e. the nature, amount and frequency of contact between parent and child. Where the child is in care by order of a court in wardship or divorce proceedings, the court

---

[78] Judicial concern that the 1986 Act remains unimplemented was expressed by Latey J. in *R.* v. *Newcastle City Juvenile Court, Ex p. S.* (1987) *The Times*, December 21.

[79] White Paper, para. 55.

[80] para. 56.

[81] para. 57.

[82] *Post*, Chap. 5.

[83] See Child Care Act 1980, s.21A as inserted by Criminal Justice Act 1982, s.25.

[84] s.12 A–G 1980 Act as inserted by s.6 and Sched. 1 of the Health and Social Services and Social Security Adjudications Act 1983.

reserves the right to give directions to the authority regarding access.[85] Considerable uncertainty has however surrounded the position where the child is in voluntary care. There is some judicial authority that the council is entitled to control access as an aspect of its statutory duty to promote the welfare of the child.[86] This seems also to have been reflected in the practice of authorities which have often proceeded on the basis that they are entitled to control access, in some cases to the extent of refusing to inform parents of the whereabouts of the child. Against this it was argued that if a parent retained the right of access even when deprived of custody then, *a fortiori*, she should retain it where she had lost only actual custody. Again, the view was expressed that if access is to be seen as a right of the *child* it should be removed only by judicial process.[87]

The unrestrained control of access by social workers became the source of many complaints and calls for greater accountability. In particular there was disquiet that an arrangement which began voluntarily could quickly take on the aura of compulsion with the control exerted over contact between parent and child. In 1983, Parliament provided for certain access decisions to be brought under the control of the juvenile court. The Health and Social Services and Social Security Adjudications Act 1983 amended section 12 of the 1980 Act to enable parents to challenge decisions terminating or refusing access. At the same time it provided for the Secretary of State to prepare a Code of Practice for local authorities to govern access to children in care. This now lays down the principles which should be applied in promoting and maintaining access and in arriving at decisions to restrict or terminate it.

Under the amended section 12 parents are entitled to receive notice of any decision to terminate or refuse them access and may appeal against this to the juvenile court. It had been thought that the new protections did not apply where the child was in care under section 2 of the Children Act 1948 (the predecessor of section 3 of the 1980 Act). This was because on its terms section 12A(1) only applies to children who enter care via the procedures mentioned in that subsection which do not include the 1948 Act

[85] See Law Com. Working Paper No. 100 paras. 2.15–2.16.
[86] *Re H.* [1975] 3 All E.R. 348; *Re Y. (A minor) (Child in Care: Access)* [1976] Fam. 125.
[87] Maidment, *op. cit.* n. 48, p. 26.

procedure. Nonetheless in *R.* v. *Corby Juvenile Court, ex. p. M.*[88] Waite J. held that this was a drafting error which Parliament could not have intended and that such children were therefore covered by the new provisions. The new provisions do not apply in those instances in which a court in family proceedings reserves the right to give directions to the local authority. In these circumstances, there is already judicial control over the access question. Neither do they extend to those in voluntary care. The rationale must be that the local authority does not in any event have power to refuse or terminate access in these circumstances. But, as we have seen, in practice authorities *do* control access to children in voluntary care and it is a defect in the law that this practice is not subject to review by the courts. An even more significant deficiency in the statutory scheme is that it does not extend to restrictions on access which do not amount to a refusal or termination. Thus it is possible for the authority to curtail access drastically in a way which, in some cases, may be tantamount to termination. This was what happened in the leading wardship case, *A.* v. *Liverpool City Council,*[89] where a mother's access was cut to one hourly visit per month under supervision at a day nursery.

It is now implicit in the intended reforms for voluntary care that termination or refusal of access would be *ultra vires* the authority and quite inconsistent with the voluntary partnership principle. The White Paper also proposes that, in compulsory cases, there should be a presumption of "reasonable access" along the lines of custody model.[90] Where possible local authorities are encouraged to agree on access with the parents at an early stage. Failing agreement, the court will have jurisdiction to define access as in custody cases. Any subsequent variation in the arrangements would then have to be brought back before the court if the parent objects to it.

Access aside, there is little opportunity for parents to contest decisions of local authorities before the courts. Wardship has been closed-off as an effective option and it is likely that an aggrieved parent will now have to fall back on the restricted basis of challenge offered by the judicial review procedure.[91] An example occurred in *R.* v. *Bolton M.B., ex. p. B.*[92] where the council failed

---

[88] [1987] 1 W.L.R. 55.
[89] [1982] A.C. 363.
[90] para. 64.
[91] *Post*, Chap. 5.
[92] [1985] F.L.R. 343.

to give the parents the requisite notice of their decision to terminate access thereby depriving them of their right of appeal. The Divisional Court granted an order of mandamus compelling the authority to comply with its statutory obligations. It should be appreciated however that this avenue of redress is a very narrow one and is not likely to be of assistance in very many cases, since it does not allow for the merits of the authority's decisions to be questioned.

The White Paper rejects a general extension of judicial control over local authority decision-making. Instead it is envisaged that authorities will be required to establish complaints procedures, with an independent element, to resolve disputes and complaints. It is proposed that the details will be left to individual authorities to decide in the light of local requirements. The procedure must be well publicised and easily accessible.[93] Some authorities already have such procedures. A scheme apparently directed particularly at complaints by the children themselves has, for example, been in operation in Bromley since 1981.[94] The procedure there has been used for many diverse complaints including dissatisfaction with placement, inability to contact a social worker in off-duty hours and concern at accommodation problems on leaving care.[95] While this type of relatively informal procedure may be very useful in dealing with comparatively minor complaints, it is questionable whether it is adequate to deal with disputes over major strategic or irreversible decisions affecting the child, e.g. which school he is to attend, whether he should undergo an operation and where he should live. It might be thought that in relation to matters as serious as this there should be a right of redress to a wholly independent tribunal outside the authority with formal procedural protections in order to satisfy the requirements of "due process." The contrary argument is that greater judicial intervention would be likely to inhibit the authority in its efforts to make positive plans for the child's long-term future. This is a particular risk with the opening up of the access question to the courts. It is on balance a disappointing feature of the Review and the White Paper that the potential contribution of the courts in this area was not recognised.

---

[93] para. 31.
[94] See Cynthia Cross, "Complaints Procedure for Children in Care in Bromley" (1986) 10 *Adoption and Fostering* 28.
[95] *Ibid.* p. 30.

5. Conclusions

The White Paper reforms should result in a more coherent theoretical framework of child care law which should achieve a better balance between the interests of parents and the state. The voluntary partnership concept may succeed in casting the role of the state in a more positive light by shifting the emphasis away from coercive intervention towards positive assistance to families in need. As we discussed in chapter 3, a change in terminology would not be enough *per se* to alter the existing distribution of powers and responsibilities. But the proposals go much further than this. In the case of voluntary care, the expectation that parents and authorities will reach agreement on the allocation of their respective powers and responsibilities, is recognition that local authorities cannot cut parents out of the decision-making process. In order to do this they must obtain a compulsory order. The reforms relating to participation in care procedings should do much to ensure that all legitimate interests in the child's future are properly represented before the court.

An issue which will still have to be decided is the weight to be attached to the wishes of children. It is not clear precisely how far their independent voice is to be recognised in what is largely conceived as an arrangement between parents and the local authority. The *Gillick* case has given rise to a new and more complex fragmentation of power in the private sphere which may well be carried over into the public arena. It conjures up the possibility that adolescents in care should be entitled to take their own decisions thereby overriding the wishes of both their parents and the local authority. The White Paper is not perhaps as responsive as it might have been to this issue. It does not for example take account of the ages of children as a factor in the degree of allowable parental involvement.

Having discussed the statutory powers and responsibilities of local authorities we must now turn to the question of how these interrelate to the jurisdiction of the courts over children.

5. Courts as Parents

1. Introduction

In this chapter we examine aspects of the role of the courts in children cases. The inherent jurisdiction of the courts to protect children is exercised mainly (but not exclusively) in wardship proceedings. The jurisdiction has its origins in feudal times and derives from the *parens patriae* function originally exercised by the Crown. The theoretical basis for this was that the King was father of the nation and had the ultimate right of supervision over all infants within the allegiance.[1] The wardship function was first delegated to the Lord Chancellor, then became exercisable by the Court of Chancery and eventually devolved on the High Court.[2]

For most of its history wardship has been associated with landed wealth. As an incident of feudal tenure it was profitable to the lord who became guardian of the land (and body) of an infant heir and thereby entitled to the profits from the land during the infant's minority. The Crown's interest in wardship during this period was also primarily financial since it became entitled to these profits on the death of a tenant-in-chief. Thus, the Court of Wards was established to enforce the Crown's rights and to discharge its protective duties. When this court was abolished in 1660 by the Tenures Abolition Act its functions passed to the Court of Chancery. Although, theoretically, the emphasis in the jurisdiction shifted to the general protection of the ward's interests, as a matter of practice it continued to be used throughout the

---

[1] The historical development of wardship is traced in Lowe and White, *Wards of Court* (1987) (2nd Ed.) Chap. 1 and Cross, "Wards of Court" (1967) 83 L.Q.R. 200.

[2] The High Court continues to retain exclusive jurisdiction over the initial warding and eventual dewarding of a child. Certain items of wardship business may now however be transferred to the County Court under s.38(2)(*b*) of the Matrimonial and Family Proceedings Act 1984.

nineteenth century and the first half of the twentieth century principally to control the property and marriages of wealthy orphans and heiresses. This characteristic of the jurisdiction was reflected in the procedural rule that the child's wardship had to be ancillary to some other issue. It became the practice to create a nominal settlement of property on the child and to begin an action to administer the trusts of that settlement.

In 1949 this procedural restriction was removed and it became possible for the first time to ward a child for the single purpose of protecting him.[3] At the same time legal aid was extended to wardship proceedings. These procedural changes marked the start of an increased use of wardship which was to be further encouraged by the transfer of the jurisdiction from the Chancery Division to the Family Division of the High Court in 1971.[4] The escalation in the use of wardship is revealed by the figures for the number of originating applications which show that these rose from 74 in 1951 to 622 in 1971 and to 2,815 by 1985.

Until comparatively recently, therefore, the use of wardship, although in theory available for the protection of *all* children, was characterised by a distinct class bias. This was in contrast to the statutory responsibilities of local authorities which have their historical roots in the Poor Law and which have been exercised primarily in relation to deprived children.[5] Today, however, the two of them are often seen, especially by local authorities themselves, as alternative means of protecting vulnerable children of whatever social background. Local authorities and the courts may now reasonably be viewed as two separate agencies of the state, each charged with the responsibility of upholding the public interest in child protection. But, as we have seen, local authorities have been given *primary* responsibility by Parliament for the protection of children. This has given rise to the much-litigated question of the proper relationship between the protective and supervisory role of the courts and the powers and responsibilities of local authorities under the child care legislation. In the first part of this chapter we consider this issue and concentrate exclusively

---

[3] s.9 of the Law Reform (Miscellaneous Provisions) Act 1949.
[4] s.1(2) and Sched. 1 of the Administration of Justice Act 1970.
[5] On the history of the child care legislation see R. Dingwall, J. M. Eekelaar and T. Murray, "Childhood as a Social Problem: A Survey of the History of Legal Regulation" (1984) 11 J.L.S. 207, particularly at 211.

on the wardship jurisdiction. The universal character of wardship and the substantially unfettered powers of the wardship court have particularly brought it into potential conflict with the statutory scheme.

If the courts' role is to act in the place of a parent in order to protect children, it is reasonable to inquire whether their authority over them should be limited to that enjoyed by natural parents. In the second section we turn to the courts' powers over children and consider the argument, given new impetus by the *Gillick* case, that these powers should be emasculated where young people possess legal capacity to take their own decisions on matters affecting their lives. This is again something which is most starkly presented in the context of wardship proceedings, but it is an issue which arises wherever a court is discharging a broadly paternalistic role. Much of what is said in this section could therefore be applied to the various statutory jurisdictions of the courts over children.

2. The Courts and Local Authorities—The Wardship and Care Debate

It is possible to identify a number of distinct functions which the courts may be thought to perform in cases involving children. We have already adverted to the *parens patriae* role but it would be a mistake to assume that the responsibility of the court ends with this. In fulfilling this particular function the courts may be seen as acting in partnership with other agencies of the state, notably local authorities. This must be immediately contrasted with the courts' public law jurisdiction to *control* the state by reviewing the legality of action taken by public bodies. Hence it has been accepted that the courts may be properly used to allege impropriety by a local authority in the discharge of its statutory duties to children in its care.[6] Another obvious function of the courts is the resolution of disputes relating to individual children. Here they are called upon to balance the competing claims of adults and institutions who have an interest in the children concerned together with those of the children themselves. It is suggested that some of the defects which have been exposed in the litigation involving wardship and care procedures can be explained on the basis the courts have

[6] This principle dates back at least as far as *Re M.* [1961] Ch. 328.

found it impossible to perform satisfactorily these different functions at the same time.

The leading decision governing the use of wardship where the child is in care is *A. v. Liverpool City Council*.[7] In this case the child was in compulsory care under an order of the juvenile court. He was boarded out with foster parents and the mother was at first allowed weekly access. In due course the council decided that there was no case for continuing with regular access and decided to restrict this to one hourly visit per month under supervision. The mother objected and wished to challenge this decision in wardship proceedings.

The House of Lords held that it was not open to the court to review the merits of the local authority's decision on access where it had resulted from a proper exercise of its statutory discretion. The issue turned on the inter-relationship of statute and the royal prerogative. While the existence of the statutory scheme could not oust completely the prerogative jurisdiction of the wardship court, the exercise of the wardship jurisdiction was circumscribed by the existence of the child care legislation. Thus wardship, it was said, should not be exercised so as to interfere with the day-to-day administration by local authorities of their statutory control. Since the control of access was a matter falling within the statutory power and responsibilities of the authority it could not be questioned in wardship proceedings. It was denied that there was any general reviewing power in the courts where a matter had been entrusted by statute to the discretionary power of the local authority.

Notwithstanding the general rule against judicial intervention, it was clear before the *Liverpool* ruling that there could be exceptional circumstances where it might be proper for the wardship jurisdiction to be exercised although the child was in care. Some commentators found within the speeches of Lord Wilberforce and Lord Roskill some hope of such intervention where the welfare of the child appeared to the court to require it.[8] The trend post-*Liverpool* was, however, to confine further the use of wardship and this culminated in the uncompromising decision of the House of Lords in *Re W. (A minor) (Wardship: Jurisdiction)*.[9]

[7] [1982] A.C. 363.
[8] See M. D. A. Freeman, "Controlling Local Authorities in Child Care Cases—A. v. Liverpool City Council Revisited" (1982) 146 J.P. 188, 202 and Bainham, "Wardship, Care and the Welfare Principle" (1981) 11 Fam. Law 236.
[9] [1985] A.C. 791.

Here the House held categorically that there remained no residual class of exceptional or unusual circumstances in which wardship would be available as a remedy against local authorities.

Following this decision it is crucially important to distinguish between those cases in which wardship is invoked *against* local authorities and those in which the wardship application is made *by* the authority.

(A) WARDSHIP AGAINST LOCAL AUTHORITIES

The use of wardship against local authorities by parents and others is no longer deserving of detailed discussion. It is only possible to recount a catalogue of failures. After the *Liverpool* decision the courts exhibited an evermore restrictive attitude to such applications. At one time it used to be thought that the restrictions only applied where the local authority had acquired parental rights,[10] but in *W.* v. *Nottinghamshire County Council*[11] the Court of Appeal held that they also applied where the child was in voluntary care. The decision supports the view that the court should not exercise jurisdiction where it can be demonstrated that the council is contemplating proceedings under the 1969 Act, but has not at the relevant time made the requisite application to the juvenile court. According to Purchas L.J. the mere existence of a local authority's statutory powers and duties requires the High Court not to interfere.

It also appears that this anti-interventionist policy applies with equal force where no action is taken under the statutory code but the child enters care via family proceedings. In *J.* v. *Devon County Council*[12] the child, aged seven, who had originally been placed in voluntary care, was formally committed to care by the divorce court under section 43(1) of the Matrimonial Causes Act 1973. The child's foster parents later applied for adoption and the mother tried to frustrate this application and to regain control of the child in wardship proceedings. Swinton-Thomas J. held that the *Liverpool* principle governed children in care under an order

---

[10] It was thought that there was no objection to wardship where the child was in voluntary care since the local authority would not have acquired parental rights and, because its powers were transient, the High Court might need to act to protect the child. See Lord Denning M.R. in *Re. S. (An infant)* [1965] 1 W.L.R. 483 at 487.

[11] [1986] 1 F.L.R. 565.

[12] [1986] 1 F.L.R. 597.

in matrimonial proceedings. The purpose of the order, like one under the 1969 Act, was to vest decision-making powers and duties in the local authority. In fact the legal position is not indentical since, unlike the juvenile court in 1969 Act proceedings, the divorce court retains the power to give directions to the authority under section 43(5)(a).

More recently it has been held that the *Liverpool* principle of non-intervention in wardship applies outside the context of care procedures. In *Re D. (A minor)*[13] the Court of Appeal held that the wardship jurisdiction should not be exercised so as to conflict with the statutory duties of local education authorities under the Education Act 1981 to make provision for children with special educational needs. On the facts no such conflict arose since the authority welcomed the intervention of the court. Again, in *Re F. (A minor)*[14] Hollings J. held that the court could not and should not exercise the wardship jurisdiction to clog the statutory machinery of the Immigration Act 1971 which had laid down a code for the control of immigrants and had entrusted its administration to the immigration authorities.

Logically there is no reason why the *Liverpool* restrictions should apply only to child care procedures and it seems likely that the principle against intervention is of general application.

This relentless policy of refusing to allow wardship to be used as a mechanism for challenging child care decisions of local authorities has had a particularly damaging effect on the legal position of "non-parents." In *Re W. (A minor) (Wardship: Jurisdiction)* the House of Lords refused to allow wardship to be used by members of the extended family who wished to present proposals for the care of a child. This was so despite their lack of standing in care proceedings and in proceedings to free the child for adoption. According to Lord Scarman the failure to provide relatives with a right to participate in these proceedings was the result of the express enactments of Parliament. The result of the decision was to leave an uncle, aunt and grandparents with no legal redress at all, notwithstanding the House's recognition of the genuine contribution which they might have made to the well-being of the child.

---

[13] [1987] 1 W.L.R. 1400. For a critical assessment of the case see Clive Lewis, "Statutory Powers and Wardship" [1988] C.L.J. 27.
[14] (1988) *The Times*, January 23.

In *Re D.M. (A minor) (Wardship: Jurisdiction)*[15] the Court of Appeal held that it was not open to short-term foster parents to resort to wardship as a means of disputing the authority's adoption panel's decision that they were not suitable as potential adopters. Unmarried fathers have fared no better. In *Re. T.D. (A minor) (Wardship: Jurisdiction)*[16] Sheldon J. rejected a father's argument that he be allowed to seek access with a view to rehabilitation in wardship proceedings since he had no standing in the juvenile court nor was his agreement to adoption or freeing for adoption required.

The standing of parents has been improved by the introduction of the access provisions into the statutory code thereby removing one of the principal reasons for resorting to wardship. This may be illustrated by comparing the two post-*Liverpool* decisions *Re J. (A minor)*[17] and *Re M. (A minor)*.[18] The former case was heard before the introduction of the access provisions. The Court of Appeal held that the wardship jurisdiction could properly be exercised to overcome a deficiency in the powers of the juvenile court under the child care legislation. This was that the court had no power, when discharging a care order, to direct a phased reintroduction of parent and child by means of a programme of experimental access. The High Court could do this in wardship by incorporating conditions as to access. The Court drew on the words of Lord Wilberforce in *Liverpool* that "the court's general inherent power is always available to fill gaps or to supplement the powers of the local authority."[19]

Re M. was decided after this "lacuna" had been at least partially filled by the access legislation. A baby boy had been removed from his mother at birth under a place of safety Order. Access was originally allowed but when the child was one month old the council applied for a care order and announced its intention to seek long-term foster parents with a view to adoption. The guardian *ad litem* favoured a trial period of access but the juvenile court nevertheless made the care order, whereupon the mother commenced wardship proceedings. The Court of Appeal upheld the judge's decision to deward the child in view of the mother's statutory right to contest termination of access in the juvenile court and the obligation on the authority to obtain a court order freeing the child for adoption. The court did however appear to

[15] [1986] 2 F.L.R. 122.
[16] [1985] F.L.R. 1150.
[17] [1984] 1 W.L.R. 81.
[18] [1985] Fam. 60.
[19] n. 7, p. 373.

recognise the continued existence of the "lacuna" principle and Slade L.J. instanced the situation where a local authority might drastically curtail access without actually terminating it. We have already noted this defect in the access legislation which will be remedied with the implementation of the White Paper proposals.[20] The reform of the statutory code will largely eliminate the defects which have been relied on in wardship. But in the meantime it is in any event unlikely, following *Re W.*, that wardship will again be allowed to fill any existing gaps since the courts are likely to take the view that they were left deliberately by Parliament. As the Law Commission comments, the implication of this decision "seems to be that where the statutory code provides no redress for an individual the absence is to be treated not as a lacuna in the scheme, but as part of the scheme itself."[21]

Until recently it was well established that wardship could be utilised to challenge *ultra vires* action on the part of the local authority. This happened in *Re L. (A.C.)*[22] where the council failed to follow the correct statutory procedures when passing a resolution assuming parental rights, thereby depriving a mother of the procedural protections in the Children Act 1948. It now seems however that the correct procedure to follow in such cases is the judicial review procedure under Order 53 of the Rules of the Supreme Court. This was the interpretation placed upon the *Liverpool* and *Re W.* rulings by Sheldon J. in *Re R.M. and L.M. (Minors)*.[23] Long-term foster parents wished to use wardship to challenge the authority's decision to remove twins from their care. They alleged that in so deciding the authority had deprived them of the opportunity of applying for legal custody under the custodianship procedure and had therefore acted in breach of its statutory duties. Sheldon J. thought that the effect of the two House of Lords decisions was to restrict such challenges to the Order 53 procedure and this view was accepted by the Court of Appeal in *Re D.M.*

There is already evidence that wardship is being abandoned in favour of judicial review. In *R. v. Hertfordshire County Council,*

---

[20] *Ante*, Chap. 4. It has recently been held by Bush J. in *Re Y (A minor) (Wardship: Access Challenge)* 1988 1 F.L.R. 299. That the "Lacuna" principle has not survived *Re W.*, and that, in any event, the Juvenile Courts inability to renew a drastic reduction in access was not a "Lacuna", but was intended by Parliament.

[21] Law Com. Working Paper No. 101, "Wards of Court" (1987) para. 3.41.

[22] [1971] 3 All E.R. 743.

[23] [1986] 2 F.L.R. 205. *Cf.* the views of Hollis J. in *D. v. X. City Council (No. 1)* [1985] F.L.R. 275.

ex p. B; *R.* v. *Bedfordshire County Council, ex p. C.*[24] the procedure was used to challenge decisions of two local authorities which were alleged to have been made in breach of the rules of natural justice. In one case Social Services had abandoned their plan to allow the children home on trial with their father solely because of an unsubstantiated allegation by the mother that he had forced her to submit to sexual intercourse and had committed buggery on a teenage boy. Ewbank J. held that the father should have been given an opportunity to answer this charge before Social Services arrived at their decision. In the other case the local authority was held to have acted fairly in deciding to abandon attempts at rehabilitation since it did not rely *solely* on a neighbour's unsubstantiated allegations of drunkenness against the mother, but took into account all the circumstances including the child's weight loss while at home, his disruptive behaviour and hyperactivity.

The suitability of judicial review in children cases has been questioned by several commentators.[25] The principal objections have been the delays involved, the lack of expertise on family matters in the Queen's Bench Division and the limited orders which can be made by the Divisional Court. The court can only quash the offending decision and cannot substitute its own solution. This contrasts with the flexible powers available in wardship to give effect to the court's view of the child's best interests. The Court of Appeal has now attempted to meet these objections in *Re D. (A minor)*.[26] In this case Woolf L.J. said that in appropriate cases arrangements could be and were made for judicial review cases to come before judges of the Family Division and that, provided the judicial review application was made promptly, it should be perfectly practicable for this and the wardship application to be heard together by the same judge on the same day. In this way it ought to be possible to deal with the narrow and technical basis of challenge afforded by administrative law while at the same time taking advantage of the flexibility of the remedies in the Family Division.

---

[24] [1987] 1 F.L.R. 239.

[25] See, for example, N. V. Lowe, "To Review or Not to Review?" (1982) 45 M.L.R. 96, 98 and M. D. A. Freeman, *op. cit.* n. 8 at p. 202. It has also been judicially criticised by Latey J. in *R.* v. *Newham L.B.C. ex p. McL.* (1988) 18 Fam. Law 125. where he suggests that wardship is a more appropriate remedy and that judges should be ready to recommend that local authorities submit to wardship proceedings in suitable cases.

[26] 1987 3 All E.R. 717.

What the case law establishes beyond doubt is that the courts will not be prepared to question the merits of local authorities' decisions whether in wardship or judicial review and will limit themselves to intervention which can be justified on a strict application of administrative law principles.

(B) WARDSHIP BY LOCAL AUTHORITIES

The refusal of the judiciary to allow wardship to be used against authorities contrasts sharply with their encouragement of authorities to seek the courts' assistance where they feel that their powers under the statutory scheme are inadequate. The *locus classicus* of this position is the judgment of Dunn J. in *Re D. (Justices' Decision Review)* where he said that

> "far from local authorities being discouraged from applying to the court in wardship . . . they should be encouraged to do so, because in very many of these cases it is the only way in which orders can be made in the interests of the child, untrammelled by the statutory provisions of the Children and Young Persons Act 1969."[27]

Wardship is therefore available to provide "supplementary assistance" to local authorities in the discharge of their statutory duties by invoking the superior powers of the High Court. For example, the power to grant injunctions and enforce them by committal for contempt may be useful in providing additional protection for children from association with undesirable adults.[28] The High Court may also be a more appropriate forum in which to resolve complex issues.[29]

The Law Comission has referred to this use of wardship as the "supportive jurisdiction." It is relatively uncontroversial when contrasted with the other uses of wardship since its purpose is merely to achieve more effectively a result which could be achieved under the statutory code.[30] In particular it must be

---

[27] [1977] Fam. 158, 166. See also the remarks of Lane J. in *Re B. (A minor) (Wardship: Child in Care)* [1975] Fam. 36, 44.

[28] In the above case the wardship was continued in order to protect the girl from her step-father.

[29] An example is *Re J.T. (A minor) (Wardship: Committal)* [1986] 2 F.L.R. 107 where the mother had converted to Rastafarianism and there were complex, cultural, environmental and dietary considerations.

[30] Law Com. No. 101, para. 3.53.

contrasted with what the Commission calls the "independent jurisdiction." Here the local authority is resorting to wardship as a means of circumventing restrictions in the child care legislation to achieve an object which it could not secure under that legislation. It may, for example, feel that it has no legal basis for obtaining a statutory care order but is nevertheless sufficiently concerned about a child to try to gain care and control in wardship. Thus in *Re P. (A minor) (Child Abuse: Evidence)*[31] the authority followed up a place of safety order with wardship proceedings where it was concerned about the risk of sexual abuse of a new born baby if left in a family in which there had been a history of such behaviour. Wardship has also been allowed where an authority had insufficient grounds for passing a parental rights resolution.[32] Also controversial is the use of wardship by the authority as a "review or appellate jurisdiction." It has been used where the authority was unable to appeal against the refusal of the juvenile court to make a care order[33] and where it tried unsuccessfully to oppose the discharge of a care order in the juvenile court.[34]

In these cases the respective authorities in reality by-passed the statutory scheme and it is not accurate to describe them as cases in which the courts provided "supplementary assistance." Closely allied to the "independent jurisdiction" is the "alternative jurisdiction." In this situation the local authority is endeavouring to secure a result which it could equally well achieve under the statutory scheme. Both the independent and alternative jurisdictions may be objected to for the same reason that the statutory code was intended to govern the factual situations which gave rise to the use of wardship. The only practical difference is that in the independent jurisdiction the local authority would have failed under the statutory provisions whereas it would have succeeded in the alternative jurisdiction cases.

---

[31] (1987) 2 F.L.R. 467. See also *Re G. (A minor)* (Child Abuse: Standard of proof) [1987] 1 W.L.R. 1461. where Sheldon J. suggested that allegations of sexual abuse by a parent might not require formal proof in wardship proceedings if there was sufficient suspicion for the court to conclude that the child's welfare required that she be removed from the home environment.

[32] *Re C.B.* [1981] 1 All E.R. 16.

[33] *Re C.* (A minor) (Justices Decision Review) [1981] 2 F.L.R. 62.

[34] *Hertfordshire County Council* v. *Dolling* (1982) 3 F.L.R. 423, where the authority had unsuccessfully appealed to the Crown Court against the order of the juvenile court. See also *Re R. (A minor) (Care: Wardship)* (1987) 2 F.L.R. 400.

There is an irony in the courts' willingness to allow the free use of wardship by local authorities when, in the context of applications by private individuals, they have constantly refused to intervene. Why they have been prepared to offer assistance outside the statutory scheme to local authorities but not to others is a question which has never been satisfactorily answered. The reasoning which the courts have put forward is that the royal prerogative must not be used in a way which conflicts with the statutory powers of local authorities, but that this conflict does not arise if the authority is itself seeking the assistance of the court. There are two difficulties with this:

First, there have been instances in which the courts have refused to exercise the jurisdiction where no apparent conflict with the statutory code exists. It is difficult to see how the refusal to allow the relatives in *Re W.* to present their views could be said to frustrate the legislative plan. This decision was justified on the basis that the failure to provide the extended family with *locus standi* in care proceedings was a *deliberate* omission of the legislature. This seems highly unlikely in view of Parliament's concern for the position of non-parents exhibited by the enactment of the custodianship procedure and the right given to grandparents to apply for access in certain proceedings.[35] The much more likely explanation is that Parliament did not apply itself at all to the standing of non-parents in care proceedings. If it had done so it might well have made provision for their participation. Its omission to do so should have been a sufficient justification for the court's intervention to fill the statutory lacuna.

Secondly, although the courts may not *interfere* with the statutory powers of local authorities where they intervene at their request, they can hardly be said to be acting in accordance with the intention of the legislature. What the courts have in effect done is to arrogate to themselves a wider basis for state intervention in the family than that established by the legislature. It is hardly surprising therefore that the argument has recently been put forward that local authorities should be obliged to proceed under the statutory scheme where the matters in question fall within it.

In *Re L.H. (A minor)*[36] (Wardship: Jurisdiction) the council decided to terminate all access between a child and his parents who

---

[35] s. 33 of the Children Act 1975 and s. 14A of the Guardianship of Minors Act 1971 respectively.
[36] [1986] 2 F.L.R. 306.

contested this decision in the juvenile court under section 12C of the Child Care Act 1980. They succeeded in obtaining an access order. The council considered an appeal to the High Court, but decided instead to ward the child. The parents applied to have the proceedings struck out and the wardship discontinued. They argued that it should not be allowed where the matters in question were within the statutory powers of the local authority or where the juvenile court or some other court had alternative powers to deal with the situation especially where, as here, there had already been recourse to that jurisdiction. Sheldon J. rejected these arguments on the basis that there was always jurisdiction where the authority was seeking the assistance of the court.

In fact this was a blatant attempt by the council to reopen the merits of the juvenile court's determination without using the more restrictive statutory appeals procedure. It is certainly arguable that this use of wardship is contrary to the intention of Parliament. If the courts are to be consistent they ought to refuse jurisdiction in such cases and may yet do so. In *W.* v. *Nottinghamshire County Council*[37] there was a guarded suggestion by Purchas L.J. that it might be necessary to decide at some future time whether wardship would be justified where an authority which obviously ought to have applied for a care order refused to do so. This was also the view of Stephen Brown and Dillon L.JJ. in *D. (A minor)* v. *Berkshire County Council*[38] where they appeared to be of the opinion that wardship was inappropriate and could not be used by a local authority where statutory care procedures covered the situation. The House of Lords held that it was unnecessary to rule on this point. This was extraordinarily unsatisfactory since the whole point of the parents' opposition to a statutory care order was that they wished to force the authority to use the wardship procedure. They recognised that a care order was necessary but wanted this to be made by the High Court since it could exercise greater control over the authority than could the juvenile court with its very limited powers. Conversely, the council was equally anxious to secure the greater independence which would be offered by a statutory care order. The failure of the House of Lords to address this issue means that local authorities are likely to continue to regard wardship as a generally available alternative to proceeding under the statutory code.

---

[37] n. 11.
[38] [1987] 1 All E.R. 27. The House of Lords decision is discussed in Chap. 4.

Another unsatisfactory feature of the courts' current policy is their attitude where a local authority decides to waive the jurisdictional point.

They have been prepared to allow wardship applications which are not opposed to continue where they would have refused to exercise jurisdiction if the authority had taken the point. In *A. and B.* v. *Hereford and Worcester Council*[39] both parents were themselves minors. The child had been taken into care at birth on the mother's request and placed with short-term foster parents. The father, who was 16, initiated wardship proceedings by his next friend and asked that care and control be given to the child's grandmother. The council favoured long-term fostering with a view to adoption but had no objection to the matter being dealt with in wardship. Sir John Arnold P. held that it was proper for the court to continue the wardship on the principle of supplementary assistance. Similarly in *Re J.T. (A minor) (Wardship: Committal)*[40] an application by the child's guardian *ad litem* was allowed to continue even though its purpose was to challenge the council's plans for the child. Again the council was prepared to endorse the use of wardship.

If the objections to wardship based on the existence of the statutory code are as fundamental as the courts repeatedly suggest, why do they not raise the jurisdictional question of their own motion? The answer seems to be grounded in policy considerations. The courts wish to be of assistance to local authorities who are experiencing difficulties in taking the action which they consider necessary under the statutory code. They have, accordingly, in some cases requested the authority to waive the jurisdictional point. This occurred in *R.* v. *Newham London Borough Council, Ex parte McL.*[41] where the authority agreed, at the request of Latey J., to the exercise of the wardship jurisdiction to investigate the merits of the authority's decision to move a child in their care from her grandmother to foster parents.

If the courts are willing to ignore the jurisdictional objections to the use of wardship where the local authority is experiencing difficulties under the statutory code, why are they not prepared to do so where parents, relatives and others have similar difficulties?

[39] [1986] 1 F.L.R. 289.
[40] n. 29.
[41] n. 25.

What meaningful distinction can be drawn between the grand-mother's predicament in the above case and that of the grand-mother and the other relatives in *Re W*? Again, the answer appears to have more to do with policy considerations than theoretical jurisdictional objections. The courts are concerned with the so-called "floodgates" argument. This is that the courts are there to assist authorities and not to hinder them in the performance of their statutory duties. The fear is that to allow wardship against the wishes of authorities would be to pave the way for a flood of applications challenging every conceivable decision which authorities can make regarding children in their care. This would result in an overloaded court system and practical difficulties for authorities in planning the long-term management of the future of these children. Later it will be suggested that these fears are unjustified and that the "floodgates" argument could be met by the introduction of a preliminary procedure to distinguish between meritorious and unmeritorious applications.

The objections to the current approach are that it is not even-handed and that it is not theoretically sound either. The argument about the relationship between statute and the royal prerogative is a convenient device for allowing the courts to refuse to hear those applications which they do not wish to entertain. That it is not a fundamental objection is apparent from the ease with which it can be set aside where the courts *do* wish to hear certain applications. If there are genuine theoretical objections, the courts stand accused of a selective application of legal theory. The fact that a local authority has no objection to extra-statutory intervention by the court is not in any event a convincing reason for feeling that this extra-statutory action would be approved by Parliament which, it should be remembered, has endeavoured to spell out the circumstances in which state intervention in the family is justified.

Where a care order is made in wardship proceedings the local authority gets care and control of the child while custody remains vested in the court.[42] The result is that responsibility for the child is shared between them and difficulties can arise concerning the precise distribution of decision-making powers.[43] It is established however that the court retains a parental jurisdiction which

---

[42] A useful general discussion is contained in D. Morgan, "Care Orders in Wardship Cases" [1984] J.S.W.L. 66.

[43] In particular the position differs as between orders made under s.7(2) of the Family Law Reform Act 1969 and those made under the court's inherent jurisdiction. See Morgan, *ibid.*, pp. 67–68.

requires the authority to return to it for authorisation of all "important steps" taken in the child's life.[44] There is a conceptual distinction between major decisions requiring the court's consent, and everyday matters which are delegated by the court to the authority. No attempt has been made to enumerate exhaustively the decisions which fall into each category, but the cases establish that the court must be consulted on whether further attempts should be made to reunite parent and child,[45] on the child's placement or change of placement,[46] and before a decision to reduce access substantially is taken.[47] The court is also able to give directions to the local authority regarding the discharge of its duties under the Child Care Act 1980.[48] How far the courts wish in practice to question seriously the decisions and plans of authorities is debatable since they see their role as a primarily supportive one. In *Surrey County Council* v. *W.*[49] Ormrod L.J. warned against the courts directing the authority except in a fairly broad way. In some instances the authority may welcome the involvement of the court in difficult or sensitive decisions such as whether an abortion should be performed on a girl in care.[50] Equally, the authority may not welcome the continuing control of the court and may prefer care proceedings in order to avoid this. As we have seen, this was the real point of the *Berkshire* case. There was no dispute that the child was in need of care and control but the parents wanted to force the authority to use wardship in order to preserve the court's control over any subsequent decision to place the baby for adoption.

The extent to which the courts are able to impose their own solutions on local authorities is illustrated by *Re E. (S.A.) (A minor) (Wardship)*.[51] In this case the House of Lords held that it was possible for the court to direct a course of action which was not contemplated by the parties themselves. The issue was

[44] Discussed by Lowe and White, *op. cit.* n. 1, para. 5.6 *et seq.*
[45] *Surrey County Council* v. *W.* (1982) 3 F.L.R. 167.
[46] *Re C.B.*, n. 32.
[47] *Stockport M.B.C.* v. *B.* and *Stockport M.B.C.* v. *L.* [1986] 2 F.L.R. 80.
[48] Family Law Reform Act 1969, s.7(3).
[49] n. 45. See also *Re B. (A minor)* (1987) *The Times*, October 6, 1987 where Anthony Lincoln J. refused to make an order assigning a social worker to a mother and baby who were both wards of court. He suggested that the courts should not interfere with the authority's plans except in cases of impropriety.
[50] As in *Re P. (A minor)* (1981) 80 L.G.R. 301.
[51] [1984] 1 All E.R. 289 discussed at [1984] J.S.W.L. 181.

whether a six-year-old child, who was a ward of court, should be placed for adoption or returned to the care and control of his father. The court welfare officer favoured a middle course consisting of experimental access to see if it was possible to re-establish the bond between father and child. Although neither the father nor the authority put forward this suggestion Lord Scarman held that the inquisitorial nature of wardship allowed the court to make an order to this effect. The wardship was therefore continued with care and control to the council, but subject to directions designed to preserve the court's control over the rehabilitation attempts.

This case is perhaps the best illustration of the potential advantages and disadvantages faced by local authorities who opt for wardship rather than the statutory procedures. It enabled a flexible solution to be adopted but also revealed the danger that the court may conceivably be unwilling to go along with the council's long-term strategy and may interfere to direct a different course of action. The price for the more flexible basis of state intervention represented by wardship is judicial scrutiny of the merits of certain of the authority's decisions. Authorities should therefore be aware when they make their election that if they choose wardship they will be "in for a penny, in for a pound."[52] Essex County Council were apparently oblivious to this in *Re E. (S.A.)* since they went so far as to refuse to allow the court welfare officer to observe father and son together, an attitude described by Lord Scarman as

> "a total and frightening misunderstanding by its social service advisers of the role of the court and of the court's officer in wardship proceedings."[53]

(C) REFORM

The existing practice of the courts results in two major contradictions. The first is that the principle of judicial control is

---

[52] The words of the Law Commission used to describe the indivisible nature of the effects of wardship proceedings, also described by the Commission as the "sledge-hammer effect." See Law Com. No. 101, para. 4.3. See also *Re. S. (Minors) (Wardship: Education)* [1988] 1 F.L.R. 128 where the local authority warded four children only to discover that it thereby lost the right to take educational decisions in relation to them. Waite J. held that they were for the court and that the authority could not pick and choose which decisions it wanted the court to take and which it would reserve to itself.

[53] n. 51, p. 292.

accepted where chronologically the child is first a ward of court and is subsequently placed in the care of a local authority, but not where the child enters care first and is later warded.

This means that the courts preserve control over the child's future where he enters care by virtue of an order in wardship or family proceedings, but not where he arrives in care under the statutory code. In the latter situation the decision-making powers of the authority are largely unchecked apart from the narrow basis of challenge afforded by judicial review. Yet the decisions which may be questioned are precisely the same in each situation and it must be bewildering to the layman that in the former instances the final say rests with the judges, while in the latter it is vested in the authorities. The absurdity of this situation is accentuated by the realisation that the route into care is now increasingly fortuitous since wardship is available to authorities as an unrestricted alternative to proceeding under the child care legislation. While therefore there may be legitimate disagreement about how much judicial involvement in child care is desirable, once the principle of judicial control is accepted it is difficult to argue that it should not apply equally to all cases of children in care regardless of how they came to be there.

The second contradiction is caused by the divergent policies of allowing wardship to be used *by* local authorities but not *against* them. The child care legislation is thus regarded as self-contained and exhaustive of remedies for parents and other individuals, but not exhaustive for local authorities. This produces an imbalance which is both illogical and untenable. The result of the courts' ambivalent attitude to wardship has been to deny elementary justice to those whose ability to test the legality of the actions of local authorities is either limited or non-existent under the statutory scheme. At the same time the authorities themselves have been allowed to dodge the statutory code where it suits them to do so.

The reforms proposed for child care law envisage that wardship will be left intact and will continue to exist alongside the statutory procedures. The Law Commission has suggested a number of possible options designed to produce a more acceptable place for wardship in the statutory code.[54] If no attempt is made to define the relationship between wardship and statutory procedures the

---

[54] The Commission's Working Paper No. 101 is concerned with wardship generally. Local authority cases are discussed in paras. 3.30–3.47.

effect could be to "drive a coach and horses" through the statutory code. In short there is little point in Parliament setting limits to public intervention in the family if these can be ignored with impunity by invoking a broad parental jurisdiction.[55]

Option A would be to retain wardship as a separate jurisdiction but with specific reforms to cure existing defects.[56] These reforms might include reversing the decisions in the *Liverpool* and *Re W.* cases by statute to enable challenges to be made in wardship to the merits of decisions relating to a child in care. A less radical reform would be to restore the "judicial review" function of wardship to enable the procedure to be used where the narrower grounds for judicial review exist. Another reform might be to restrict the grounds for committal to care in wardship proceedings to those for a statutory care order thereby preventing wardship being used as a mechanism for wider state involvement in family life.[57]

The main advantage of preserving wardship in its current form could be that it would provide a remedy for giving effect to the welfare principle as a rule of substantive law.[58] The principal contrary argument is that "the continued existence of a universal jurisdiction may make nonsense of the statutory codes."[59]

Option B would be to make wardship a residuary jurisdiction.[60] Its *raison d'être* would then be solely to make good deficiencies in the statutory code. It would not be allowed where to exercise jurisdiction would be inconsistent with the statutory scheme. Hence the alternative and appellate jurisdictions would be removed. The independent jurisdiction would only be exercised where to do so would be consistent with the child care legislation and the primary use of wardship would be as a supportive jurisdiction.[61] The main advantages of this option would be to redress the imbalance in the use of wardship by local authorities and others while at the same time eliminating duplication and conflicts of jurisdiction which might be perpetuated under Option A.[62] The main disadvantage is that it might be difficult to devise a statutory test for distinguishing between those apparent gaps

---

[55] para. 4.9.
[56] paras. 4.6–4.14.
[57] para. 4.13.
[58] para. 4.8.
[59] para. 4.9.
[60] paras. 4.15–4.20.
[61] para. 4.15.
[62] para. 4.16.

which were deliberately left by Parliament and those which arose inadvertently because the legislature was unable to foresee and provide for every eventuality which might justify judicial involvement.[63]

Option C is the most radical and would entail the abolition of wardship as a separate jurisdiction.[64] Its better features would instead be incorporated into the statutory jurisdictions. This would "preclude people or authorities from acquiring rights in relation to children which they could not acquire under the statutes, while improving the machinery available under those statutes for the protection of children."[65] Particularly germane to the present discussion is the suggestion that the statutory code might incorporate in certain cases provision for continued supervision by the court following an order giving powers and responsibilities over the child to an individual or authority.[66] The advantage of this option would be that the desirable features of wardship would be available in all custody and care jurisdictions.[67] The argument against abolition of wardship is that it might not be possible to make the statutory schemes sufficiently flexible to cover every conceivable situation in which a child might require protection.[68]

Possibly the best solution would be a combination of options B and C. It is obviously desirable that the useful features of wardship should be made more generally available under the statutory jurisdictions and that unnecessary duplication of proceedings and conflicts of jurisdiction should be eliminated. At the same time it is important that the courts should never find themselves unable to act in the best interests of a child solely because of some technical argument arising under the legislation. The more flexible parental jurisdiction of wardship should be preserved for this purpose as a residual long-stop for exceptional cases. Anyone seeking to institute wardship proceedings for this purpose could be required to obtain leave by demonstrating the defect in the child care legislation which makes it imperative that the court should intervene.

However wardship is reformed it should be equally available to local authorities and private applicants. Returning to the functions

[63] para. 4.17.
[64] paras. 4.21–4.25.
[65] para. 4.21.
[66] para. 4.23.
[67] para. 4.24.
[68] para. 4.25.

which, it was suggested, the courts discharge in children cases, current practice over-emphasises the *parens patriae* role and attaches too little weight to the courts' pivotal position in maintaining a balance between the conflicting claims of children, adults and local authorities. Underlying this practice is the judges' appreciation that they are essentially acting in partnership with the authorities in the sphere of child protection. This may provide the rationale for the open-door policy which has been operated whenever an authority seeks the court's assistance in wardship. The danger of this approach is that the courts may be seen to be abdicating from their responsibility as neutral arbitrators of disputes. Moreover the existence of a partnership between the courts and the state (as represented by local authorities) ignores the importance of the courts in *controlling* the state. The fundamental issue which needs to be addressed is the *level* of control which it is desirable to vest in the courts. Apart from access questions and the use of secure accommodation, this level is pitched according to orthodox principles of administrative law. It is questionable whether these principles should be transplanted into the context of family life where the aim is to provide for the welfare of children and where technical jurisdictional arguments should not be allowed to predominate. It would be preferable for the courts' involvement with local authority decision-making to be determined by an application of the welfare principle, albeit subject to a preliminary filter to identify unmeritorious applications. The need for such applications would of course be greatly diminished if the reformed statutory code were to incorporate adequate mechanisms for the independent review of major decisions affecting children in care. Problems of definition are likely to remain, but in general terms it is suggested that there ought to be distinction between day-to-day decisions and those which affect the long-term management of the child's future or which have potentially irreversible effects. Only the former should be the exclusive preserve of the local authority. The latter should be under formal legal control and it is doubtful whether the suggested internal complaints procedures go far enough in this respect.[69] It is in this area that wardship might continue to perform a useful residual function.

[69] *Ante*, Chap. 4.

3. The Courts and Young People

Following *Gillick* an argument has been advanced by Eekelaar that the courts, in particular the divorce court and those exercising the wardship jurisdiction, should re-orient their approach in cases involving older children. Instead of merely *having regard* to their wishes, they should first decide whether the child has sufficient capacity to take her decision. If so, Eekelaar contends that *the child's decision should determine the matter* whether or not the court agrees with it applying the welfare test.[70] The basis of the argument is that the Crown, as *parens patriae* should not claim a right to intervene in the lives of children which it denies to those children's parents. Applying this theory to the divorce court, Eekelaar contends that, since the right to possess a child falls within the ambit of parental rights, it should not be asserted against the child's wishes. Thus where the child has capacity to decide where she wishes to live this should be determinative of the issue, and a custody order could not operate to transfer rights which no longer exist.[71] He cites *Re D.W.*[72] (A minor) (Custody) as a case which should be decided differently in the aftermath of *Gillick*. There the judge had ordered the transfer of a 10 year old boy from his step-mother to his natural mother, against the boy's expressed wishes and despite recognition of his maturity, because the judge thought the order was in his best interests.

The crux of the matter is whether the courts can enjoy a degree of authority which exceeds that conferred by natural parenthood. The courts' jurisdiction in children cases is undoubtedly a parental jurisdiction. It has been said that the effect of wardship is that the court becomes the child's guardian or alternatively the child's parent.[73] Since the predominant consideration (albeit not the "paramount" consideration in some proceedings) in all children cases must be their best interests, it is thought that it would be accurate to describe the courts' role in all of them as broadly parental. Looked at in this way Eekelaar's thesis has a certain attraction since, if the natural parents' rights or powers are superseded where a child has capacity, so by analogy ought the powers and authority of a court when acting as a substitute parent.

[70] John Eekelaar, "The Eclipse of Parental Rights" (1986) 102 L.Q.R. 4, 8.
[71] John Eekelaar, "Gillick in the Divorce Court" (1986) 136 N.L.J. 184.
[72] (1984) 14 Fam. Law 17.
[73] See the discussion in Lowe and White, *op. cit.* n. 1, para. 1.8.

123

If accepted, this extrapolation of the *Gillick* result would mark a significant shift in the existing practice of the courts in relation to custodial dispositions.

It is felt however that there are stronger counter-arguments. First, Ekelaar's arguments are grounded in the radical interpretation of *Gillick* that the child's maturity produces complete autonomy for the child and the termination of parental powers. If the interpretation preferred in Chapter 3 is applied to this issue the child would have only a *relative* claim to independence which should be taken into consideration, but not necessarily followed, by the court. Secondly, the existence of legal rights in one member of a family unit has not hitherto precluded the courts from superseding those rights where they form the view that this is necessary in order to protect another member of the family. The obvious situation is where they interfere with the parent's powers in order to protect a child. Another example is the acceptance by the courts that a partner's property rights may be overridden to protect the other partner and/or the children from domestic violence.[74] Logically, therefore, the courts should also have power to depart from the wishes of a mature child where this is felt necessary in the interests of her welfare. Thirdly, it is submitted that the analogy between natural parenthood and judicial parenthood is at best an imperfect one. Sachs L.J. said as much in *Hewer* v. *Bryant*. Referring to the father's personal power to control his child he said: "In truth any powers exercised by way of physical control in the later years of infancy were not the father's personal powers *but the more extensive ones of the Crown*[75] . . . and hence the father's right was really no more than that of applying to the Courts for the aid he required as guardian."[76] The courts' authority does not depend on them obtaining parental rights in any technical legalistic sense and they clearly possess legal powers which natural parents do not have, *e.g.* the power to grant injunctions. More fundamentally, the parental function itself is, as we have seen, only one aspect of the courts' responsibilities. It is difficult to see how they could effectively perform the balancing exercise, which requires them to weigh the autonomy interest of children alongside parental claims to independence in child-rearing and the public interest in child protection, if they were obliged to act as a rubber-stamp for children's preferences.

[74] *Davis* v. *Johnson* [1979] A.C. 264.
[75] Emphasis added.
[76] [1970] 1 Q.B. 357, 372.

The acceptance of an obligation to follow mature children's wishes would be a retrograde development since it would mark a return to the notions of absolutism (in this case the absolutism of self-determination for children) which Mrs. Gillick and the Court of Appeal tried unsuccessfully to resurrect for parents. Moreover, as Eekelaar recognises, a requirement that the courts should always give effect to the desires of mature children could be easily circumvented by subjective and artificial determinations that particular children lack the requisite capacity where their opinions happen to disagree with those of the judge or welfare officer.[77] For all of these reasons it is felt that the effect of *Gillick* is limited to a requirement that the courts should inquire as a matter of course into the maturity of children in every case and should take account of their views to an extent commensurate with their age and understanding. This would of itself be a significant development. Although the courts frequently do take children's wishes into account, there is a good deal of inconsistency of approach in reported decisions.

At present the relevance of children's wishes depends on the particular legal context. As we have seen, local authorities are obliged to take account of children's wishes under section 18 of the Child Care Act 1980. A similar provision applies to adoption agencies.[78] These requirements do not however apply in other types of proceedings notably custody and wardship proceedings. The mandatory requirements relating to care and adoption may now be thought to have been impliedly extended by *Gillick* to *all* proceedings affecting children. Even where children's wishes are definitely a factor to be taken into account it is not clear what weight should be attached to them relative to other factors. In practice courts disagree on the importance of children's views. In *W. v. A.*,[79] for example, the children were aged 10 and 12 respectively. The Court of Appeal upheld the judge's decision not to allow a change of their surname even though both of them said that they wished to be known by their stepfather's surname and despite their proposed emigration to Australia. Dunn L.J. said that the judge had been "entirely right not to attach decisive

---

[77] *Op. cit.* n. 71, p. 185.

[78] Adoption Act 1976, s.6. It would seem however that the child's personal attendance is not always required in adoption proceedings where the court is content to rely on the report of the guardian *ad litem* as to the child's wishes. See *Re P. (A minor)* (1987) *The Times*, August 1.

[79] [1981] Fam. 14.

importance to the views of two young children of 12 and 10 who were about to embark on the excitement of going to Australia with their mother and their new step-father."[80] More recently, in *Re C. (A minor) (Adoption)*[81] Sir John Arnold P. approved the judge's view in adoption proceedings that a child aged 10 might not be able to appreciate the legal distinctions between adoption and long-term fostering. For this reason the child's express wish to be adopted was thought to be a less than compelling factor in the court's decision.

In a number of cases the courts have expressed scepticism of the value of children's views, especially in custody proceedings where suspicion of parental pressure and anxiety about the long-term interests of children are important factors.[82] The courts do however regard the settled opposition of an older child to contact with a parent as a potentially decisive factor in resolving disputes over custody and access. Thus in *B.* v. *B.*,[83] where a boy of 16 refused to see his father, the court felt that an order compelling him to do so would be ineffective.

It may be that, following *Gillick*, failure to give proper weight to the wishes of an older child may constitute a ground of appeal. This was held to be so in *M.* v. *M. (Minor: Custody Appeal)*[84] where the judge had failed to take into account the adamant view of a 12-year-old girl that she was not willing to live with her mother. A positive legal requirement that children's wishes be taken into account is desirable for, where this is the case, as Maidment puts it, "the decision-making process will respect the child as an individual, and may produce more child-appropriate or child-centred decisions."[85]

Again adopting the analysis in Chapter 3, it may be suggested that in certain cases the courts should nevertheless be obliged to *comply* with the wishes of older children or indeed to decline to exercise jurisdiction over them at all. We saw that in relation to certain activities Parliament has evinced its intention that *all* children in a specified age group should be regarded as autonomous adults. It is arguable that the courts should not defeat this

---

[80] *Ibid.* p. 21.
[81] (1988) 18 Fam. Law 13.
[82] Discussed by Susan Maidment "Child Custody and Divorce" (1984), p. 275.
[83] [1971] 3 All E.R. 682.
[84] [1987] 1 W.L.R. 404.
[85] *Op. cit.* n. 82, p. 277. For the different means of ascertaining children's wishes in legal proceedings see Maidment, (1986) 136 N.L.J. 233.

intention by purporting to overrule such a child's exercise of independence.

In *Re G.U. (A minor) (Wardship)*[86] a girl aged 16 was a ward of court in the care of the local authority. Late in 1983 she became pregnant and the authority arranged for her to have an abortion. In April 1984 they brought the matter back before the High Court, by which time of course the operation had been performed. Balcombe J. ratified the authority's decision taking the view that it had been in the girl's best interests, but he criticised the council for failing to return to the court earlier since what was proposed was a major step in the child's life necessitating the court's prior authorisation. This decision may be criticised in that the judge assumed that the abortion decision was one for the court. In view of section 8 of the Family Law Reform Act 1969 it is arguable that *neither* the consent of the court *nor* that of the council was required since the girl had attained the statutory age for taking independent medical decisions. The unambiguous intention of the legislature is that *all* young people of 16 or over should have capacity to take medical decisions. The only exception is where a child of that age suffers from a degree of mental handicap which has the effect of impairing the reality of consent.[87] Young people in the relevant age group are to be treated as adults and there ought to be no room for arguments about maturity or for paternalistic interventions by the courts. It is therefore extraordinary that Balcombe J. makes no reference to section 8 or to the wishes of the girl. The likelihood is that she wanted the abortion and was of one mind with the local authority and the court. But it must be implicit in this decision that the court could, if it felt it necessary, override her wishes. It is submitted that this would be a genuine illustration of the court overstepping its powers in the face of the contrary intention of Parliament. To allow the courts a free hand to intervene in this way would be to neutralise completely the effect of section 8. In particular the child's independence from her parents would be wholly illusory if they could resort to wardship for the express purpose of maintaining "parental" control over the child. Moreover, as we saw in relation to children

[86] (1984) 5 F.L.R. 811, *sub. nom. H. v. Lambeth L.B.C.* discussed at [1984] J.S.W.L. 290.
[87] See the discussion of *Re B. (A minor)* [1987] 2 W.L.R. 1213 *post*, Chap. 6.

in care, to allow the court to impose its view necessarily entails discrimination against certain categories of adolescents, in this case those who happen to be wards of court.

Another situation in which it is suggested the courts should not attempt to interfere with the independence of older children is where Parliament has specifically sought to lay down legal limits to official control. It may do this by indicating that children of a particular age are not subject to the jurisdiction of the courts. In *Re S.W. (A minor) (Wardship: Jurisdiction)*[88] the parents of a girl aged 17 years and four months warded her and invited the court to place her in the care of the local authority on the grounds that she was beyond their control. The judge found that, after leaving school, she started to "kick over the traces." Amongst other things she was sexually active, had shaved her head and tatooed her body and had run away from home several times. She pleaded guilty to a theft charge for which she received a conditional discharge, but the following day she took her mother's jewellery. Later her parents discovered her in possession of a sheath knife and razor. It was also suspected that she had been introduced to drugs.

In view of her age the girl could not be placed in the care of the authority under the statutory code.[89] Neither was the court empowered to make a care order under the statutory wardship jurisdiction.[90] But Sheldon J. held that these statutory age restrictions did not prevent the court from exercising its inherent jurisdiction to make a care order where this was considered to be in the best interests of the ward. He also thought that it would be open to the court at some future point to direct placement in secure accommodation, notwithstanding the statutory provisions requiring the authorisation of the juvenile court for the use of such accommodation.[91]

---

[88] [1986] 1 F.L.R. 24 and see the commentary by Eekelaar, "Parents' rights to punish—further limits after Gillick" (1986) 28 *Childright* 9, 10.

[89] Care proceedings may not be initiated in relation to a person who has attained 17 (s.1(1) and s.70(1) of the Children and Young Persons Act 1969). Neither can a person of that age be committed to care in the various family proceedings in which care orders may be made (*e.g.* s.43(4) of the Matrimonial Causes Act 1973).

[90] Family Law Reform Act 1969, s.7(3).

[91] After some considerable judicial disagreement it is now established that only the authority of the High Court is required where the child is a ward of court (The Secure Accommodation (No. 2) (Amendment) Regulations 1986 (S.I. 1986 No. 1591)).

This decision also seems to fly in the face of the declared intention of Parliament that young people of 17 should not be placed in local authority care. In so far as the girl's behaviour was criminal it could have been dealt with by prosecution. This was done with respect to the theft and it would also have been open to the police to consider prosecutions for possession of offensive weapons or a drugs offence provided that sufficient evidence was available. But the other complaints related to behaviour which might incur "official" disapproval but which was not of itself criminal and which fell within the sphere of legal autonomy allowed to those over 16. Sexual intercourse is not an offence and the girl herself commits no offence by being tatooed or by shaving her head. As for running away from home, she was well within the age of discretion recognised at common law for the purposes of determining where she should live. It has been observed that there is an important distinction between the operation of the criminal law, which recognises the capacity of young people to engage in certain activities subject to punishing the exercise of that capacity in certain instances, and the paternal jurisdiction of wardship which denies capacity and lacks the procedural safeguards which are designed to safeguard the liberty of the subject.[92]

We saw in Chapter 3 the extent of independence which the law allows to young people over 16. In the light of this it is questionable whether the traditional jurisdiction of the wardship court over "Teenage Wards' can continue to be justified at all.[93] Autonomy includes the right to make mistakes which should perhaps not be removed by the inculcation of "official" values, especially where these may be unrepresentative of those held by the population at large. The objection to the courts exercising control over recalcitrant teenagers may be based on the analogy with diminishing parental powers.[94] The stronger objection is that Parliament has determined that in a number of areas they should be free from official control except where they transgress the criminal law.

[92] Eekelaar, *loc. cit.* n. 88.
[93] The involvement of the courts in such cases is discussed by Lowe and White, *op. cit.* n. 1, para. 12.1. *et seq.*, and by Cross, *op. cit.* n. 1, pp. 209–211. See also Law Com. No. 101, paras. 3.48–3.51.
[94] This is Eekelaar's reasoning, *loc. cit.* n. 77.

6. Health Care

1. Introduction

No area better illustrates the competing interests of children, parents and the state than that of medical care. In North America there has been extensive litigation concerned largely with the question of who should decide what medical treatment a child should undergo.[1] In England some of the more significant and well-publicised cases involving children have been concerned with health-related issues.

The child's right to receive appropriate health care is reflected in a correlative duty in parents to ensure that he receives it. The state has an interest in protecting the well-being of individual children and a general interest in the health of the community of which children form an important part.[2] There is substantial agreement that there must be some circumstances in which the state, through its various agencies, should step in to override parental discretion in order to safeguard the health of a child. At the same time it is widely felt that parents should be permitted some latitude in determining what is the appropriate manner of caring for their child's health. Goldstein, Freud and Solnit argue that state intervention based on medical neglect should take place only in extreme circumstances, and in particular would confine it to life-threatening situations.[3] Their position has

---

[1] Useful collections of materials are contained in W. Wadlington, C. H. Whitebread and S. M. Davis, *Children in the Legal System* (1983), pp. 893–965 and R. H. Mnookin, *Child, Family and State* (1978), Chap. 4.

[2] The state's interest is evidenced by the existence of the National Health Service and the statutory duty imposed on the Secretary of State for Health and Social Services to promote it under the National Health Service Act 1977.

[3] In their view public intervention should take place only where parents refuse to authorise medical care and "(i) medical experts agree that treatment is non-experimental and appropriate for the child; (ii) denial of that treatment would result in death; and (iii) the anticipated result of treatment is what society would want for every child—a chance for normal healthy growth or a life worth living." See *Before the Best Interests of the Child* (1980), p. 91.

been widely criticised as tilting the balance too far in favour of parents.[4] The difficulty, as always, is knowing where to draw the line.

It may be readily accepted that it is both a practical necessity and right in principle that parents should have first claim to decide health issues affecting their child where that child lacks capacity to give a valid consent himself. But implicit in this parental discretion is the power to *withhold* consent or veto medical procedures. It is at this point that the question of parental duties arises. The existence of a legal duty to ensure that the child receives adequate medical aid circumscribes the parental discretion. In cases of controversy it therefore becomes necessary to determine whether, in withholding authorisation of treatment, parents are in breach of their legal duty or whether they are acting within the sphere of discretion which is preserved for them under the law.

In this area, as in others, the law does not draw any obvious distinction between children of different ages, at least until they attain 16. Yet there are clearly important practical differences between the position of a newly-born infant and an adolescent. Different considerations again apply to the situation of the developing foetus, where there is sharp disagreement on what legal measures (if any) should be taken to safeguard its health. It may therefore be helpful for analytical purposes to draw a distinction between unborn, newly born, young, mentally immature or retarded children on the one hand, and older children or mature adolescents on the other hand. Since the former category lack the capacity to resort to self-help the emphasis is on the enforcement of parental duties rather than the exercise of parental discretions. Conversely, the second category of children may possess the capacity to consent on their own behalf. In those cases the issue is the relationship between their own powers of independent action and their parents' discretion to arrange medical care on their behalf. The child or young person is here not seeking to enforce his parents' duties but rather to by-pass parental involvement altogether by arriving at his own decision in conjunction with professional medical advice.

---

[4] See, for example, Freeman, *The Rights and the Wrongs of Children* (1983), pp. 255–259; Dickens, "The Modern Function and Limits of Parental Rights" (1981) 97 L.Q.R. 462, pp. 466–485.

The issue of consent is fundamental to any discussion of medical decision-making.[5] At common law any unauthorised touching constitutes a battery. Thus, a doctor who performs an examination or a surgeon who carries out an operation without the patient's consent is liable in tort. The patient's right to give or withhold consent is founded on the idea of self-determination which implies that every person should be able to decide what is or is not done to his body. The principle of patient autonomy is however a qualified one which exists alongside a strong tradition of medical paternalism in England. Accordingly, although the final decision on whether to submit to various medical procedures rests with the patient, the tortious doctrine of informed consent has not taken root in England. It was rejected by the House of Lords in *Sidaway* v. *Board of Governors of the Bethlem Royal Hospital and the Maudsley Hospital*[6] in the context of a negligence action brought by an adult patient. Where this doctrine applies a doctor is required to provide enough information about the risks involved in various procedures and the available alternatives to enable the patient to arrive at a reasoned decision on whether to submit to them. Failure to provide sufficient information can give rise to tortious liability if the risk subsequently materialises. In England, however, the doctor will be regarded as having discharged his duty to provide information if he can show that he has acted "in accordance with a practice accepted as proper by a responsible body of men skilled in the particular art."[7]

The law seems to be more concerned in the case of adults with the fact rather than with the quality of consent. It is sufficient that the patient should understand in general terms the nature of the proposed treatment. In the case of a child, however, the law must concern itself with qualitative assessments of consent since the doctor *must* satisfy himself that the child fully understands the nature and implications of the proposed treatment before proceeding without parental consent.[8] As we have seen, Lord Scarman in *Gillick* took the view that a high level of maturity would be

---

[5] See, for example, Mason and McCall Smith, *Law and Medical Ethics* 2nd Ed. (1987) Chap. 9.

[6] [1985] A.C. 871 H.L. See also Robertson, "Informed Consent to Medical Treatment" (1981) 97 L.Q.R. 102; Teff, "Consent to Medical Procedures: Paternalism, Self-determination or Therapeutic Alliance?" (1985) 101 L.Q.R. 432; *cf.* Lee, "Operating Under Informed Consent" (1985) 101 L.Q.R. 316.

[7] *Bolam* v. *Friern Hospital Management Committee* [1957] 1 W.L.R. 582, 587.

[8] *Gillick* v. *West Norfolk and Wisbech A.H.A.* [1986] 1 A.C. 112.

required of a girl under 16 before she could give a valid consent to contraception. She would be required to understand not only the medical implications but also the moral and family considerations surrounding contraception. It has been suggested that Lord Scarman is here propounding his own doctrine of informed consent, the effect of which may be to deprive people of reduced abilities, such as the mentally handicapped or child patients, of the right to choose.[9] If this is so, it is also arguable that the extent of the doctor's legal duty of disclosure of risks may vary depending on the age and capacity of the patient.

Since child autonomy, parental powers and medical paternalism coexist, a legal model of participatory decision-making has emerged. The important questions concern the relative extent of involvement of the various participants in the decision-making process, and under what circumstances the state may intervene through a local authority or the courts to take the decision itself.

2. The Unborn, the Newly-Born and the Immature

Where a child lacks mental capacity to consent to necessary medical treatment and the parents refuse to provide a proxy consent, public intervention may be necessary. One way in which the state may respond to this situation is to prosecute the parents under the criminal law for failing to provide adequate medical aid. In *R. v. Senior*[10] it was held that a parent's failure to call medical aid for a dangerously ill child who died of diarrhoea and pneumonia amounted to manslaughter by gross negligence. This was so even though the parent's decision was grounded in genuinely held religious convictions and it was accepted that the accused had otherwise done all that he could in terms of attention to the child's food and diet.[11] A specific statutory offence embracing medical neglect by persons *in loco parentis* has existed since the Poor Law Amendment Act 1868 and is now contained in section 1 of the Children and Young Persons Act 1933. This is

[9] Brenda Hoggett, "Parents, Children and Medical Treatment: The Legal Issues" in *Rights and Wrongs in Medicine* (Ed. Peter Byrne) (1986), pp. 165, 173.
[10] [1899] 1 Q.B. 283.
[11] The accused belonged to a sect known as "The Peculiar People" whose specific objection to the use of doctors was based on their interpretation of the Epistle of James, Chap. 5 verses 14 and 15.

committed by any person over the age of 16 years having the custody, charge or care of any child or young person who "wilfully assaults, ill-treats, neglects, abandons or exposes him ... in a manner likely to cause unnecessary suffering or injury to health."

By subsection (2) the offence is deemed to include failure to provide, *inter alia*, adequate medical aid, or failure to take steps to procure it to be provided. Whether the degree of neglect required is established is a question of fact for the jury but, following *R. v. Sheppard*[12] it is established that the requirement of wilfulness implies a subjective rather than objective test. In that case the majority of the House of Lords held that the use of the verb "neglect" could not import into the criminal law the civil concept of negligence. Hence it must be proved that the accused appreciated the risk to the child's health or was reckless about this, and it could be a defence to show that this appreciation was absent in parents of low intelligence. Failure to comply with the objective standard of reasonableness might however ground a tortious action by the child against his parent. Criminal prosecution does not of course provide the solution to the immediate problem of procuring medical attention for a child. It may be necessary to resort to wardship or care proceedings for this purpose.

Wardship has been used in a number of leading cases either to authorise or prohibit proposed medical operations. In *Re B. (A minor) (Wardship) Medical Treatment*[13] a baby girl, "Alexandra," was born with the double disadvantage of Down's Syndrome and an intestinal blockage. The medical evidence was that, unless she underwent surgery, she would die within a few days. Her parents objected to the operation taking the view that, bearing in mind her mongolism, it would be kinder to allow her to die. The hospital staff notified the local authority which warded the child. The council obtained care and control and the court's authorisation for the surgery to be performed, but the surgeon whom the council approached refused to operate against the parents' wishes. Other surgeons were prepared to operate and the council brought the matter before the court. Ewbank J. having refused to order the operation, the council took the issue to the Court of Appeal. Allowing their appeal Templeman L.J. held that the judge had erred in attaching too much importance to the parents' wishes and in concluding that they should be respected. The sole issue for the

---

[12] [1981] A.C. 394.
[13] [1981] 1 W.L.R. 1421.

court was the best interests of the child and, in particular, whether her life was demonstrably going to be so awful that she should be condemned to die, or whether it was so imponderable that she should be allowed to live. The evidence established only that, if the operation took place and succeeded, the child might live the normal life span of a mongoloid child with the handicaps and defects of mongolism. The Court concluded that it was not for it to say that life of that description ought to be extinguished.

Hoggett and Pearl raise the interesting question of whether the welfare principle should be allowed to govern life and death situations such as this.[14] They ask whether such an approach can be reconciled with the criminal liability of parents (and others) who wilfully fail to secure adequate medical aid for children. The implication appears to be that the court may not have had any choice in *Re B.* but to authorise the surgery.

There are a number of responses which could be made to this suggestion. First, the argument was presented in Chapter 3, in relation to *powers*, that the courts' powers over children need not necessarily be limited to those of natural parents since the analogy between natural and judicial parenthood is an imperfect one. This argument could be applied equally to *duties*. The fact that parents have a legal duty to take certain action in relation to their child does not automatically produce the conclusion that a commensurate duty is placed upon the judiciary. Secondly, it may be argued that section 1 of the Children and Young Persons Act 1933 was not intended to apply to situations in which parents take decisions in relation to seriously ill children in conjunction with professional medical advice. The failure to provide adequate medical aid, deemed by subsection (2) to constitute neglect, may be thought not to apply where proper medical assistance has been sought. The section, it may be argued, is designed to catch those parents who fail to summon medical attention *at all*. It is unlikely, therefore, that the parents themselves could be said to have been in breach of their statutory duty in the circumstances of *Re B.*

Medical aid for defective newborns is an issue on which there is no societal consensus. It involves subjective moral evaluations about the quality of life and what constitutes appropriate medical aid. The reason why the welfare principle is an inadequate principle *per se* for the resolution of these issues is that it may

---

[14] Brenda M. Hoggett and David S. Pearl, *The Family, Law and Society*, 2nd Ed. (1987) p. 377.

allow the individual preferences of the judge or other decision-maker to intrude. Later it will be suggested that a primary objective should be to establish standard procedures and principles to govern cases like this.

A similar situation to *Re B.* arose in the United States in 1982 in the case of "Baby Doe."[15] The child was born with Down's Syndrome and a blocked oesophagus. Again the infant's parents declined to authorise life saving surgery and were supported by their physician. The hospital notified the local authorities who brought the matter before the state courts. The state courts refused to order removal of the child from the parents with a view to surgery. While attorneys were preparing an appeal to the Supreme Court, the child died six days after birth. The case highlighted the deficiencies of the legal system in providing the kind of immediate protection required in life threatening situations and the absence of guiding principles to govern such cases. The result was action at the federal level. First, an anti-discrimination statute was applied with a view to preventing discrimination in the denial of medical treatment and nourishment to handicapped children with life-threatening conditions.[16] Secondly, the Child Abuse Prevention and Treatment Act[17] was amended to require states to establish specific procedures for dealing with complaints of medical neglect of these infants. These legislative initiatives, which attempted to establish equality of treatment for all handicapped children in life-threatening situations, were criticised for falling short of creating standards which were enforceable against individuals.[18] In any event the federal anti-discrimination regulations were subsequently invalidated by the Supreme Court in *Bowen* v. *American Hospital Association*.[19] It was held that the relevant department of State had provided no evidence of a discriminatory withholding of medical care to newly born infants on the basis of their handicap. Where care had been withheld this was invariably because of lack of parental or other appropriate consent. The statute did not authorise the use of federal resources to save the lives of handicapped newborns,

---

[15] For a discussion of the case and its aftermath see Jessica Dunsay Silver, "Baby Doe: The Incomplete Federal Response" 20 Fam.L.Q. 173 (1986).
[16] Rehabilitation Act 1973, s.504; 29 U.S.C., s.794.
[17] 42 U.S.C., s.5101.
[18] Silver, *op. cit.* n. 15, p. 195.
[19] 90 L. Ed. 2d 584 (1986).

without regard to whether they were victims of discrimination by recipients of federal funds or not.

Despite the practical result in Baby Doe it is well-established in the United States that parents' constitutional privacy rights are not entitled to *absolute* respect where their child's life is threatened. In *Custody of a Minor*[20] the Supreme Court of Massachusetts recognised that these rights "do not clothe parents with life and death authority over their children." Accordingly, the court was prepared to override parental preferences in the manner of treatment for their three year old son who was suffering from leukemia. The evidence revealed that chemotherapy could save the child's life, but the parents wished to persist with metabolic therapy including laetrile despite proof that this was not only useless but dangerous. However the opposite conclusion was reached by the Court of Appeals of New York in *Matter of Hofbauer*.[21] The court upheld the parents' choice of treatment of their seven year old son who had Hodgkin's disease. The court held that the limit of the parents' duty to arrange medical assistance for their child was to provide "a treatment which is recommended by their physician and which has not been totally rejected by all responsible medical authority."

These two cases show that while there may be general agreement that parents are not invested with absolute powers over life and death, beyond this there is disagreement on the precise weight to be attached to their wishes.[22]

If no consensus exists in life-threatening cases, it is not surprising that this has been even more difficult to achieve where life itself is not at stake. American courts have traditionally shown greater respect for parents' wishes in these cases. For example, in *Matter of Seiferth*[23] a New York court declined to order surgical correction of the split lip and cleft palate of a 14 year old boy, although these defects substantially impaired his speech. His father's view that nature should take its course was upheld by the court. Eventually, however, in *Re Sampson*[24] another New York

[20] 379 N.E. 2d 1053 (1978).
[21] 393 N.E. 2d 1009 (1979).
[22] For the arguments that there should be standard procedures governing life and death decisions relating to newly born infants see Robertson, "Involuntary Euthanasia of Defective Newborns: A Legal Analysis" 27 Stan.L.Rev. 213 (1975).
[23] 127 N.E. 2d 820 (1955).
[24] 278 N.E. 2d 918 (1972).

court was prepared to order corrective surgery in a non life-threatening case. Kevin Sampson was 15 years old at the time of the proceedings and had suffered since early childhood from a congenital facial deformity known as neurofibromatosis. His condition could be alleviated, but not cured, by a dangerous operation to be followed by prolonged treatment. The surgery required transfusions of the whole blood but the boy's mother, owing to her religious convictions, would authorise only the use of plasma. All the state courts held that this refusal constituted parental neglect, not of a generalised nature, but in relation to this one controversial decision.[25] The decision should be contrasted with *In Re Green*[26] where the Supreme Court of Pennsylvania upheld the religious beliefs of a Jehovah's Witness who refused to assent to corrective surgery on a child's collapsed spine. This case is regarded by some as the high water mark of respect for parental autonomy and religious freedom, the court offering the opinion that "the State does not have an interest of sufficient magnitude outweighing a parent's religious beliefs when the child's life is not immediately imperiled by his physical condition."

In England the most controversial non life-threatening issue has proved to be the sterilisation of mentally handicapped minors. The question first came before the courts in 1976 in *Re D. (Sterilisation).*[27] The child, aged 11 at the relevant time, suffered from "Sotos' Syndrome" of which the symptoms were accelerated growth during infancy, epilepsy, generalised clumsiness, emotional instability, aggressive tendencies and an impairment of mental function. Her widowed mother was concerned that the girl might become pregnant and give birth to an abnormal child which she would be unable to look after. She wished to have her daughter sterilised and was supported in this by a paediatrician. Together they arranged with a gynaecologist to perform the operation. This course was however opposed by certain individuals who had had involvement with the child, including the plaintiff who was an educational psychologist. The plaintiff commenced wardship proceedings and succeeded in obtaining an order prohibiting the operation. Heilbron J. thought that what was proposed was an irreversible procedure which involved "the deprivation of a basic

---

[25] See also *In Re Karwath* 199 N.W. 2d 147 (1972) where the Supreme Court of Iowa authorised the surgical removal of tonsils and adenoids, the parents having refused consent.

[26] 448 Pa. 338, 292 A. 2d 387 (1972).

[27] [1976] Fam. 185.

human right, namely the right of a woman to reproduce." This was not medically indicated nor in the girl's best interests since it was not possible to predict accurately her future role in society, nor her subsequent development. Although it was accepted that she presently lacked capacity to give or withhold consent, the evidence was that she would almost certainly understand the implications of the treatment by the time she reached 18. On the facts the operation was of a nontherapeutic nature and could not therefore be within the doctor's sole clinical judgment.

One of the interesting features of this case was that the judge talked in terms of basic human rights. At the same time the case was decided on an individualistic application of the welfare principle and it was obvious from the outset that its value as a precedent was limited.[28] This was because the judge did not purport to lay down general principles to govern the circumstances under which sterilisations could be justified. The court's sole concern was whether this particular child's best interests justified the operation. It left open the possibility that in another case the same welfare criterion might be invoked to justify a sterilisation operation. So it was that in *Re B. (A minor)*[29] the House of Lords upheld a sterilisation operation for contraceptive purposes on a mentally handicapped girl ("Jeanette") aged 17.

Jeanette had a mental age of five or six. The expert evidence was to the effect that she could not appreciate the causal connection between sexual intercourse and childbirth and would never be capable of consenting to marriage. It was also said that she had no maternal instincts, would be incapable of understanding the pains and stresses of pregnancy and would be unable to look after a child. At the same time it was feared that she was becoming sexually aware and that there was a significant danger that she would become pregnant as a result of casual sexual activity. Most forms of contraception had been rejected as impracticable in her case. The only feasible method was an oral contraceptive which was estimated to have only a 40 per cent. chance of success and which might have undesirable sideeffects. The local authority, who had the care of Jeanette, decided with the support of her mother, to sterilise her by a method involving occlusion of the fallopian tubes.

---

[28] The evidence in the case itself indicated that the consultant paediatrician at the Sheffield Northern General Hospital had already performed sterilisation operations on two handicapped girls in that city.

[29] [1987] 2 W.L.R. 1213. For a discussion of the decision see Bainham, "Handicapped Girls and Judicial Parents" (1987) 103 L.Q.R. 334.

The House of Lords decided to sanction the operation on the sole basis that it was in her best interests. The House rejected the view that any general issues of public policy were involved and denied that the case had anything to do with eugenics. The Law Lords refused to accept the Canadian distinction between therapeutic and non-therapeutic sterilisation. In the Canadian case *Re Eve*[30] La Forest J. had held that sterilisation should never be used for non-therapeutic purposes. Lord Oliver thought that it did not matter whether protective measures were described as therapeutic and Lord Hailsham felt that to draw such distinctions would be meaningless and would represent a "startling contradiction" to the welfare principle. He also thought that it was not proper to talk in terms of a "basic human right to reproduce" in relation to an individual who lacked the capacity to make an informed choice in matters of pregnancy and childbirth. Lord Templeman emphasised that sterilisation was a procedure of last resort and should never be carried out without the leave of a High Court judge since only in wardship would the matter receive the full and informed investigation which it required.

This case has many interesting features. On its facts it *does* appear to be distinguishable from *Re D.* to the extent that the future mental capacity of Jeanette was much easier to predict than the more speculative position of the younger girl in *Re D.* It is not proposed however to express an opinion on whether sterilisation was right in this particular case, although that in itself is a question which has provoked considerable controversy.[31] The decision, taken with *Re D.*, exposes the need for established principles or standards, together with adequate procedures, to achieve a measure of consistency in the treatment of children in comparable situations. One way of partially achieving this might be to adopt the distinction between therapeutic and non-therapeutic procedures.[32] The essential difference is between procedures which are *medically* indicated and those which are not. If the issue is defined in terms of the best interests of the child, operations should be confined to those which could be justified in accordance with the child's best *medical* interests.[33]

The result of applying this test is that the operation in *Re B.* would have been authorised, but not the operation in *Re D.* In the former

[30] (1986) 31 D.L.R. (4th) 1.
[31] For an assessment of the merits of the decision as applied to Jeanette herself see Alison Wertheimer, "Sterilisation: for better or for worse?" (1987) 38 *Childright* 17.
[32] For an illuminating discussion see Andrew Grubb and David Pearl, "Sterilisation and the Courts" [1987] C.L.J. 439, particularly at 442–445.
[33] *Ibid.*

case there were sound medical reasons for the operation. In particular it was predicted that Jeanette would, in the event of pregnancy, have to be delivered by Caesarian Section and that there was a risk that she would thereafter pick at the operational wound and tear it open. By contrast no such considerations applied to the girl in *Re D*. Neither was it demonstrated in that case that there were no reliable contraceptive alternatives to sterilisation. As we have seen, these results were in fact achieved by the respective courts on an unqualified application of the welfare principle.

The therapeutic test requires that the medical procedure in question be necessary to preserve the life or physical or mental health of the child. Therapy for these purposes would extend beyond an *existing* malfunction or disease to include *anticipated* disease, illness, disability or disorder. Non-therapeutic procedures would include those motivated by considerations of convenience as opposed to medical need. The desire to avoid pregnancy and to relieve the anxiety and the burden which might be placed on the child's family would fall into this category.[34]

Re D. was a good illustration of the inadequacy of existing legal procedures. The girl in that case was protected because of the fortuitous intervention of an interested third party. Following that case, it was thought that the wardship procedure could not protect the vast majority of children who do not profit from such interventions. In the case itself Heilbron J. specifically rejected the contention that the Official Solicitor's department had the authority to act as a public watchdog by instituting wardship proceedings of its own volition. Nonetheless, Lord Templeman's view is that the authority of the court is a condition precedent to a lawful operation. Thus, although the operation was authorised in *Re B.*, the case offers (in theory at least) automatic protection to *all* mentally handicapped minors by requiring judicial scrutiny of their individual circumstances. It has been suggested elsewhere however that the theoretical basis of Lord Templeman's new procedure is highly suspect.[35] Moreover his remarks are clearly *obiter* since none of the other Law Lords concurred with his opinion on this point. In the United States a number of states have enacted sterilisation statutes empowering the courts to authorise sterilisation operations on the mentally retarded. But, significantly, it has been held there that in the absence of such a statute

[34] *Ibid.* pp. 444–445.
[35] Bainham, *op. cit.* n. 29.

there is no jurisdiction to do so.[36] As we saw in Chapter 5, there is growing concern that wardship is a largely unrestrained jurisdiction. It is not self-evident that judges are better qualified to pronounce definitively on the merits of sterilisation in individual cases than are parents or doctors (or both of them acting in concert).[37]

These objections could be met in part by the adoption of clear principles. While it may be that judicial referral provides the best safeguard in this area, this should be a matter for Parliament to decide and sterilisation should be governed by statutory principles.

The English wardship cases have all been concerned with single, albeit fundamentally significant, medical issues. In some cases however wardship may not be the preferred procedure, quite apart from its high cost and associated delays, since it may be alleged that a parent is generally unfit to have the care of a child because of evidence of unwillingness or inability to safeguard the child's health on a continuing basis. In these circumstances a local authority may wish to remove the child from parental care in care proceedings and itself resume responsibility for the child's health. Although this could also be achieved in wardship proceedings, a statutory care order offers greater independence to the authority.

We saw in Chapter 4 that the House of Lords in *D. (A minor)* v. *Berkshire County Council* considered the circumstances under which a care order might be made to safeguard the health of a newly born child. The case also gave rise to a certain amount of speculation about the status of the unborn child under the civil and criminal law. Since the health of the embryo/foetus is inextricably connected to the mother's own state of health, the question arises as to how far the law should demand that pregnant women so conduct themselves that they avoid the risk of harm to their unborn children. It might be argued that the mother who abuses or neglects her body while pregnant should render herself liable to criminal prosecution for consequential damage to the health of the foetus which may become apparent at birth.

In general, the criminal law does not protect the unborn child since offences against the person require that the victim should have an

---

[36] See the discussion in C.A.P. Finch-Noyes, "Sterilisation of the Mentally Retarded Minor: The Re K. Case" [1986] 5 Can.J. of Fam. Law 277, 286. For U.S. cases on sterilisation see *A.L.* v. *G.R.H.* 325 N.E. 2d 501 (1975) and *Re Grady* 426 A. 2d 467 (1981).

[37] See Charles H. Baron, "Medicine and Human Rights: Emerging Substantive Standards and Procedural Protections for Medical Decision-Making Within the American Family" in *The Resolution of Family Conflict* Ed. John M. Eekelaar and Sanford N. Katz (1984) 575 at pp. 588–591.

independent existence at the time of the commission of a criminal act. It is not strictly necessary however that, in order to offer protection to the foetus, it must be brought within the legal definition of a "child." It would be possible, as recognised by the Warnock Committee, to invest the human embroy/foetus with a special status in law giving rise to certain legal protections.[38] Deciding on the appropriate level of protection is a subject upon which it is exceptionally difficult to find agreement. The process of balancing the conflicting interests of children and parents, difficult enough in relation to living children, is even more vexing where the argument is that restraints should be imposed on the cherished autonomy interests of adults in order to protect the health of the foetus.

In the United States the Supreme Court has refused to extend the personal constitutional rights enjoyed by living children to the unborn child. In *Roe* v. *Wade*[39] it was held that the foetus was not to be regarded as a person under the constitution. Any specific legal protections which states see fit to enact may be examined for their constitutionality in that they will, by definition, involve some restriction on the privacy rights of women. Certain states it appears have assumed powers to order compulsory blood transfusions or caesarean sections in the interests of the foetus. Others have created specific criminal offences relating to the unborn or have amended existing criminal statutes to ensure their equal applicability to the unborn.[40] Opinion is sharply divided on whether these developments are justifiable.[41] Ultimately these questions involve value judgments about the relative weight which should attach to potential life and personal autonomy.

Certain limited protections exist in English law. Abortion is a criminal offence except where performed in the circumstances laid down by the Abortion Act 1967. The offence of child destruction is committed "by any person who, with intent to destroy the life of a child capable of being born alive, by any wilful act causes a child to die before it has an existence

---

[38] Report of the Committee of Inquiry into Human Fertilisation and Embryology (1984) Cmnd. 9314, para. 11.17.

[39] 410 U.S. 113 (1973).

[40] Some of these developments are discussed by Dawn E. Johnsen, "The Creation of Foetal Rights: Conflicts with Women's Constitutional Rights to Liberty, Privacy and Equal Protection" 95 Yale L.J. 599 (1986).

[41] See Johnsen *ibid.*, *cf.* Jeffrey A. Parness, "The Abuse and Neglect of the Human Unborn: Protecting Potential Life" 20 Fam.L.Q. 197 (1986).

independent of its mother."[42] In *C.* v. *S.*[43] a postgraduate student at Oxford University applied for an injunction on his own behalf and as next friend of his unborn child to prevent his former girlfriend from terminating her pregnancy. He argued that the proposed abortion constituted a threatened offence of child destruction contrary to section 1 of the Infant Life (Preservation) Act 1929. The critical question was whether the 18 week old foetus was "capable of being born alive" within the meaning of the Act. Both Heilbron J. and the Court of Appeal answered this question in the negative.

The Court of Appeal did not go on to consider the further questions as to the father's *locus standi* and whether a foetus was a juristic person capable of suing. The court did indicate however that if it had been required to rule on these issues it would have given strong consideration to the words of Sir George Baker P. in *Paton* v. *British Pregnancy Advisory Service Trustees*[44] where he said that " ... not only would it be a bold and brave judge ... who would seek to interfere with the discretion of doctors acting under the Abortion Act 1967, but I think he would be a really foolish judge ... ."

More recently, in *Re F. (In Utero)*[45] Hollings J. and subsequently the Court of Appeal held that there was no jurisdiction to make an unborn child a ward of court. The action was instigated by a local authority which was concerned about the welfare of the "child." The mother suffered from delusions that doctors and nurses would harm her baby. She had disappeared from her flat and it was feared that she might return to her "hippy" nomadic lifestyle. No doubt Social Services were concerned that an unconventional birth with no adequate medical supervision might take place unless they took pre-emptive action to prevent this.

In this case the foetus was much closer to term than was the foetus in *C.* v. *S.* so that no issue arose as to whether it was capable of being born alive. Neither was the court presented with the *locus standi* problem since in wardship proceedings it is not necessary that the "child" be made a party. It was nonetheless held that wardship was confined to a living child because of the application

---

[42] See I. J. Keown, "The Scope of the Offence of Child Destruction" (1988) 104 L.Q.R. 120.

[43] [1987] 1 All E.R. 1230.

[44] [1979] Q.B. 276, 282.

[45] (1988) *The Times*, 20 January, 1988 (Hollings J.); (1988) 138 N.L.J. 37 (Court of Appeal).

of the welfare principle. The Court of Appeal took the view that there was an inherent incompatibility between this and the rights and welfare of the mother. May L.J. said that any order made to protect the welfare of an unborn child would be bound to affect the mother. There would have to be an order authorising the tipstaff to find her and perhaps an order that she live in a certain place and attend a certain hospital. All these orders would be restrictive of the mother's liberty. There might also be medical problems since the mother might wish one course of action to be taken while it might be in the interests of the child that an alternative procedure should be followed. The court rejected the invitation of counsel to accept that the wardship jurisdiction could be limited to a viable unborn child of 28 weeks' pregnancy taking the view that under the law as it stands the jurisdictional line was drawn at birth.

The reasoning of both Hollings J. and the Court of Appeal based on the welfare principle is unconvincing. While this principle governs the vast majority of decisions in wardship it is not universally applied. Where, for example, considerations of public policy are involved the court sometimes has to weigh the interests of the ward against the interests of others.[46] There would seem to be no compelling reason why the court could not have taken it upon itself to weigh the autonomy interests of the mother in determining the manner of the birth against the interests of the unborn child in the prevention of unnecessary risks to its health which might be occasioned by an unsupervised birth. The court's decision in effect accords paramountcy to the interests of the *mother*. With respect to the Court of Appeal, the fact that the exercise of the wardship jurisdiction would expose the existence of a conflict between the interests of the mother in taking personal decisions and the health and welfare interests of the foetus/newly born child is *the whole point* and the principal argument in favour of judicial intervention.

It appears, for the moment at least, that English law is not ready to acknowledge the claims of the foetus *qua* foetus. But the above cases may nonetheless serve to heighten public consciousness on the potential conflict of interest between women and their unborn children.

---

[46] See, for example, *Re X. (A minor) (Wardship: Jurisdiction)* [1975] Fam. 47.

3. Adolescents

The issue of medical care becomes yet more complex where the child in question is an adolescent. Here there is the added dimension and complication that the child herself may represent another location of decision-making power. Health care may be seen as a private matter between the child and her doctor, obviating the necessity of parental involvement and transcending the instructions of parents where they happen to conflict with the joint decision of the child patient and her medical advisers. After all, as Hoggett has observed, "parental consent is required, not because the treatment would otherwise be an invasion of the rights of the parent, but because it would otherwise be an invasion of the rights of the child."[47] It is therefore a serious question whether parental authority should be limited to providing consent on behalf of incapable children or whether parents should be able to provide an *alternative* consent even when the child is capable.[48] As we saw in Chapter 3, the House of Lords held in *Gillick* that a mature child could give a valid consent for the purposes of contraception. The majority speeches were expressed at a fairly broad level of generality, although the minority confined themselves to discussing the narrow issue of contraception. The better view would therefore seem to be that the *Gillick* principles should now govern the provision of all forms of medical treatment to children under the age of 16. It also seems likely that Lord Fraser's conditions for proceeding without parental consent will be considered to represent the existing state of the law, certainly as far as contraception is concerned. Thus, they are incorporated in the revised D.H.S.S. Circular.[49]

Lord Fraser's formulation rejects the idea of an absolute right to decide being vested in children, parents or the medical profession and is best characterised as supportive of rights of participation in the decision-making process. It is envisaged that, in the ordinary case, the doctor will be at liberty to discuss the matter with his child patient without prior parental consultation, but that thereafter the parents will be notified. Only where all of his conditions are satisfied should the parents be excluded from a say in the

---

[47] *Op. cit.* n. 9, p. 161.
[48] *Ibid.* p. 165.
[49] Health Circular H.C. (86) 1; H.C. (F.P.) (86) 1 and Local Authority Circular L.A.C. (86) 3.

discussions leading up to a final decision. The result of *Gillick* also seems to be to vest the ultimate right to decide not in the parent, nor in the child but in the medical profession.[50] As such it is arguable that the decision has more to do with the English tradition of medical paternalism than with child liberation. This seems to be confirmed by the revised circular which states that decisions about whether to prescribe contraception in cases covered by *Gillick* guidelines are for a doctor's clinical judgment.

In the United States the reconciliation of the competing interests of children, parents and the state in the matter of medical treatment has given rise to a number of Supreme Court decisions. In some cases the court has been concerned with intrusive state action which curtails the child's right of privacy arising from substantive due process guaranteed by the fifth and fourteenth amendments. This right implies independence in personal decisions on matters such as marriage, procreation and conception. In these cases the interests of parent and child may well coincide and unite under the umbrella of *family* autonomy. In another type of case the court has had to resolve an apparent conflict of interest between parent and child which arises under state laws.[51]

Carey v. *Population Services International*[52] is an example of the first variety. Here a New York statute proscribing the distribution of contraceptives to children under 16 was struck down as unconstitutional. The majority held that it violated privacy rights. The decision whether or not to beget a child was considered to be at the very heart of the cluster of constitutionally protected choices, and the state restriction could not be validated by the presence of a significant state interest. The court held that it was not open to the state to demonstrate its disapproval of teenage sexual activity by deliberately increasing the hazards attendant upon it. Stevens J. likened this to a desire to dramatise disapproval of motorcycles by prohibiting the use of safety helmets![53]

Planned Parenthood of Central Missouri v. *Danforth*[54] illustrates the second type of case. Here Missouri had imposed a requirement

---

[50] This interpretation is put forward on the basis that Lord Fraser's guidelines are couched in permissive rather than mandatory language. Nowhere is there any suggestion that a doctor is ever *obliged* to provide contraceptive advice or treatment.

[51] See H. Wingo and S. N. Freytag, "Decisions within the Family: A Clash of Constitutional Rights" 67 Iowa Law Rev. 401 (1982).

[52] 431 U.S. 678 (1977).

[53] *Ibid.* p. 715.

[54] 428 U.S. 52 (1976).

of parental consent before an abortion might be performed on an unmarried woman under the age of 18, except where a licensed physician certified that the operation was necessary to preserve her life. Invalidating the statute, the Supreme Court held that the state lacked the authority to give a third party, including a parent, an "absolute, and possibly arbitrary veto over the decision of the physician and his patient to terminate the patient's pregnancy."

The state's contention that the veto furthered a significant state interest in safeguarding the preservation of the family unit was rejected. The court felt that absolute parental power could not achieve this aim and that the very existence of the pregnancy would in some cases already have fractured the family unit. In effect, the court had to decide between giving precedence to the constitutional rights of children or parents. It chose the latter in that any independent interest which a parent might have in the termination of the pregnancy was no more weighty than the privacy right of the competent minor who was mature enough to have become pregnant.

This decision was followed by the Supreme Court's ruling in *Bellotti II*[55] that a Massachusetts statute requiring parental consent or judicial consent before an abortion might be performed on an unmarried minor was unconstitutional. Its lack of constitutionality turned on the width of its application. The plaintiff represented a class of mature minors and the highest state court had interpreted the statute as allowing a court to overrule the informed and reasonable decision of a mature minor. The statute also provided for mandatory notification of parents irrespective of the child's maturity. The cumulative effect was to create a veto either in a parent or judge.

Danforth and *Bellotti* left open the possibility that some less invasive requirement of parental notification or consultation might be constitutional. The issue came before the Supreme Court in *H. L.* v. *Matheson*.[56] In contrast to *Bellotti* the case was concerned only with the application of a statute to immature, unemancipated minors.[57] The State of Utah passed a statute requiring a doctor to "notify if possible" the parents of a minor upon whom an abortion was to be performed. The court upheld its constitutionality in

---

[55] 443 U.S. 662 (1979), following *Bellotti* v. *Baird*, 428 U.S. 132 (1976).

[56] 450 U.S. 398 (1981).

[57] The "mature minor rule" and the doctrine of emancipation are discussed in Chap. 3.

relation to a girl of 15 living at home with her parents and dependent on them. The court did not decide whether it would be constitutional if applied to mature and emancipated minors since neither the plaintiff nor any member of her class were in that category. The majority reasoned that the statute furthered both family integrity and a significant state interest by enhancing the potential for parental consultation concerning a decision that has potentially traumatic and permanent consequences.

The *Matheson* case is interesting from the English perspective since it raises directly the issue of parental consultation as distinguished from parental veto. This distinction is not made in *Gillick*, neither is it drawn in the guidance of the D.H.S.S.[58] Is there a case for saying that, while parents should not have absolute powers over decisions such as abortion and contraception, they should have a right to receive notice of them and be brought into the decision-making process? *Gillick*, it will be recalled, merely requires the doctor to *attempt* to persuade the girl to agree to parental notification. It clearly visualises that treatment could take place in some circumstances without it.

The case against mandatory notification of parents is both theoretical and practical.

In theory such a requirement would be difficult to reconcile with the principle of medical confidentiality which is thought to derive from the Hippocratic Oath.[59] The legal basis of the requirement of confidentiality may be either contractual or equitable.[60] Whatever the strict legal position may be, the British Medical Association's *Handbook of Medical Ethics* states that "a doctor must preserve secrecy on all he knows."[61] The obligation is however qualified by the existence of five recognised exceptions, including the patient's consent and the doctor's overriding duty to society. In relation to mature adolescents there is a strong case for saying that the duty of confidentiality exists to the same extent as it applies to adult patients. The difficulty arises in relation to those children deemed immature under the *Gillick* principles. In America, the *Matheson* case supports the principle that a law in effect requiring a breach of

---

[58] The revised circular refers in several places to the doctor proceeding "without parental knowledge or consent," and the advice is intended to apply to both of these situations equally.

[59] Discussed by Mason and McCall Smith, *op. cit.* n. 5, Chap. 8.

[60] The theoretical position is explored in Andrew Grubb and David Pearl, "Medicine, Health, the Family and the Law" (1986) 16 Fam. Law 227, 240.

[61] Para. 1.6.

confidentiality in cases involving immature children *is* constitutional. The same position has been taken in England by the General Medical Council which has issued guidance that doctors may notify a girl's parents of her visit if they consider it in her best medical interests having regard to the trust that she has placed in them.[62] Although disputed by the B.M.A. the advice has not been withdrawn and it has been argued that it has a sound legal basis. No contract, it is said, can exist between the girl and the doctor in view of her mental capacity. It has also been suggested that equity would not intervene to prevent disclosure to parents where the doctor reasonably took the view that it was in her best medical interests. Moreover it is said that this is consistent with the concern expressed in *Gillick* for respect of parental responsibility.[63]

These technical legal arguments are not perhaps as convincing as the more pragmatic approach of Marshall J. in the United States which would support confidentiality in *all* cases. Dissenting in *Matheson* (and dealing specifically with the abortion question) he makes what is surely the most telling point when he observes that not all families conform to the ideal in which a child will naturally turn to her parent for comfort and support. In many cases family relations will be strained and this is precisely why the girl wishes to preserve confidentiality. Denial of this right may well be likely to result in many adverse consequences which Marshall J. describes as follows:

> "In addition to parental disappointment and disapproval, the minor may confront physical or emotional abuse, withdrawal of financial support, or actual obstruction of the abortion decision. Furthermore, the threat of parental notice may cause some minor women to delay past the first trimester of pregnancy, after which the health risks increase significantly. Other pregnant minors may attempt to self-abort or to obtain an illegal abortion rather than risk parental notification. Still others may foresake an abortion and bear an unwanted child . . . "[64]

Another difficulty thrown up by the *Gillick* decision surrounds the position of the 16 or 17 year old who would, hypothetically, fail the

---

[62] *The Times*, February 12, 1986.

[63] Grubb and Pearl, *loc. cit.* n. 60. *Cf.* Jonathan Montgomery, "Confidentiality and the Immature Minor" (1987) 17 Fam. Law 101.

[64] *Op. cit.* n. 56, pp. 438–440.

Gillick test of maturity. We have seen that section 8(1) of the Family Law Reform Act 1969 provides that minors of that age should be invested with adult capacities as regards medical, dental or surgical procedures. Since adult capacities are not dependent on evaluations of emotional or intellectual maturity, the young person should be able to consent despite being immature in the *Gillick* sense. This produces the rather odd conclusion that a higher level of understanding is required by the law of those under 16 than that required of those over 16. Where a 16 year old suffers from a degree of mental handicap which would prevent an adult from providing a real consent it will remain necessary to seek a substituted consent for treatment. In the case of sterilisation, *Re B.* suggests that this must be provided by a court. In other cases it may be that parental consent would suffice.

Taking *Gillick* and *Re B.* together the position would therefore seem to be that when considering the position of a minor under 16 the question will be whether or not she is mature, applying *Gillick* principles. When considering the situation of the 16-year-old a different test must be applied. This is whether the person in question has a level of understanding which would be sufficient to enable an adult to provide a valid consent. This may involve some difficult line-drawing between degrees of intellectual attainment.

What is the position where the adolescent is a ward of court and/ or in the care of a local authority? Where the child is in care (and assuming that the authority has acquired parental rights by court order or resolution) it is the authority rather than the parent which should be approached for a proxy consent to treatment. If the authority shares parental rights with another person (*e.g.* where it has assumed only one parent's rights), the consent of the authority will be sufficient unless that other person signifies an objection. Where the child is a ward of court, the court's consent must be obtained and this applies equally where the child has been committed by the court into the care of a local authority.[65] The precise relationship between the court and the authority is however unclear. Lowe and White, discussing the effect of wardship generally, at one time offered the view that consent to medical treatment was not something which *must* be referred to the court. They saw this as a day-to-day decision which should be within the control of the person having *de facto* care of the child. They acknowledged however that the court's consent might be

[65] See footnote to the revised D.H.S.S. circular, n. 49.

required for non-therapeutic procedures such as sterilisation.[66] They later reconsidered their view and now draw a distinction between minor matters of routine care and major issues.[67] The distinction is easier to state than to apply but it would seem that the person with actual care of a ward would be unwise, emergencies apart, to authorise significant medical procedures whether therapeutic or non-therapeutic without first contacting the court.[68]

In practice the council may welcome the assistance of the court in dealing with sensitive medical questions. For example, in *Re P. (A minor)*[69] the issue was whether an abortion should be performed on a 15 year old girl where her parents objected to it on religious grounds. The girl was in the compulsory care of the local authority, so that the council in fact had the legal authority to determine the matter. They elected however to ward the child and, in due course, Butler-Sloss J. authorised the operation as being in the girl's best interests. A surprising feature of the decision is that no mention is apparently made of the girl's own wishes. It is probably fair to assume that she wanted the abortion but her capacity to consent seems to have been regarded as irrelevant. Whether such an approach is correct, following *Gillick*, is very doubtful as discussed earlier.[70] A related issue is whether the person with actual care of a ward, or a doctor dealing with her, would be justified in by-passing the court if he considers that the child is sufficiently mature to take the decision herself without the court's assistance. It is a moot point whether the doctor's duty of confidentiality owed to the mature ward would take precedence over his duty to bring significant medical questions back before the court. As matters stand he would certainly risk being held in contempt of court if he chose to ignore the court.

4. Who Decides? — The Quest for Standards

Whether we are concerned with young or immature children or mature adolescents, the primary objective must be to achieve a

---

[66] "Wards of Court" 1st Ed. (1979), p. 64.

[67] 2nd Ed. (1987) paras. 5.21–5.22.

[68] Support for this view is found in the decision of Butler-Sloss J. in *Re C. (Minors) (Wardship: Medical Evidence)* [1987] 1 F.L.R. 418 where the judge emphasised the continuing role of the court and the Official Solicitor's department where the child was in hospital.

[69] (1982) 80 L.G.R. 301.

[70] *Ante*, Chap. 5.

societal consensus on the principles and procedures which should govern their health care. Many of the reported cases, both here and in the United States, have been decided on an individualistic basis and are not binding precedents. These cases show first, that there is a need for the mutual powers and duties of parents, medical personnel and children themselves, which arise by operation of law, to be spelt out in legislation. Secondly, they indicate that provision should be made for an objective review of decisions relating to major medical procedures on children, in order to avoid a state of affairs in which these matters are determined entirely on the basis of the individual predilections of parents or doctors.

The difficulty in establishing principles acceptable to everyone is that there is never likely to be total agreement on who is the proper person to have the final say. Most of the more sensitive questions are not purely medical concerns, but are a complex amalgam of medical, legal, social and ethical issues. Moreover they arise not as abstract intellectual challenges, but in the context of particular children who are members of particular families. While therefore it may be accepted that doctors should inevitably take a dominant position in relation to specifically medical questions, it is by no means clear that they should be allowed to rule on moral issues,[71] or that they are better placed than parents to decide what is best for a particular child. Abortion, contraception and sterilisation are all concerned with teenage sexuality and, as such, are especially likely to bring the child into conflict with her parents and the official policies of the state. They are all decisions with a medical component, but it is impossible to sever or isolate this from the other social and moral considerations involved. The *Gillick* ruling does represent, in relation to contraception, a genuine attempt to recognise the legitimate concerns of children, parents and the medical profession. It encourages the various interested parties to endeavour to arrive at a joint decision on the best course of action for the individual child.

The participatory model, which forms the basis of *Gillick*, appears in various manifestations in most attempts to formulate

---

[71] For example, in *Carey*, Brennan J. at p. 699 thought that the decision whether or not to make contraceptives available to adolescents was a *moral* not *medical* decision. As such he thought that it was not a suitable decision to leave in the hands of doctors and feared that it might be exercised arbitrarily. The *Gillick* decision is discussed in the context of the debate on the relationship between law and morality in Simon Lee, *Law and Morals* (1986) Chap. 9.

standards or principles.[72] The American Bar Association's Juvenile Justice Standards provide some valuable and detailed standards relating to the medical care of minors.[73] They provide that, subject to exceptions, "no medical procedures, services or treatment should be provided to a minor without prior parental consent."[74]

These exceptional situations are, however, very significant and cover in addition to emergency treatment, drug or alcohol dependency, venereal disease, contraception and pregnancy. In short, special provision is made for all the more controversial areas of activity which are calculated to bring the child into conflict with her parents. In these situations the standards provide that a child *of any age*[75] should be able to consent to medical services, treatment, therapy or counselling, and that the minor's permission should be sought before parents are notified. If the minor objects, notification should not take place unless the physician concludes, after taking into account specified factors,[76] "that failing to inform the parent could seriously jeopardise the health of the minor."

Special provision is made in the standards for mental or emotional disorder.[77] The standards also prescribe that a mature or emancipated minor should have capacity to consent to *all* forms of medical treatment "on the same terms and conditions as an adult." Parental notification should not take place in the case of an emancipated minor, but should in the case of a mature minor except in relation to the forms of treatment discussed above.

These guidelines add up to a substantial respect for the autonomy interests of adolescents and the fundamental rights of

---

[72] See, for example, the three alternative sets of guidelines in Madzy Rood-de Boer, "Decision Making about Health Care and Medical Treatment of Minors" in *The Resolution of Family Conflict—Comparative Legal Perspectives*, Ed. John M. Eekelaar and Sanford N. Katz (1984), p. 557. The guidelines cover such matters as obligations on the medical profession to inform parents and children of proposed treatment, requirements as to consent and special forms of decision-making.

[73] A.B.A. Juvenile Justice Standards Project Standards relating to the Rights of Minors (1980).

[74] *Ibid.* para. 4.1.

[75] Emphasis added.

[76] The factors are—(a) the impact that such notification could have on the course of treatment; (b) the medical considerations which require such notification; (c) the nature, basis, and strength of the minor's objections; (d) the extent to which parental involvement in the course of treatment is required or desirable.

[77] para. 4.2.B. A minor aged 14 or over may consent to three sessions with a psychotherapist or counsellor for diagnosis or consultation, but thereafter the parents should be notified and their consent to further treatment obtained.

parents to freedom from State interference in their child-rearing practices. They are an attempt to strike a balance between the two. They reflect to some extent the laws in operation in various states.[78] The constitutionally protected liberty rights of adolescents is a dimension lacking in England where the orientation, even after *Gillick*, is largely paternalistic. The English solution of leaving the final decision in the hands of doctors rather than giving it to the adolescent is a questionable policy. There is much to be said for a scheme which seeks to encourage young people to seek the assistance of their parents and of professional advisers in arriving at difficult decisions. But, having acquired advice and assistance, it is suggested that the ultimate decision should rest with the child. Those who suggest otherwise must live with the practical consequences of allowing external interference with the child's wishes. Can it ever be right that a doctor, judge, social worker, parent or any other third party should be legally entitled, for example, to force a pregnant girl either to abort or, worse still, bear a child against her wishes? Surely this would be fundamentally repugnant to the concept of children's rights. The case against a third party dictating to the child in the matter of contraception is equally strong. How can it ever be sensible that contraceptives should be withheld from a young person who is known or suspected to be engaging in sexual intercourse? These considerations take on an even greater significance with the spread of the AIDS virus. Moreover it would seem discriminatory for the state to restrict the availability of female contraceptives at a time when official policy is to exhort everyone involved in casual sexual activity to have recourse to male contraceptive devices. The case for providing contraceptives to *all* young people who seek them, *regardless* of age is a strong one. This result could have been achieved quite simply by the adoption, as the sole consideration for the doctor, of Lord Fraser's third condition in *Gillick*, that the girl "is very likely to begin or to continue having sexual intercourse with or without contraceptive treatment."

The self-help which may be exercised by adolescents is a more difficult exercise for an immature child and an impossible one for a baby or very young child. In these situations, the emphasis has to

---

[78] The standards are not "law" themselves but were formulated to achieve uniformity in the law with a view to greater fairness, efficiency and predictability. They are highly influential in the development of child law across the United States and are regularly cited as persuasive authority in the courts. For some illustrations of individual state laws see Mnookin, *op. cit.* n. 1, p. 376.

be on devising standard procedures for obtaining proxy consents and standard principles to govern the circumstances in which a doctor may proceed without consent in order to secure the delivery of necessary medical care. One of the most unsatisfactory aspects of *Gillick* is the apparent assumption that where a child is adjudged to lack capacity to consent there should be a reversion to the principle of parental autonomy and resurrection of the parent's right to provide or withhold consent. This is completely unsatisfactory. The immature or mentally retarded girl who is having sexual intercourse is equally at risk, as far as unwanted pregnancy, abortion or sexually transmitted diseases are concerned, with her more mature counterpart. If anything she is more vulnerable. How then can it be sensible to vest in parents the power to veto the use of contraceptives or some other necessary medical care? Some other, more rational solution needs to be devised. One possibility would be to embody in legislation a requirement that medical personnel bring the issue before a court for review. At present judicial interventions are a matter of chance although they may now be mandatory in relation to proposed sterilisations depending on whether Lord Templeman's views are followed. It is felt however that a better solution would be to find a legal basis for allowing medically indicated treatment to be provided *automatically*, without the requirement of referral to a court or other body. The theoretical justifications for such action are usually considered to be either implied consent or necessity.

The theory of implied consent is that the patient may be presumed to have wished for the treatment were it not for his incapacity to consent. The obvious example is the admission of an unconscious patient to the casualty ward of a hospital. It is reasonable to assume that if he were conscious he would consent to those medical procedures required to save his life.[79]

The doctrine of necessity holds that an otherwise unlawful act may be justified where the good which results from it outweighs the consequences of complying with the strict legal requirements as to consent.[80]

In *T. v. T.*[81] Wood J. found a third legal basis for proceeding without consent preferable to either of the above justifications.

[79] See Mason & McCall Smith, *op.cit.* n. 5, p. 142.
[80] *Ibid.* p. 143. See also P.D.G. Skegg, "A Justification for Medical Procedures Performed Without Consent" (1974) 90 L.Q.R. 512.
[81] [1988] 2 W.L.R. 189.

The case concerned a 19 year old severely mentally handicapped girl who was found to be 11 weeks pregnant. She was an epileptic, destructive, unable to comprehend her condition and would be unable to look after a child. Both her mother and her medical advisers were of the opinion that it was in her best interests that the pregnancy be terminated and that a contemporaneous sterilisation be performed. The girl, however, was unable to give a consent to these operations and the hospital was unwilling to perform them without the court's authority.

Wood J. granted a declaration that the requested procedures would not amount to an unlawful act by reason only of the absence of the girl's consent. He held that there was no power vested in anyone to provide consent. The provisions of the Mental Health Act 1983 did not apply and the *parens patriae* jurisdiction of the courts did not extend to persons who had attained the age of majority. It was not possible to invoke the doctrine of implied consent since the young woman could never *in fact* consent on her own behalf. Neither was it appropriate to regard the case as one of necessity since the use of that word was not sufficiently precise as a test of what the court would consider to be a justification for the anticipated operative procedures in this case. He preferred rather to base the declaration on the principle of the best interests of the patient. He found that it was in her best interests that she should undergo the surgery without delay and that, in the exceptional circumstances of the case, the medical advisers were justified in proceeding without express or implied consent.

It would appear that Wood J. had in mind here the best *medical* interests criterion discussed above since he referred to a medical adviser as being justified in taking such steps as good medical practice demanded. It is submitted that the declaration here could also have been supported by either the implied consent or necessity theories. The fact that the young woman would never *in fact* have been able to consent would not seem to have precluded a presumption that if she had been able to consent she would have done so. Wood J. also refers to this as a situation in which upon good medical practice there were really no two views on what course was for the best.[82] This is surely only another way of stating necessity.

In *T.* v. *T.* the mother was in complete agreement with the proposed treatment but was unable to provide a valid consent

[82] *Ibid.* p. 199.

herself since her daughter had attained majority. The above grounds for proceeding without consent could also be applied in the face of parental opposition and in relation to a minor child. Acting in this way the doctor would be doing no more than enhancing, on behalf of the public interest, the parental duty to provide medical treatment. This approach would be consistent with the analysis of parental authority presented in Chapter 3. The reasoning there was that parents are obliged to exercise their powers reasonably and in accordance with the best interests of their children and a failure to do so entitles a third party to ignore their wishes on the ground that they are acting unlawfully. This principle would be confined to those forms of treatment which could properly be classified as therapeutic.

7. Education

1. Introduction

The child's right to education has received international recognition. Article 26(1) of the Universal Declaration of Human Rights provides:

> "Everyone has the right to education. Education shall be free, at least in the elementary and fundamental stages. Elementary education shall be compulsory."

The child's right to receive an education exists alongside the parents' right to determine the nature of that education. Thus, Article 26(3) states that "parents have a prior right to choose the kind of education that shall be given to their children."

These provisions are mirrored in the European Convention on Human Rights which states:

> "No person shall be denied the right to education. In the exercise of any functions which it assumes in relation to education and to teaching, the State shall respect the right of parents to ensure such education and teaching in conformity with their own religious and philosophical convictions."[1]

These international statements of principle apparently assume an identity of interests between parents and children. The observance of parental preferences is not perceived to be inconsistent with the discharge of the state's obligations towards children. This chapter is concerned with the relationship between the wishes of parents, the independent interests of children and the responsibilities of public authorities in the educational sphere.[2] Education law is a

---

[1] Article 2, Protocol 1.

[2] For a discussion of the competing interests of children, parents and the state in the sphere of education see Patsy Marson, "Parental Choice in State Education" [1980] J.S.W.L. 193.

vast area and we shall therefore examine this relationship in the context of a few selected issues.[3]

2. School Attendance

The principle of universal compulsory education is expressed in the Education Acts by the imposition of legal duties on parents and the local education authority (L.E.A.).

(a) PARENTS' OBLIGATIONS

The parental duty to educate is contained in section 36 of the Education Act 1944. This provides:

> "It shall be the duty of the parent of every child of compulsory school age to cause him to receive efficient full-time education, suitable to his age, ability and aptitude, either by regular attendance at school or otherwise."

Compulsory school age is currently between 5 and 16.[4] In relation to children of that age parents are therefore deprived of the right *not* to educate them. The obligation to educate may be discharged otherwise than by attendance at school. It is unlikely however that most attempts by parents to educate at home would be sufficiently structured as to comply with the requirements of section 36 and L.E.A.s are known to question the suitability of the curriculum offered in the home environment.[5]

The parents' duty is usually discharged initially by securing the registration of the child at a particular school and then by ensuring his regular attendance.[6] Where parents fail to comply with their initial duty of registration the L.E.A. must serve them with a notice under section 37 which requires them to inform the authority, within a period of not less than 14 days, whether or not the child is being educated in accordance with section 36. Under

---

[3] The standard work on Education law is Taylor and Saunders, *Law of Education* 9th Ed. (1984) by Peter Liell and John B. Saunders. For a more succinct and critical analysis see D. Milman, *Educational Conflict and the Law* (1986).

[4] 1944 Act, s.35.

[5] The issue is discussed by Milman, *op. cit.* n. 3, p. 41.

[6] Enforcement of parental duties is discussed by N. Harris in "The Legal Enforcement of School Attendance" [1986] *Legal Action* 69 and "Tackling Truancy: The Legal Options" (1987) 17 Fam. Law 21.

the statutory procedure, as amended by sections 10 and 11 of the Education Act 1980, the L.E.A. will give notice of the school which they propose to name in any subsequent school attendance order (S.A.O.). If the named school is not acceptable the parents may, within the period specified in the notice, apply for admission to another school. If this application succeeds, that school becomes the named school for the purpose of enforcement procedures. Where the application fails, the parents are entitled to appeal under section 7 of the 1980 Act. Where the parents fail to comply with the notice, an S.A.O. may be served under section 37(2) which requires them to cause the child to become a registered pupil at the school named in the order. Under section 37(5) breach of this order is a criminal offence, punishable under section 40 initially by a fine and in the case of a third offence by a fine and/or imprisonment. The effectiveness of criminal proceedings has however been doubted and the procedure is unduly cumbersome in the case of repeated offences. This is because where a parent has been convicted of one offence under section 37 it seems that any subsequent failure to register the child at school has to be the subject of a fresh notice and a second S.A.O. It was held in *Enfield L.B.C.* v. *F. and F.*[7] that on its proper construction section 37(5) created only one offence of failure with regard to any particular S.A.O. and that a parent could not be prosecuted for a second offence with reference to the same S.A.O.

Parents commit an alternative offence under section 39(1) where their child fails to attend school regularly. It has been held that this is an offence of strict liability so that ignorance of the child's truancy is no defence.[8] Further, the child's persistent late arrival at school may amount to non-attendance.[9] But under section 39(2) certain statutory excuses for non-attendance are specified. Thus, no offence is committed where absence is due to the child's sickness or some other unavoidable cause. The sickness or unavoidable cause must however be an emergency and must relate to the child's position rather than the parents'.[10] Another exemption relates to days of religious observance and is consistent with the general policy in education law of respect for the religious convictions of the parents. A further statutory excuse, recently

---

[7] [1987] 2 F.L.R. 126.
[8] *Crump* v. *Gilmore* (1970) 68 L.G.R. 56.
[9] *Hinchley* v. *Rankin* [1961] 1 W.L.R. 421.
[10] *Jenkins* v. *Howells* [1949] 2 K.B. 218.

interpreted by the House of Lords, is that the School is not within walking distance of the child's home and no suitable arrangements have been made by the L.E.A. regarding the child's transport or alternative schooling arrangements.

In *Essex C.C.* v. *Rogers*[11] the issue was the proper interpretation of "walking distance." The expression is partially defined in section 39(5) as meaning "in relation to a child who has not attained the age of eight years two miles, and in the case of any other child three miles, measured by the nearest available route."

Mr. and Mrs. Rogers were convicted by Colchester justices of the offence under section 39 arising from the failure of their 12 year old daughter, Shirley, to attend regularly the comprehensive school at which she was registered. The distance between the school and the Rogers' home, as measured by the shortest public route, was 2.94 miles. Part of this included an isolated unmade and unlit track which represented a considerable danger to a young girl, especially in winter. The question was whether "availability" was to be measured by what was reasonable for an *accompanied* or *unaccompanied* child to use. The Divisional Court accepted the parents' argument that the route must be such as a responsible parent would allow his child to follow. The House of Lords disagreed, taking the view that this test would be too vague and was not warranted by the statutory language. It held that the nearest available route was the nearest along which the child could walk to school with reasonable safety when accompanied by an adult. A route did not fail to qualify because of dangers which would arise if the child were unaccompanied.

In fact there was no question of Shirley Rogers being required to walk to school at all. Transport was available and the real issue was whether the cost of this should be met by the parents or by the L.E.A. The authority had exercised its discretion under section 55 of the 1944 Act[12] to offer the parents concessionary fares on the school bus, being satisfied that they did not qualify for free transport applying the relevant means test. This statutory duty has been modified by section 53 of the Education (No. 2) Act 1986. Section 55 as amended now provides:

---

[11] [1987] 1 A.C. 66. For an assessment of the decision see Simon Lee, *And So to School* (1987) 103 L.Q.R. 162.

[12] s.55 requires L.E.A.s to "make such arrangements for the provision of transport ... as they consider necessary for the purposes of facilitating the attendance of pupils at schools ... "

"In considering whether or not they are required by subs. (1) above to make arrangements in relation to a particular pupil, the local education authority shall have regard (amongst other things) to the age of the pupil and the nature of the route, or alternative routes, which he could reasonably be expected to take."

If, therefore, it can be shown that the L.E.A., in any individual case, has failed to take the specified matters into consideration this might be challenged by way of judicial review and could also constitute a defence to proceedings under section 39.[13]

As an alternative to prosecution of parents the L.E.A. is obliged by section 40(2) of the 1944 Act to consider whether it is appropriate, instead of or as well as prosecuting, to bring care proceedings under section 1(2)(e) of the Children and Young Persons Act 1969. Here it must be established that the child is of compulsory school age and is not receiving suitable education, but also "that he is in need of care and control which he is unlikely to receive unless the court makes an order."

In *Re S. (A minor)*[14] the Court of Appeal held that a child could be in need of care and control simply because he was not receiving a suitable education and despite the fact that he was otherwise well looked after in a good home. In that case the failure to educate arose from the parents' implaccable opposition to comprehensive education. There appears to be some doubt whether the effect of this decision is to render the care and control test redundant. Since proper "care" requires education then, if condition (e) is proved, the second condition should be automatically satisfied. Research in a Sheffield court indicated however that "the two legs of the procedure still had to be formally acknowledged and satisfied."[15]

In recent years, the appropriateness of "penal" intervention as a method of combating the rise in truancy has been seriously questioned. In particular the practice, pioneered in Leeds, of adjourning care proceedings has become widespread. The purpose

---

[13] For a successful parental appeal against the refusal of free transport under the amended s. 55 see the Court of Appeal decisions in *R.* v. *Devon County Council, Ex. p.* G. (1988) *The Times*, March 22, 1988.

[14] [1978] Q.B. 120.

[15] John Pratt and Roger Grimshaw, "An Aspect of 'Welfare Justice': Truancy and the Juvenile Court" [1985] J.S.W.L. 257, 262.

is to allow for an improvement in school attendance before a care order is countenanced.[16] It now seems likely that in the foreseeable future care proceedings will be removed as a direct option for L.E.A.s. The Government has accepted the recommendations in the "Review of Child Care Law" that L.E.A.s should no longer be qualified applicants in care proceedings, but should instead be able to apply in separate proceedings for an education supervision order limited to securing school attendance. It would not be necessary in order to obtain a supervision order to prosecute under section 37 or section 39 but the order would be available in criminal proceedings in addition to or as an alternative to a sentence. Breach of section 37 or section 39 would be a sufficient ground for the order and it would not be necessary to prove the more complex harm condition envisaged for making a care order.[17]

The rationale of these proposals is that care proceedings should take place in truancy cases only where the educational problems form part of a wider risk to the child's immediate or long-term welfare which justifies taking the child into care. Where this is the case it is expected that the L.E.A. will cooperate with Social Services who alone will be the appropriate applicant in care proceedings. If enacted, these reforms should have the effect of overruling *Re S.* since failure to attend school will not *per se* be a sufficient basis for care proceedings. The powers of the education welfare officer (who would be the likely supervisor) would be increased in relation to parents since the order would be binding on them as well as the child.[18]

(B) THE DUTIES OF THE L.E.A.

The Secretary of State for Education has the general duty under section 1 of the 1944 Act "to promote the education of the people of England and Wales." At the local level statutory duties are imposed on L.E.A.s by section 8 of the Act which requires them to secure that there shall be available for their area sufficient schools.[19] The duty is

---

[16] See Roy Hullin, "The Leeds Truancy Project" (1985) 149 J.P. 488.
[17] Review, para. 12.22. See also White Paper, para. 44.
[18] Review, paras. 18.6–18.13. See also Law Com. Working Paper No. 100 "Care, Supervision and Interim Orders in Custody Proceedings." (1987) para. 3.32.
[19] s.8 goes on to provide that the schools for an area shall not be deemed to be sufficient unless they are sufficient "in number, character, and equipment to afford for all pupils opportunities for education offering such variety of instruction and training as may be desirable in view of their different ages, abilities and aptitudes . . . "

defined so broadly that it is difficult to allege that the L.E.A. has failed to comply with it. A successful challenge was however mounted where an authority attempted to introduce a charge for music lessons which were part of the syllabus. This was struck down in *R. v. Hereford and Worcester L.E.A , ex. p. Jones*[20] as offending the central principle of free education reinforced in section 61. This prohibits any charge for lessons which form part of the syllabus at the relevant school. But the width of discretion allowed to L.E.A.s in discharging the statutory duty recognised in this case resulted in some of them circumventing the rules by deciding to axe music from the curriculum.

Complaints to the Secretary of State under sections 68 and 99 of the 1944 Act have invariably failed for the same reason and because of the restrictive attitude taken by the Secretary of State to the basis for challenge under these procedures.[21] An attempt by the minister to invoke these procedures to compel a local education authority to implement a plan for comprehensive education in all its schools failed in *Secretary of State for Education and Science v. Tameside Metropolitan Borough Council.*[22]

The plan to bring all the schools in the area under the comprehensive principle was approved by the minister in November 1975 for implementation by September 1976. In May 1976 the local government election took place and retention of the grammar schools in the area was a strongly fought issue. The opposition gained control of the authority and considered that they had a mandate to reconsider their predecessors' education policy. They proposed, *inter alia*, to postpone the conversion of three grammar schools arguing that an immediate change would cause grave disruption to the education of the children affected. They proposed an interim selection procedure for these schools consisting of a combination of reports, records and interviews.

The minister purported to direct the L.E.A. to implement the November plans and the arrangements previously made for the allocation of pupils to secondary schools for the coming year

[20] [1981] 1 W.L.R. 768.
[21] s.68 enables a complaint to be made to the Secretary of State alleging that the L.E.A. or governing body are acting or proposing to act unreasonably in the discharge of any of their statutory functions. Where satisfied that the complaint is substantiated he may give directions as to the performance of the relevant duty. s.99 gives the Secretary of State a similar power to give directions in cases where the L.E.A. or governing body is failing to perform its statutory functions.
[22] [1977] A.C. 1014.

on a non-selective basis. He argued that a change of plan at that stage of the academic year would be bound to give rise to considerable difficulties. He then sought an order of mandamus to compel the L.E.A. to comply with his direction.

The House of Lords found in favour of the L.E.A. It was held that they were entitled to have a policy and that section 68 did not entitle the Secretary of State to require them to abandon it because he disagreed with it. A direction could only be properly given where the L.E.A. were acting unreasonably. The critical question was whether in June 1976 the minister had a sufficient factual basis for believing that the proposed change would lead to educational chaos and undue disruption. On the facts no such defects as there were in the L.E.A.'s proposed selection procedure enabled it to be said that no reasonable authority would have attempted to carry it out. Thus, the minister had no grounds for his direction under section 68.

In recent years unsuccessful complaints have alleged that the standard of educational provision has fallen so low under public expenditure cuts as to constitute a breach of section 8. Reliance has been placed on adverse criticisms of the state of schools in H.M.I. Effects Reports.[23] Attempts to challenge the legality of school closures owing to industrial action have met with mixed fortunes.[24] In general it must be concluded that parents have no realistic means of enforcing the general duties of L.E.A.s in the matter of educational provision.

(C) CHILDREN—RIGHTS OR DUTIES?

The principle of compulsory education may be interpreted as creating a legal right in the child to receive education and correlative duties in parents and L.E.A.s to provide it. The question is whether it also gives rise to a legal duty in the child himself to attend school. We have seen that the Education Acts place the statutory duties regarding school attendance on the *parents* and it is against them that enforcement proceedings are taken. A legal duty in the child may perhaps be implied from the existence of the care option since the child is the defendant in care

---

[23] See the discussion in Paul Meredith, "Individual Challenge to Expenditure Cuts in the Provision of Schools" [1982] J.S.W.L. 344.

[24] Discussed by Milman, *op. cit.* n. 3, p. 10.

proceedings. But even this implied duty may disappear if the care option is removed for non-attendance.[25]

The point is not purely academic since, following *Gillick*, it is possible to contend that a child under 16 (*i.e.* compulsory school age) with the requisite level of maturity and understanding of what is involved in school attendance, has sufficient legal capacity to elect not to attend and that parental rights and duties are terminated by the existence of this capacity. Moreover the issue has enormous practical significance since many children clearly *do* decide to stay away from school. It is a virtual certainty that if this question ever came before the courts a legal duty would be implied from the existence of the compulsory education system. It would however be sensible, for the avoidance of doubt, to place the child under a specific statutory obligation to attend school.

This issue is discussed at length by Grenville.[26] She points out that the existing law is based on the questionable assumption that there is a community of interest between parent and child in the matter of receiving education.[27] She argues that the independent powers and duties of both children and parents should be spelled out in legislation.

As to the parental position, she observes that the 1944 Act gives parents no specific powers to enable them to enforce their duty to ensure the child's school attendance. Further, since *Gillick*, it might, in her view, be possible for a parent to raise as a defence to prosecution the argument that an older child's autonomous decision to stay away from school is an "unavoidable cause" within section 39(2)(*a*) so far as the parent is concerned. She concludes that statute should clarify what powers a parent is to have over the child for the specific purpose of ensuring school attendance. She suggests that in relation to older children parents should either be exempt from legal responsibility or should be able to raise the child's independent duty as a good defence where they have done everything within their powers to ensure that the child attends. She rejects the imposition of strict liability on parents arising purely from the child's non-attendance.[28]

---

[25] It should be noted however that supervision orders are binding on the child and require him to cooperate with the supervisor.

[26] Maureen P. Grenville, "Compulsory School Attendance and the Child's Wishes" [1988] J.S.W.L. 4.

[27] *Ibid.* p. 10.

[28] *Ibid.* p. 18.

Grenville's treatment of the child's independent duty to attend school is rather more questionable. It is difficulty to disagree with her that the child should be placed under an independent statutory duty, but she goes on to suggest that the present age limit of 16 is higher than the age at which many children are capable of making up their own minds and acting on their decision.[29] She tentatively suggests that the statutory age should be reduced to 13, "since under present social conditions most children below that age are still within the effective control of their parents whereas many children above it are not."[30] It seems that she was influenced in this view by the apparent lack of efficacy of legal sanctions to ensure school attendance. She criticises all of these, including supervision orders which are, in her view, based on the optimistic notion that the supervisor will be able to persuade the child to attend.

The difficulty with this view is that it tends to assume that because a legal duty is incapable of enforcement it is not worth having. We have argued earlier, in relation to custody and access orders, that it is a proper function of law to affirm a standard of behaviour which is considered desirable even though its practical realisation may be imperfect.[31] It is therefore arguable that the existence of a legal duty in the case of older children could perform a similar function in giving statutory expression to societal expectations for the education of young people. Certainly there is a risk that a reduction in the statutory age might serve to encourage non-attendance. This assumes, of course, that school attendance is still regarded as a desirable policy objective. It might be argued that the child's autonomy interest dictates that he be allowed to decide. It is felt however that there are good reasons why, in the sphere of education, the child's right of recipience should prevail over his autonomy interest. Essentially this is because it is through the process of education that the child acquires the capacity to exercise meaningful independence.[32] The consummation of autonomy is therefore dependent on the curtailment of independence during earlier stages of development. But, as in other contexts, respect for children's rights does require that they should be allowed to participate to an extent

[29] *Ibid.* p. 16.
[30] *Ibid.* p. 18.
[31] *Ante*, Chap. 2.
[32] See, *e.g.* Freeman, *The Rights and Wrongs of Children* (1983) pp. 40–43.

commensurate with their age and understanding in educational decisions affecting them.

3. Choice of School

The principle of parental choice in education is enshrined in section 76 of the 1944 Act which provides:

"In the exercise and performance of all powers and duties conferred and imposed on them by this Act [the Secretary of State] and local education authorities shall have regard to the general principle that, so far as is compatible with the provision of efficient instruction and training and the avoidance of unreasonable public expenditure, pupils are to be educated in accordance with the wishes of their parents."

Parental involvement in education is recognised in a variety of ways. For example, in *R.* v. *Brent L.B.C., ex. p. Gunning*[33] the Divisional Court held that parents have a legitimate expectation tantamount to a statutory right to be properly consulted by the L.E.A. prior to its making proposals affecting the closure and amalgamation of local schools. A brief consultative document containing little information and sent to parents barely three weeks before the deadline for written representations was regarded as wholly inadequate. Accordingly, the L.E.A.'s decision announcing revised plans regarding the future of education in the area was quashed as *ultra vires*.

It is in relation to choice of school that the status of parental preferences is most often raised. It has long been recognised that the L.E.A.'s duty under section 76 is not an absolute one in the sense that the authority is obliged *to give effect* to parents' wishes. In *Watt* v. *Kesteven C.C.*[34] the Court of Appeal held that a parent was not entitled to insist that his children be sent to an independent fee paying school at the expense of the L.E.A. The latter's duty was limited to considering the parent's wishes along with other factors. The wording of section 76 impliedly recognises the potential conflict between giving effect to individual parents' wishes

[33] (1986) 84 L.G.R. 168.
[34] [1955] 1 All E.R. 473.

and providing efficient education for all children in the area within the constraints of public expenditure.[35]

The Education Act 1980, often described as a "parents' charter," attempts to entrench the principle of parental choice of school by giving it specific statutory recognition and to inject greater accountability into L.E.A.'s admissions procedures. Section 6(1) places L.E.A.s under a legal duty to make arrangements for parents to express a preference with reasons on choice of school. Under subs. (2) L.E.A.s and the governors of a county or voluntary school are obliged to comply with any preference expressed in accordance with admissions arrangements. Prima facie, it appears that parental wishes have been elevated from the status of a factor to be taken into consideration to a conclusive determinant of the admissions decision. Parental choice is not, however, guaranteed since subs. (3) contains escape clauses for the L.E.A. Compliance with the parents' preference is not required where it would prejudice the provision of efficient education or the efficient use of resources; or where it would be incompatible with the arrangements for admission made between the L.E.A. and the governors of a voluntary aided school; or where the school involved is selective and the child does not meet its requirements as to ability and aptitude.

The generality of these exceptions is reminiscent of the language of section 76. Nonetheless the 1980 Act has enhanced the parental position in a number of respects. First, section 8 requires L.E.A.s to publish information about, *inter alia*, admissions policy and appeal rights in order that parents may be assisted in making an informed choice of school. Secondly, under section 7 there is a right of appeal to an appeal committee constituted under Schedule 2 of the Act.[36] These provisions have at least achieved greater uniformity in the administrative procedures of L.E.A.s where previously such matters were dealt with informally.

---

[35] Other unsuccessful challenges under s.76 occured in *Cumings* v. *Birkenhead Corporation* [1971] 2 W.L.R. 1458 and *Winward* v. *Cheshire C.C.* (1971) 77 L.G.R. 172, discussed by R. G. Lee at (1980) 10 Fam. Law 44.

[36] For assessments of the statutory appeals procedure see David Bull, "Monitoring Education Appeals: Local Ombudsmen Lead the Way" [1985] J.S.W.L. 189 and Trevor Buck, "Schools Admission Appeals" [1985] J.S.W.L. 227. For a descriptive account of the entire procedure from expressing a preference to the conclusion of an appeal and beyond see Neville Harris, "Exercising Parental Preference under the Education Act 1980" [1984] *Legal Action* 32.

The central issue, both before and after the 1980 Act, has been how to accommodate individual rights within a system which requires L.E.A.s to provide an efficient education system for all children within their catchment area. Clearly a balance has to be struck and commentators have highlighted this "preference *v.* policy" conflict.[37] The potential for conflict has been accentuated in a climate of public expenditure cuts and falling rolls where the enforced closure or amalgamation of schools may operate as a further *de facto* restriction on parents' choices.[38]

Most of the debate in this area has been concerned with whether policy considerations should predominate over individual preferences or vice-versa. The Act itself does not deal directly with the relative weight to be attached to each of these factors. Schedule 2 paragraph 7 simply provides that an appeal committee shall take into account "(a) any preference exrpessed by the appellant in respect of the child . . . and (b) the arrangements for the admission of pupils published by the local education authority or the governors . . . " Put starkly the question is whether it is open to the L.E.A., in pursuance of its admissions policy, to fix admissions ceilings for particular schools and then to refuse parents' applications where an individual school is full.[39] A literal reading of section 6 would suggest that the L.E.A. must give effect to parental wishes unless it can establish the existence of one of the statutory reasons for not doing so. This interpretation seems to have been accepted, first by local ombudsmen, and later by Forbes J. in *R. v. South Glamorgan Appeals Committee, ex. p. Evans.*[40]

In this case Forbes J. adopted an "individualist approach." The L.E.A. argued that compliance with the parent's wish to enrol his children in an over-subscribed Welsh speaking primary school would "prejudice the provision of efficient education." In

---

[37] Paul Meredith, "Executive Discretion and Choice of Secondary School" [1981] *Public Law* 52 and Jack Tweedie, "Rights in Social Programmes: The Case of Parental Choice of School" [1986] *Public Law* 407.

[38] Paul Meredith, "Falling Rolls and the Reorganisation of Schools" [1984] J.S.W.L. 208.

[39] The L.E.A.'s powers to fix artificial limits on the number of pupils which individual schools can admit are removed by Clauses 17–22 of the Education Reform Bill. Schools will be required to admit pupils up to a prescribed "standard number." This reform is intended to have the effect of enhancing parental choice but critics fear that unpopular schools will cease to be viable as a result.

[40] May 10, 1984, Transcript No. CO/197/1984, discussed by Meredith at [1985] J.S.W.L. 162.

quashing the appeal committee's decision which had upheld the authority view, the judge held that the committee had failed to follow the correct procedure which entailed a two-stage process. First, the onus was firmly placed on the L.E.A. to show that admission of the individual child would prejudice efficient education at the chosen school. If the authority succeeded at this stage, the committee should move on to consider the second question, whether the prejudice was of a sufficient degree to outweigh the parental factors. At this second stage it was not clear where the onus should lie, but the tenor of the judgment is that it should continue to rest on the L.E.A. since the Act's "primary object is to support parental choice."

This decision suggests that the individual claims of parents should take precedence over collective policy considerations. The interpretation adopted by Forbes J. is, however, only one of a number of different interpretations which might be adopted by appeal committees and in practice it seems that they more often favour a policy orientated approach. Tweedie identifies two variants as the "policy rights approach" and the "substantial justice approach."[41] Both are fundamentally supportive of the L.E.A.'s general admissions policy for the area. Under the former, appeal considerations are restricted to whether or not the L.E.A. has followed its own declared policy in determining the individual parent's application. In the latter, the appeal committee again considers the application within the general framework of the L.E.A.'s policy, but takes into account any exceptional circumstances justifying a departure from that policy in the particular case. The appeal is then allowed if it would not significantly damage the L.E.A.'s policy.[42] An estimated success rate of about one-third of appeals suggests that the Act may have done little in reality to strengthen the parents' position.[43] Complaints to local ombudsmen alleging maladministration offer an alternative avenue of redress.[44] It should be remembered however that the vast majority of parental preferences will in any event be accommodated under the ordinary admissions procedures operating in the area.

---

[41] *Op. cit.* n. 37, p. 410.

[42] Tweedie identifies a possible fourth approach which he calls the "administrative justice approach" under which the applicant is afforded the opportunity of challenging the legal basis of the L.E.A.'s policy itself as well as arguing for an exception to be made in his case.

[43] See the assessment of Meredith, *op. cit.* n. 37, p. 68.

[44] Discussed by Bull, *op. cit.* n. 36.

It is questionable whether parental wishes should be allowed to prevail over policy considerations since, as Tweedie observes,

> "an L.E.A.'s inability to control its rolls can have serious effects on its schools because some schools might become too large and overcrowded and others might become too small and so not able to offer a comprehensive education."[45]

It is also interesting to observe that the policy *v.* preference debate has been entirely concerned with reconciling the interests of parents with the interests of the State (represented by L.E.A.s). Nowhere in the legislation is provision made for taking into account the wishes of the children themselves. Their interests are assumed to coincide with those of their parents.

4. School Government

L.E.A.s have a statutory obligation to produce instruments of government and articles of government for state schools within their area.[46] The instrument of government provides for the constitution of the governing body of the school and must contain the provisions required by Part II of the Education (No. 2) Act 1986 regarding its size and composition and the procedures for electing members and filling vacancies.[47] The articles of government must contain the provisions required by Part III of the Act which is concerned, *inter alia*, with the manner in which schools are to be conducted and the allocation of functions between the L.E.A., the governing body and the head teacher.[48] The intention is to produce a better definition of these respective functions and to produce greater uniformity. At the same time the underlying philosophy is to increase parental involvement in the educational system. This process will be carried a stage further by the Education Reform Bill which obliges L.E.A.s to delegate control over financial spending to the level of individual schools. L.E.A.s will have a general schools' budget and will be responsible for

---

[45] *Loc. cit.* n. 41.
[46] s.1(1), Education (No. 2) Act 1986. For a general assessment of the Act see Neville Harris, "Regulation of Schools Under the Education (No. 2) Act 1986" (1987) 17 Fam. Law 287.
[47] s.1(3).
[48] s.1(4).

delegating to governing bodies of individual schools the management of their school's budget share.[49] Since parents now have greater representation on governing bodies the intention is to increase their influence in the spending of particular schools and to wrest control from L.E.A.s.

Milman notes that historically there has been little enthusiasm for involving parents in the management of schools except in relation to the fund raising activities of parent teacher associations.[50] But in 1977 the Taylor Report on School Governors[51] recommended the appointment of at least two elected parent governors and this proposal was introduced by section 2 of the Education Act 1980. The Conservative Government later proposed in its Green Paper "Parental Influence at School"[52] that parental representation on governing bodies should be increased to give them a majority. This was strongly opposed and withdrawn when the Government published its White Paper, "Better Schools"[53] which now forms the basis of Part II of the 1986 Act. The composition of governing bodies is to depend on the status and size of school. Section 3 relates to county controlled and maintained special schools and provides for parity of representation between parent governors and L.E.A. representatives, replacing the majority previously enjoyed by the latter. The head teacher and one or two other teachers, depending on the size of school, will also have membership. The appointed governors have power to co-opt up to three or six further governors, again depending on the size of school. Under section 4 aided and special agreement schools are to have a similar composition of governors but with foundation governors in the majority and comparatively less parental representation.[54]

Parents' interests are further represented by the introduction of other measures designed to make governing bodies more accountable to them. Section 30 provides that the articles of government

[49] Clauses 23–36 incl.
[50] *Op. cit.* n. 3, p. 37.
[51] "A New Partnership for our Schools," published by the Department of Education and Science.
[52] May 1984, Cmnd. 9242.
[53] March 1985, Cmnd. 9469.
[54] The Act allows for progressive implementation of the school government provisions which must be achieved in relation to all county schools and maintained special schools by September 1, 1988 and in relation to all voluntary schools by September 1, 1989.

must require the governors to prepare an annual report for parents, while section 31 requires the articles to impose a duty on the governors to hold an annual parents' meeting.

A striking feature of these reforms is the conspicuous absence of any allowance for the participation of pupil representatives in school government. In 1977 the Taylor Committee had advocated that school pupils of 16 or over should be eligible for membership of governing bodies.[55] It is understood that many authorities acted on this recommendation and appointed pupil governors. The 1986 Act reverses this trend by expressly prohibiting the appointment of persons under 18.[56] Prior to the Act, the Department of Education and Science apparently took the view that there were legal impediments to the appointment of persons under 18. It relied on section 20 of the Law of Property Act 1925, which prevents an infant from becoming a trustee in relation to any settlement or trust, and section 1(1) of the Family Law Reform Act 1969, which fixes the age of majority at 18. Certain old common law authorities were also thought to preclude an infant from holding a public office.

These supposed legal objections have been convincingly met by Pannick in his advice to the Children's Legal Centre.[57] The principal counter-argument is that the age of legal capacity is not fixed *for all purposes* at 18. In the absence of express statutory regulation capacity to act as a school governor should depend, applying the *Gillick* test, on the understanding and intelligence of the individual pupil candidate. This could mean that pupils of 16 *or under* possessing the requisite level of maturity, would have sufficient legal capacity to stand for election. It might also be argued that those *over 16* should be presumed to have capacity in the light of the amount of legal independence already enjoyed by that age group.[58] Indeed, it might even be contended that to deny them participation in school affairs is tantamount to discrimination bearing in mind how much control the law allows those who have left school to exercise over their lives. The absence of an appeal procedure which can be invoked by children who have been permanently excluded from school under disciplinary procedures may be criticised for similar reasons. Section 26 of the 1986 Act

[55] para. 4.26.
[56] s.15(14).
[57] David Pannick, "School Student Governors—no legal obstacle" (1986) 25 *Childright* 15.
[58] *Ante*, Chap. 3.

175

only obliges L.E.A.s to make arrangements conferring appeal rights on pupils over 18 and on the *parents* of pupils under that age.

These arguments are now academic since *Gillick* cannot apply where the matter in issue is expressly governed by statute. The change in the law is a retrograde step, but one which is entirely consistent with the Conservative Government's preference for parent power and the scant attention which it has paid to the independent claims and interests of children.

5. The Curriculum

(A) GENERAL

The 1944 Act vested control of the content of the secular curriculum in L.E.A.s. Parents were given no statutory right to be consulted apart from that arising from the general duty of L.E.A.s to have regard to their wishes under section 76. There was some judicial authority that a right of consultation could be implied from this,[59] but the difficulties involved in parental enforcement of this duty have already been noted. Central control of the curriculum was limited to religious education although the Education Reform Bill now introduces for the first time a National Curriculum.[60] The 1986 Act shifts the balance of power over the curriculum away from L.E.A.s and towards governing bodies. Since parents have increased representation on the latter, the effect is again to increase their influence. The Act also contains several provisions designed to exert central control over the sensitive areas of politics and sex education in schools. The Act requires L.E.A.s, governing bodies and head teachers to forbid "the pursuit of partisan political activities" by junior pupils under the age of 12 and the "promotion of partisan political views in the teaching of any subject" in any maintained school. They must also "take such steps as are reasonably practicable to ensure that where politics is presented pupils are offered a balanced presentation of opposing views."[61] Sex education is discussed below.

[59] See Goff J. in *Wood* v. *Ealing L.B.C.* [1966] 3 W.L.R. 1209, 1221.
[60] Clauses 1–16 incl.
[61] ss.44 and 45. The prohibition on political activity may be seen as unduly authoritarian and might well be unconstitutional in the United States. See *Tinker* v. *Des Moines Independent Community School District* 393 U.S. 503 (1969). For a criticism of the new provisions see "Political Issues in Schools" (1987) 38 *Childright* 10.

The hallmark of the 1986 legislation is consultation between the L.E.A., governing bodies and head teachers. Section 17 requires L.E.A.s to keep under review their policy in relation to the secular curriculum and to publish and keep up-to-date a written statement of it. Under sections 18 and 19 articles of government must place governing bodies under a duty to consider the L.E.A.'s policy and, in the light of their opinion as to the aim of the secular curriculum at their school, to consider whether and if so how it should be modified in its application to that school. The head teacher is responsible for determination and organisation of the curriculum. He must ensure that it is compatible with the L.E.A.'s policy as amended by the governing body (where relevant) and with the general law. It is his responsibility to ensure that the curriculum is followed at his school. In fulfilling their respective functions they are all enjoined to have regard to any representations made to them by "any persons connected with the community served by the school" and specifically (and somewhat controversially) those made by "the Chief Officer of Police and which are connected with his responsibilities."

We shall now consider two aspects of the curriculum which illustrate particularly well the respective interests of children and parents and the public interest.

(B) RELIGIOUS INSTRUCTION

Statutory regulation of religious education exists under the 1944 Act. Section 25(1) provides that the school day in every county and voluntary school shall begin with "collective worship on the part of all pupils in attendance at the school." The Education Reform Bill amends these arrangements for daily worship to enable them to be organised at times other than the beginning of the day and to allow for separate acts of worship for pupils in different age groups or different school groups.[62] Section 25(2) makes religious instruction, in accordance with an agreed syllabus, a compulsory subject in every county and voluntary school. The Education Reform Bill confirms this and places the L.E.A. and the governing body under a duty to secure compliance with this requirement.[63]

---

[62] Clause 79.
[63] Clause 6.

Under section 25(4) parents may withdraw their children from both the collective act of worship and religious education classes. The school authorities are obliged to comply with a parental request by excusing the child from attendance. Parental choice in religious education is further enhanced by section 25(5). This provides that, where the parent wishes his child to receive religious instruction which cannot be provided in the school which the child attends or by transfer to another school, the parent can require the L.E.A. to make alternative arrangements for the child to receive the instruction during school hours elsewhere, provided that the L.E.A. are satisfied that the arrangements will interfere with his attendance only at the beginning or end of the school day.

These provisions have been unaffected by legislation on education in recent years. The Government recognised in 1985 the special contribution which religion has made to the education of all pupils and proposed that it should continue to receive "the significance which it deserves within the curriculum." Its view was that "within the statutory framework an introduction to the Christian tradition remains central to the religious education provided in our schools," and that the government would look to L.E.A.'s and schools to ensure that the statutory requirements were met.[64]

Religious education therefore appears to have been considered by Parliament to have an importance exceeding that of any other subject in the curriculum. Prima facie, it ought to be possible to interpret the duties of L.E.A.s as creating a correlative right in individual children to receive religious instruction. But this analysis quickly breaks down in the light of the unqualified deference which the Act accords to parental choice in this sphere. In contrast to the parents' entitlement on choice of school, which is essentially limited to expressing a preference, parents have a right to *require* their wishes in the matter of religious instruction to be observed. Parental wishes are therefore paramount in this context and have direct effect on the education which the child receives. Moreover religious education differs from secular education in that there is no legal duty on parents to ensure that their child receives the former. Their discretion extends to a decision to raise the child outside any religious faith. Ironically, such a decision

[64] "Better Schools" para. 55.

might historically have been a reason for depriving a father of the custody of his child.[65]

Respect for parental wishes in the United States is grounded in freedom of religion as a fundamental right. This is protected by the Constitution under the "Free Exercise" and "Establishment" clauses of the First Amendment.[66] Early Supreme Court decisions have been interpreted as supporting the principle that the state is not entitled to interfere with the religious liberty of parents without an unusually strong reason for doing so.[67]

The "Free Exercise" and "Establishment" clauses have also been interpreted as requiring official neutrality as between different religions. Thus, the Supreme Court has held unconstitutional the practices of daily Bible reading and prayer in state schools.[68] More recently, the United States Court of Appeals, Third Circuit held unconstitutional the use of school premises by a students' club which proposed, *inter alia*, to conduct prayers and scripture reading. The students' interest in free speech was held to be outweighed by Establishment clause concerns.[69] Two interpretations of these decisions have been suggested. First, the Supreme Court may have taken the view that the exercises put pressure on non-believing students to participate despite provision for them to be excused, or that there was an unavoidable risk of favouring some religions over others. Secondly, the Court may have viewed the existence of the practices as governmental support for religion in general, being an issue upon which there was no national consensus.[70]

The extent of the restrictions on religious practices in schools imposed by the First Amendment is illustrated by the Supreme Court's decision in *Wallace* v. *Jaffree*.[71] Here the Court held unconstitutional an Alabama statute authorising a moment of silence in public schools for "meditation and voluntary prayer."

[65] See, for example, *Shelley* v. *Westbrooke* (1817) Jac. 266, discussed in Chap. 1.
[66] This provides: "Congress shall make no law respecting an establishment of religion, or prohibiting the free exercise thereof . . . "
[67] See particularly *Meyer* v. *Nebraska* 262 U.S. 390 (1923) and *Pierce* v. *Society of Sisters* 268 U.S. 510 (1925).
[68] *Abington School District* v. *Schempp* 374 U.S. 203 (1963) and *Engel* v. *Vitale* 370 U.S. 421 (1962)
[69] *Bender* v. *Williamsport Area School District* 741 F. 2d 538 (1984).
[70] Michael E. Smith, "Relations Between Church and State in the United States: With Special Attention to the Schooling of Children" (1987) 35 Am.J. of Comp. Law 1, 30.
[71] 472 U.S. 38 (1985).

This constituted a violation of the Establishment clause since its sole purpose was held to be to return voluntary prayer to the schools. Justice O'Connor expressed the view that the clause did not prevent states from affording school children an opportunity for voluntary silent prayer, but the Alabama law intentionally and improperly crossed the line between creating a quiet moment in which those so inclined could pray, and affirmatively endorsing the religious practice of prayer.

The English compulsory act of collective worship would therefore be unconstitutional in the United States. The difference in approach reflects a commitment to religious pluralism in the United States in order to take account of the enormous diversity of religions which exists there. This commitment is absent in England owing to the existence of an established church. It is true that the 1944 Act does contain provisions designed to avoid practices in schools which are distinctive of any particular religious denomination.[72] But it is likely that the reference to different denominations refers to different *Christian* churches and does not embrace other religions. Moreover, representatives of the Church of England are alone automatically entitled to participate in the conference convened for the purposes of agreeing a local syllabus for religious instruction. Other religious denominations may send representatives only at the discretion of the L.E.A.[73] As we have seen the government has endorsed the primary place for *Christian* traditions in religious education. It is arguable however that the current statutory position constitutes discrimination against non-Christian parents which is not adequately removed by the opting-out procedure. There is some evidence that the existing system has given rise to discontent among the ethnic minorities.[74]

The system of religious education in schools is nonetheless strongly supportive of the parental right to determine religion. It cannot however reasonably be interpreted as creating rights in children themselves. Indeed the argument has recently been advanced that it is a breach of the rights of children under the European Convention on Human Rights.[75] In essence the contention is that linking the child's religious participation in school to

---

[72] s.26.

[73] s.29 and Sched. 5, para. 2.

[74] See Milman, *op. cit.* n. 3, p. 134.

[75] See the letter by Alan Nelson, "School religion law may break Convention" (1988) 44 *Childright* 7.

parental wishes is tantamount to a denial of the child's right to freedom of religion protected by the Convention. This, it is said, arises in one of two ways. A student may wish not to attend any, or particular, acts of worship for a number of valid reasons but is obliged to do so unless his parents have requested withdrawal. Conversely, he may wish to attend all, or particular, acts of worship but is unable to do so because his parents have exercised the withdrawal option. This is not, as yet, an issue which has been brought before the European Court.

Outside the educational context there is perhaps more direct concern for the independent interests of children. In particular statute provides that local authorities who have the care of children do not acquire the power to change their religion.[76] The courts also have been most reluctant to allow the child's religion to be changed following custody or adoption proceedings.[77]

In such proceedings the courts have adopted the principle of non-discrimination as between different religions.[78] They have however been prepared to intervene in the interests of the child's welfare where they consider that the social practices which form part of the faith are such that they would have a deleterious effect on the child.[79] It may therefore be correct to say that the law recognises the child's independent interest in religious upbringing in the negative sense of restricting interferences with his settled religion and in protecting him from religious practices which represent a risk of harm. It stops short of creating a positive right of recipience, at least one which is capable of taking precedence over parental claims.

The right of parents to exercise the withdrawal option in relation to religious education raises the issue of how far (if at all) they may legally resort to this device in relation to other aspects of the curriculum and other practices which they find objectionable. The issue is particularly acute where the parental objection to school activities is founded on strongly held religious beliefs or

[76] Child Care Act 1980, s.10(3).
[77] See for example *Stourton* v. *Stourton* (1857) 8 De G.M. & G. 760 and *Re M. (Infants)* [1967] 3 All E.R. 1071.
[78] The *locus classicus* is the speech of Scrutton L.J. in *Re Carroll* [1931] 1 K.B. 317, 336.
[79] See for example *Hewison* v. *Hewison* (1977) 7 Fam. Law 207 (Exclusive Brethren); *Jane* v. *Jane* (1983) 4 F.L.R. 712 (Jehovah's Witnesses); *Re B. and G. (Minors) (Custody)* [1985] F.L.R. 493 (Scientology) and *Re J.T. (A minor) (Wardship Committal)* [1986] 2 F.L.R. 107 (Rastafarianism).

philosophical convictions. There is no better illustration of this problem than the controversy surrounding sex education in schools.

(c) SEX EDUCATION

As we have seen, Article 2 Protocol 1 to the European Convention on Human Rights requires states to respect the right of parents to ensure the education and teaching of their children in conformity with their own religious and philosophical convictions. The parents' right to withdraw their children from religious activities is based on the offence which attendance would cause to their basic values and beliefs. The converse argument is that parents who *do* hold strong religious beliefs should be able to shield their children from what they consider to be anti-religious views or information which is antithetical to the morality of their churches.[80] The classic objection to sex education is that it is alleged to encourage extra-marital sexual activity among the young.

The issue came before the European Court of Human Rights in 1976 in the case of *Kjeldsen, Busk Madsen and Pedersen*.[81] In 1970 the Danish Parliament decided to follow the example of Sweden and passed legislation amending the State Schools Act in order to introduce compulsory sex education into primary schools. Because of the way in which such education would be integrated into other subjects on the curriculum the inevitable result was that Danish parents would lose their existing rights to exempt their children from sex education classes. The parents applicants contended that the new system was contrary to the beliefs which they held as Christians and constituted a violation of Article 2, Protocol 1.

While acknowledging the parents' right to require the state to respect their religious and philosophical convictions the Court took the view that the setting and planning of the curriculum was within the competence of the individual state authorities. In fulfilling their functions in this respect it was incumbent on states to take care that the information or knowledge included in the curriculum was conveyed in an objective, critical and pluralistic manner. It was not open to states to pursue a policy of indoctrination.

---

[80] For a good discussion of anti-religious challenges in the United States see Smith, *op. cit.* n. 70, p. 34.
[81] December 7, 1976, Series A no. 23.

However, the Danish legislation was aimed at presenting knowledge to children more correctly, precisely, objectively and scientifically than they would acquire informally from various other quarters.[82] In no way did it, in the Court's view, amount to an attempt at indoctrination aimed at advocating a specific kind of sexual behaviour, nor did it affect the right of parents to enlighten and advise their children protected by Article 2.

This case is authority that states which are signatories to the European Convention *may* introduce compulsory sex education which overrides parental wishes provided that it is presented in a balanced and objective manner. It is *not* authority that children themselves have a right to receive sex education under the Convention. Again the focus of attention has been on the *parents'* position rather than the child's. In order to establish the principle of universal sex education it would be necessary to obtain a ruling on whether the child's general right to education, protected by Article 2, implies a duty in states to introduce compulsory sex education in schools. Meanwhile it is open to states to leave the question of the inclusion and form of sex education to regional and individual school authorities. This is essentially the position in England, albeit subject to a new statutory directive on the manner in which sex education is presented. Whether sex education is included at all is a matter for the collective consideration of L.E.A.s, governing bodies and head teachers. Under section 18(2) of the 1986 Act the articles of government must provide for it to be the duty of the governing body to consider separately whether sex education should form part of the secular curriculum. The inevitable result is bound to be widespread regional variation on whether it is included in the curriculum and, if so, what its content and form of teaching is to be. However, statute now requires steps to be taken by those responsible to secure that where sex education is given to any registered pupils at the school it is given "in such manner as to encourage those pupils to have regard to moral considerations and the value of family life."[83]

The Department of Education and Science has issued a detailed circular on Sex Education at School to all L.E.A.s.[84] This accepts

---

[82] The Swedish system of integrated sex education is described in Carl Gustaf Boethius, "Swedish Sex Education and Its Results," *Current Sweden* No. 315, March 1984, published by the Swedish Institute.

[83] Education (No. 2) Act 1986, s.46.

[84] No. 11/87, September 25, 1987, as to which see "DES call for 'Moral' Sex Education in Schools" (1987) 42 *Childright* 4.

that "appropriate and responsible sex education is an important element in the work of schools in preparing pupils for adult life."[85] It affirms the primary responsibility of parents for educating their children in sexual matters and the "complementary and supportive" role of schools.[86] Importantly, it is expected that, although they have power to decide that no sex education should be provided in their school, "governing bodies will be strongly influenced by the widely accepted view that schools have a responsibility to their pupils to offer at least some education about sexual matters."[87] Governors have a discretion to accept or reject requests from parents that their children be withdrawn from any sex education to which they object. Although parents have no statutory right of withdrawal, the circular advises that where there are strong objections on religious grounds governing bodies should fully appreciate this in exercising their discretion.[88]

The principal objection to the current position is that it fails to attach sufficient weight to the acquisition of sex education as a legitimate claim which *all* children have. The L.E.A. together with the governing body and head teacher may effectively veto sex education at certain schools. It is interesting to compare the law on sex education with the development of the law relating to corporal punishment in schools. The European Court of Human Rights held in *Campbell and Cosans* v. *United Kingdom*[89] that Article 2, Protocol 1 was infringed where corporal punishment was inflicted in Scottish schools contrary to the wishes of parents based on their philosophical convictions. The British Government's initial response to the ruling was the Education (Corporal Punishment) Bill 1985 which sought to introduce a mechanism to enable parents to exempt their children from corporal punishment. There was widespread opposition to the idea of two separate categories of school children comprising respectively "beatables" and "unbeatables." The Bill was lost and in July 1986 Parliament voted narrowly in favour of the complete abolition of corporal punishment in state schools.[90] Abolition is effected by sections 47 and 48 of the Education (No. 2) Act 1986 which came into force on

[85] Para. 1.
[86] Para. 2.
[87] Para. 7.
[88] Para. 9.
[89] (1982) 4 E.H.R.R. 293.
[90] The chequered history of the campaign for abolition is traced in "When the Beating has to Stop" (1986) 30 *Childright* 11.

August 15, 1987. The end result is the creation of a universal right in children not to be subjected to corporal punishment in state schools, but the impetus for abolition was not the vindication of *children's* rights but rather the rights of *parents*. It is the same concentration on parents' rights, implying choice in education, which results in sex education being relegated to the level of an optional extra.

It may be however that the argument over sex education is concerned more with the subject matter and method of teaching than with the question whether it should be offered at all. Some courses have been criticised for taking a narrow biological view, while those which offer guidance on the use of contraceptives are criticised for encouraging promiscuity. Section 46 of the 1986 Act is an attempt to dictate centrally the content of such courses by requiring them to emphasise sexual responsibility as a moral value and the place of sexual activity within the context of family life. This provision is itself open to criticism for singling out one (admittedly important) aspect of sex education. The circular, also, may be criticised for its emphasis on the "moral framework" for sex education[91] and for its diatribe against "teaching which advocates homosexual behaviour, which presents it as the "norm," or which encourages homosexual experimentation by pupils."[92] Further, its advice on the effect of the *Gillick* decision on teacher's relationships with pupils is highly suspect. It takes the position that the ruling is confined to advice on sexual matters in the medical context and that the principles governing the child's relationship with the medical profession "have no parallel in school education." It therefore proffers the advice that, "the general rule must be that giving an individual pupil advice on such matters without parental knowledge or consent would be an inappropriate exercise of a teacher's professional responsibilities, and could, depending on the circumstances, amount to a criminal offence."[93] This is an unjustifiably narrow interpretation of the decision which is widely regarded as having general application to the capacities of adolescents for various decisions. The legal capacity to exercise self-help in seeking advice from educational professionals is an important (perhaps essential) requirement of schoolchidren who have a poor quality of family life with their

[91] Para. 19.
[92] Para. 22.
[93] Para. 26.

EDUCATION

parents. Despite what the circular says, *Gillick supports* rather than detracts from the legal entitlement of mature adolescents to approach professionals for advice. There is a strong case for compulsory sex education embracing reproductive biology, advice on contraception and discussion of the role of sexual activity within the context of caring relationships and family life. The Swedish experience shows that its introduction may serve to reduce the incidence of teenage pregnancies, abortion and sexually transmitted diseases.[94] The issue has acquired a new urgency with the appearance of the AIDS virus. Apart from these practical considerations it may be supported by reference to the child's fundamental right to accurate knowledge of the facts about sexual activity. The potential dangers which attend sexual involvement make it too important an issue to leave exclusively in the hands of parents who may discharge the duty imperfectly or not at all. Neither should it be left in the hands of individual governing bodies for the same reasons. A compulsory system is the only way of universalising the rights of schoolchildren in this vitally important matter.

6. Conclusions

Education law provides a striking illustration of the identity of interests doctrine which subsumes the interests of children under those of their parents. The legal arguments continue to revolve around the statutory responsibilities of the state (vested in L.E.A.s and school authorities) and the rights and responsibilities of parents. Throughout, there is little or no acknowledgment of the independent claims of children.

There is no better illustration of this phenomenon than the American case *Wisconsin* v. *Yoder.*[95] Here the Supreme Court

[94] It has not been possible to establish a direct correlation between the availability of compulsory sex education in Swedish schools and the reduction in teenage pregnancies, abortions etc. Nevertheless it is the case that, following the intensification of school information measures concerning gonorrhoea in 1970, the incidence of gonorrhoea among the high risk age groups declined by about 40 per cent. in five years. Equally, there has been a consistent decline in the number of teenage pregnancies and abortions in Sweden. See "Sex Education in Swedish Schools" May 1986, published by the Swedish National Board of Education pp. 10–12.
[95] 406 U.S. 205 (1972).

struck down a state compulsory education law to the extent that it required Amish children to remain in state schools beyond the eighth grade (attained at the age of 14). The court upheld the parents' claim that state education could be detrimental to the Amish way of life which the children would lead. The majority of the court failed to deal with the potential conflict of interest between Amish parents and their children in the manner of their education. Douglas J. dissented, however, on the basis that the childrens' *independent* rights were at stake. He pointed out that an individual student might wish to opt out of the Amish tradition and that the effect of allowing his parents to keep him out of school might be to bar him from entry into the "new and amazing world of diversity that we have today." He thought, therefore, that the individual child should be given an opportunity to present his views before parents were permitted to withdraw him from the state system.

The failure to isolate the independent interests of children has resulted in neglect of their claims to autonomy. This now runs counter to the spirit, if not the letter, of *Gillick* which surely requires adequate opportunity for children to express their views on educational issues affecting them. The proposal of the Inner London Education Authority to appoint an educational ombudsman to handle complaints from parents and school students over 16 is an interesting innovation in this respect.[96] Similarly, fundamental rights of recipience such as sex education may be denied to children where parental wishes are regarded as inviolable.

The difficulty in asserting the independent interests of children is that in many instances they may *in fact* coincide with their parents'. It would be folly to assume that a conflict of interest *necessarily* exists between parents and children. Where this coincidence is a reality, the parents may legitimately be regarded as the child's representatives in what is a conflict between the family and the state. If the parents then succeed in an action against the state it may not be clear whether it is primarily the child's right or the parents' rights over upbringing which is being upheld.

This is illustrated by the American case of *Tinker* v. *Des Moines Independent Community School District*.[97] Here the Supreme

---

[96] I.L.E.A. report, "Complaints Procedure and I.L.E.A. Ombudsman" (1987). It is understood that extension of the scheme to *all* children of secondary school age is under consideration.

[97] n. 61.

Court held that public school authorities were acting unconstitutionally in prohibiting students from wearing black armbands in protest at the Vietnam war, unless they could show that the practice would result in substantial disruption of, or material interference with, school activites. The decision is couched in the language of children's rights. For example, Forbes J. observed:

> "It can hardly be argued that either students or teachers shed their constitutional rights to freedom of speech or expression at the school house gate."

But the students' protest was directly supported by their parents and has led one commentator to interpret the decision as support for the parents' right "to teach and influence their children against state claims that would limit the exercise of such parental prerogatives."[98]

Likewise the European cases of *Campbell and Cosans* and *Kjeldsen* were unashamedly actions by parents against the state. In so far as children's own rights were promoted this was an incidental by-product of the legal process. Both corporal punishment and sex education are areas in which there may indeed be a conflict of interest between parent and child. The aftermath of *Campbell and Cosans* testifies to the inequality and arbitrary treatment of children which might have resulted from a failure to recognise this conflict.

[98] B. Hafen, "Children's Liberation and the New Egalitarianism: Some Reservations about Abandoning Youth to their Rights" (1976) Brigham Young Univ. Law Rev. 605, 646.

8. Financial Support

1. Introduction

The provision of financial support for children is an obligation primarily discharged by parents in the context of a functioning family. But even where the family remains intact it is widely accepted that the state should bear some part of the financial burden of raising children. This view is based on the philosophy that children represent an economic investment as future productive adults and that the community should therefore share in the economic cost of supporting them during childhood. The principle was accepted by the Government in its Green Paper, "Reform of Social Security" where it stated that "we should give financial support to those who bear the extra responsibility of bringing up children." Acceptance of this principle "acknowledges not only the duty to ensure that children should not face hardship, but also the importance of supporting family life and those who are ensuring our own future by caring for the next generation."[1]

Where the family unit breaks down the role of the state in maintaining a minimum level of income for children is much increased. It is an established fact that a high proportion of single parents with dependent children rely primarily on state support.[2] In these cases the issue is the correct balance of responsibility between the state, the custodial and the non-custodial parent. The matter is complicated by the consideration that in a large number of cases any payments made by the absent parent will be of no direct benefit to the recipients. This is because maintenance payments count as income for the purposes of Income Support (formerly Supplementary Benefit) entitlement and will simply

---

[1] "The Reform of Social Security" (1985) Vol. 1, para. 8.1. Cmnd. 9517.
[2] See, *e.g.* the discussion in Eekelaar and McClean, *Maintenance after Divorce* (1986) Chap. 6, pp. 93–94.

result in a *pro tanto* reduction of benefit.[3] Accordingly, it is only where the absent parent is able to pay maintenance at a rate significantly above the level of his former family's benefit entitlement that it will be of real value to them.[4] This is only likely to occur in two types of case *viz.* where the non-custodial parent has a substantially above average income, or where the custodial parent is in employment and the combined effect of her remuneration and maintenance is to pull her away from the margins of poverty.

Prima facie, therefore, it might seem advantageous for the custodial parent and children to look exclusively to the state for support in the post-breakdown situation and to accept a "clean-break" from private financial support. This would especially be so where there is the possibility of enhanced property rights or other capital provision. We consider below whether the "clean break" principle is consistent with the concept of continuing parental responsibility, but in any event these private considerations are only one aspect of the debate since the state's interest in recouping part of the cost of social security payments from "liable relatives" is also of great importance. It is this relationship between private and public support for children which is the subject of this chapter.

2. The Parental Support Obligation

Parents have both private and public law obligations to support their children. The history of the private obligation is traced by Eekelaar and McClean.[5] Surprisingly, child maintenance was ignored as a separate principle in the nineteenth century and was first acknowledged in the Married Women (Maintenance) Act 1920. The exception was the father's obligation to maintain his illegitimate child which was recognised during the nineteenth century by the existence of affiliation proceedings dating from the Poor Law. Child maintenance in the Magistrates' Courts then remained subject to financial limits which were finally removed in 1968. Orders for periodical payments and lump sums for children as well as for one party to a marriage may now be made, where the

[3] s.2(1)(*b*) of the Social Security Act 1986.
[4] This is because the effects of the "poverty-trap" may still be felt where a family is marginally above subsistence level. The amount by which income exceeds this level may be off-set by the loss of other state benefits which go with entitlement to Income Support.
[5] *Op. cit.* n. 2, pp. 19–28.

marriage continues, under sections 1 and 2 of the Domestic Proceedings and Magistrates' Courts Act 1978. They may also be made on divorce under section 23 of the Matrimonial Causes Act 1973. Financial orders for children only may be sought by one parent against the other under the Guardianship of Minors Act 1971 or in wardship proceedings. Parents may also be ordered to pay maintenance in wardship or custodianship proceedings in respect of a child in the actual care of a third party.

Where parents are unmarried the position until recently was that the mother could seek an order for periodical payments for the child from the alleged father in affiliation proceedings. The father, however, had no means of seeking an order against her in the minority of cases in which he had the actual care of the child. Father and mother have now been placed on an equal footing. The Family Law Reform Act 1987 abolishes affiliation proceedings but empowers the court to make an order against either parent for the benefit of the child in proceedings under the Guardianship of Minors Act 1971.[6] It is not necessary that the order sought should be ancillary to a claim for custody or access and this jurisdiction now applies equally to married and unmarried parents.

The public law obligation arises under section 26 of the Social Security Act 1986. This places both parents under a liability to maintain their children and, while they remain married, each other. The latter obligation terminates where their marriage is dissolved or annulled, but their liability to the children survives until the children attain majority. This public liability to maintain children applies equally to married and unmarried parents.

At this stage it is necessary to address what is a fundamental issue. This is whether it is appropriate to recognise *independent* support rights in the parent with care of the children and the children themselves, or whether it is more appropriate to regard their claims as inextricably linked and to think in terms of *family* support rights. The traditional approach has been to conceptualise the claims of parent and child as independent elements of support. As noted above, this distinction is necessarily made for the purposes of public support obligations. The private obligation to both the children and the former spouse continues following divorce, but the distinction between these two elements resurfaces in the event of the latter's remarriage since this has the effect of

---

[6] Family Law Reform Act 1987, s.12, inserting a new s.11B into the Guardianship of Minors Act 1971.

terminating automatically spousal support but not child support.[7] Most significantly, the dichotomy is illustrated by the situation of unmarried parents who have no public or private support rights *inter se*, but who are both now liable under public and private law to provide support for their children.

The basic distinction has however been subjected to a penetrating analysis by Eekelaar and McClean who conclude that there exists no rational basis for it.[8] The essence of their argument is that in reality the child's standard of living is bound up with that of the caregiver who is responsible for attending to the child's food, clothing, accommodation and everyday needs. Although, therefore, periodical payments may be formally earmarked for the child, they are usually received on behalf of the child by the caring parent. In this sense they are similar in nature to spousal support payments since both payments may be applied partly towards providing for the parent's living requirements and partly towards the child's living requirements. In short, "the elements constituting the child's economic well-being are indivisible."[9] They cite the case of *Northrop* v. *Northrop*[10] as an illustration of the technical difficulties which can arise from separation of the respective support claims of the wife and the children. There the Court of Appeal strained to find a theoretical basis for awarding spousal support in addition to child support in order to boost the total award of maintenance which could be made for them.[11]

The authors therefore suggest that the distinction is cosmetic except in relation to certain fiscal advantages which may accrue in some circumstances where payments are designated for children.[12]

[7] Matrimonial Causes Act 1973, s.28.

[8] *Op. cit.* n. 2, p. 106.

[9] *Ibid.* p. 106.

[10] [1967] [1968] p. 74.

[11] *Op. cit.* n. 2, pp. 23–24.

[12] These fiscal advantages were first, that an order for payment to a child would have the effect of transferring the income from the payer to the child so that the payer would cease to be liable to tax on it and, secondly, that the child would be unlikely to be liable for tax on the payment either since he would have the benefit of a personal allowance which in most cases would exceed the amount of maintenance. The House of Lords had held that these advantages might be secured by a custodial parent seeking an order against himself in relation to payment of school fees. See *Sherdley* v. *Sherdley* [1987] 2 All E.R. 54. The decision had wide-ranging implications for different types of custodial arrangements, discussed by Susan Maidment at (1987) 137 N.L.J. 393. The 1988 Budget has, however, radically altered this position by removing tax relief on maintenance payments for children on orders made after March 15, 1988.

They conclude:

> "If a clearer set of principles can be developed regarding the child support obligation, it may be that, in cases where the adult claimant is caring for children, the principles of child support will be sufficient to conclude the matter."[13]

The issue is an extraordinarily difficult one. From a practical point of view it is irrefutable that maintenance payments for parent and child together form a common purse which is utilised for the benefit of that family unit. Clearly there is no practical way of ensuring that child support is applied in satisfaction of the child's needs, but equally money intended for an adult's benefit may well be applied in whole or in part in satisfaction of the child's needs. The effect of refusing to recognise the adult claim may therefore be simply to reduce the size of the common purse. In low income cases the result will be to increase the burden on the state by reducing the amount recoverable from the liable relative. These practical considerations do suggest that there is no good reason for perpetuating the distinction.

There may, however, be sound theoretical reasons for preserving it. The ideology of modern divorce law is to encourage a clean break between the adults involved. The Matrimonial and Family Proceedings Act 1984 introduced a number of provisions designed to encourage this and to promote the principle of self-sufficiency.[14] Hence the thrust of the law, albeit subject to qualifications, is against the notion of persisting support rights between former spouses.[15] But this philosophy cannot readily be applied to the relationship between the non-custodial parent and the children of the family since it clashes directly with prevailing ideas on continued parenting following divorce. A clean break in relation to *child* maintenance may be thought inconsistent with this basic orientation. This was a widely held view before the Act and one

---

[13] Op. cit. n. 2. p. 107.
[14] The Act followed the Reports of the Law Commission "Family Law: The Financial Consequences of Divorce: The Basic Policy. A Discussion Paper" (Law Com. No. 103 (1980) and "Family Law: The Financial Consequences of Divorce. The Response to the Law Commission's Discussion Paper, and Recommendations on the Policy of the Law" (Law Com. No. 112 (1981)).
[15] The termination of spousal support obligations is a controversial matter and it is clear that there will be many instances where this is not appropriate. See the discussion on the background to the Act in Stephen M. Cretney, "Money After Divorce—The Mistakes We Have Made?" *Essays in Family Law* (1985) p. 34, University College, London.

which seemed to be reinforced by the new priority which the Act attached to the welfare of children. Henceforth this was to be the court's "first consideration" when considering how to exercise its powers in relation to property and financial adjustment under sections 23 and 24 of the Matrimonial Causes Act 1973 as amended by the 1984 Act.[16] Can it therefore be said that the priority to be accorded to children's interests precludes the termination of maintenance in *all* cases in which children are present?

In *Suter* v. *Suter and Jones*[17] H. had been ordered to pay £100 per month to W. in periodical payments. The judge had taken the view that a clean break was impossible until the children had grown up. The issue for the Court of Appeal was the relationship between section 25(1) and section 25A of the Matrimonial Causes Act 1973. The former provision requires the court, in deciding whether to exercise its powers, to give first consideration to the welfare of any children. The latter provision imposes a duty on the court, in every case in which an order in favour of a party to the marriage is sought under section 23 (even where there are children), to consider whether a termination of maintenance is appropriate immediately or at some future date.[18]

The court held that the cumulative effect of these two provisions was not such as to render a clean break impossible in children cases. On the evidence, however, the court decided that it would be premature to terminate H.'s obligations and that a nominal order was appropriate. Sir Roualeyn Cumming-Bruce took the view that, although parents might have to cooperate with one another over their children, it might be possible to recognise a date when the parent in whose favour the order was made would be able to adjust without undue hardship to the termination of financial dependence on the other party. Since the child's welfare was the "first" but not "paramount" consideration[19] it could not

---

[16] For a case perhaps reflecting the shift in emphasis see *Roots* v. *Roots* (1987) 17 Fam.Law 387.

[17] [1987] Fam. 111.

[18] s.25A(2) provides that where the court is considering an order for periodical payments in favour of a party to the marriage it shall "consider whether it would be appropriate to require those payments to be made or secured only for such term as would in the opinion of the court be sufficient to enable the party in whose favour the order is made to adjust without undue hardship to the termination of his or her financial dependence on the other party."

[19] On the distinction between the two statutory expressions see M. D. A. Freeman, "A Guide to the Matrimonial and Family Proceedings Act 1984" para. [620].

override considerations of the clean break which had to be looked at under section 25A.

This case establishes that the court is bound to consider the clean break option in relation to *adult* support even where there are children. It does *not* decide that the court must consider it in relation to *child* support. Section 25A itself only expressly requires the court to consider termination of the former. Indeed, in *Suter* itself there was no question of a termination or reduction in *child* support. The sole issue was whether H's financial obligations to W should be terminated. In deciding to reduce the order in her favour to a nominal amount the court took an overall look at her financial situation and took into account the value of child maintenance (totalling £200 per month in respect of the 2 children) and the value of the capital transfer which H had already made. Both the Act and the decision are therefore predicated on the assumption that adult support and child support are distinct.

Is it implicit in this decision that, although under no statutory obligation, the court would be acting properly in considering the termination of child support? The court lacks power to terminate formally maintenance for children,[20] but it could decide to make no order or a nominal order. As we have seen such an order might be advantageous to all concerned. If compensated by a generous agreement on the matrimonial home or other capital order it might be argued that it would be quite consistent with the promotion of the child's welfare as the first consideration.

The difficulty with this approach is that it ignores the interest of the state in the enforcement of H.'s public law obligation. In *Hulley* v. *Thompson*[21] there was a consent order that no maintenance be paid by F. for M. or the children. Instead he agreed to transfer his half interest in the matrimonial home to M. Later the Supplementary Benefits Commission brought proceedings against him to recover a contribution to the benefit being paid for M. and the children. F. contended that he had discharged his liability towards them by the property transfer. The Court of Appeal disagreed. Waller L.J. held that a consent order which might be effective to impose a clean break between two adults, could not avoid the public liability to maintain children. Whether, in considering the appropriate amount of the order, the court

---

[20] This is because the new power of termination in s.25A(3) is restricted on its terms to periodical payments in favour of the adult parties to the marriage.
[21] [1981] 1 All E.R. 1128.

should take account of the value of the property transfer was left open.

Thus, it would appear that it is impossible to achieve a complete discharge from maintenance liability towards children, even where sanctioned by court order, since the public law obligation endures. The argument for preserving the private law obligation towards children is discussed below. The conclusion to be drawn from this discussion is that it may be necessary to continue to separate in theory the support claims of parent and child, while at the same time recognising that maintenance payments are practically indistinguishable in the hands of the recipient parent. This appears to have been the approach of Sir George Baker P. in *Haroutunian* v. *Jennings*,[22] a case concerning the extent of the financial liability of an unmarried father in affiliation proceedings. Here the father was ordered to pay £20 per week for the child. It was not contested that this was an amount well within his capacity to pay, but he argued that in reality the order was intended to be for the maintenance of the mother rather than the child. Since the mother was wholly dependent on state benefits, any sum which she received by way of maintenance for the child would serve only to reduce her overall entitlement by virtue of the aggregation principle. The President rejected this argument as fallacious since it sought to equate the amount allowed under the then supplementary benefit scheme for the child's maintenance at subsistence level with what was reasonable for the father to pay for his child's support. In his view, the fact that money earmarked for the child might find its way into the mother's pocket for caring for the child was not something which the father could rely on to bring down the amount of the order for the child.

What will matter to the custodial parent and the children is not the label which attaches to the payments which they receive but the global level of support. It is in relation to this that the clean break is potentially damaging to children's interests. Even if theoretically it applies only to spousal support and does not affect child support, the reality may be that the loss of spousal support is not compensated by an increase in child support. Thus, the practical effect may be a diminution in the standard of living of the family unit directly affecting the children. Consequently, it is arguable that the clean break should be reserved for childless marriages unless financial obligations towards children can be met

[22] (1977) 1 F.L.R. 62.

in advance by appropriate capital provision. In order to preserve equity between liable relatives some attempt should be made to ensure that such provision is broadly commensurate with the amount of maintenance which would have been likely to be payable for the children.

3. State Benefits for Children

The state's contribution to the financial support of families with children is most directly reflected in the provision of Child Benefit. Beveridge recognised in 1942 that the community interest in the well-being of the future generation should give rise to a partnership between parents and the state.[23] He was influenced by social surveys which had indicated that, after income loss, the failure to relate income to the size of families was the major cause of poverty. His report led to the introduction of Family Allowances in 1945, the historical precursor of Child Benefit. Until 1975 a dual system had existed comprised of family allowances and tax allowances for children. This was criticised for benefiting the higher income groups (who could take advantage of the tax concessions) over the lower income groups (whose tax liability was either much lower or non-existent). The Child Benefit Act 1975 replaced this system with a new flat-rate universal benefit payable to every family in which there was at least one child.[24] The current rate of child benefit is £7.25 per week for each child and, unlike certain other provisions for children, is not age-related. The Conservative Government has stated its commitment to Child Benefit as a universal non-means tested benefit but has nevertheless allowed its value in real terms to be eroded.[25] Critics of the recent social security reforms[26] see them

[23] "Report of the Committee into Social Insurance and Allied Services" (1942) Cmnd. 6404.

[24] The benefit is payable to any person who is "responsible for one or more children in any week," Child Benefit Act, 1975, s.1(1).

[25] See, e.g. Mother's Lifeline by Alison Walsh and Ruth Lister, (1985) C.P.A.G. and "Of Little Benefit—A Critical Guide to the Social Security Act 1986" Social Security Consortium (1986).

[26] The basis of the reforms was the Green Paper, "The Reform of Social Security" (1985) Vol. 1, Cmnd. 9517, Vol. 2 Cmnd. 9518 and Vol. 3 Cmnd. 9519, and the White Paper, "The Programme for Action" (1985) Cmnd. 9691. The proposals were substantially embodied in the Social Security Act 1986 which received the Royal Assent on July 25, 1986. The Act has been implemented progressively, the principal changes taking effect on April 11, 1988.

as prioritising means-tested benefits at the expense of maintaining the value of child benefit.

Elsewhere in the social security system children's needs are recognised by way of additions to the amounts of benefits payable to their adult carers. In relation to Social Security benefits[27] the additions are known as dependant increases. Their value has been gradually eroded over a period of years and in 1984 they were abolished in relation to the short-term unemployment and sickness benefits, except where the adult claimant is over pensionable age.[28] For the long-term benefits of retirement pensions, widows benefits, industrial death benefit, invalidity pensions, invalid care allowance and severe disablement allowance a standard addition is payable for a child dependant at the current rate of £8.40 per week. The 1984 Act removed entitlement to these increases where the claimant's spouse or cohabitant earns more than a specific figure.[29] The abolition of child increases for short-term benefits is one of the reasons why the short-term unemployed may find it necessary to top-up unemployment or sickness benefit with Income Support under which an allowance is made for the presence of children in the family unit.

Until April 11, 1988 the principal means-tested benefits available to families with children were Supplementary Benefit (SB) and Family Income Supplement (FIS). As from this date they were replaced by Income Support and Family Credit respectively.[30]

Income Support is payable to a person over 16 years of age who is not engaged in remunerative work and whose spouse or unmarried partner is also unemployed, who either has no income or whose income does not exceed the "applicable amount."[31] Formerly, SB was payable in respect of an "assessment unit" comprising a husband and wife or unmarried couple living together as husband and wife, together with any child dependants living in their household. This principle of aggregation has been unaffected by the transition to Income Support. The income and capital of all members of the family are, subject to certain qualifications, aggregated for the purposes of computing

---

[27] The term is used here to distinguish contributory benefits under the National Insurance Scheme which arise under the Social Security Act 1975 from means-tested benefits.

[28] Health and Social Security Act 1984, s.13 and Sched. 5.

[29] Sched. 5, paras. 3 and 4.

[30] The Social Security Act 1986 (Commencement No. 8) Order 1987.

[31] s.20(3) of the Social Security Act 1986.

entitlement to benefit. The applicable amount comprises an amount in respect of the claimant, his married or unmarried partner and an amount in respect of each child in the family unit. The needs of children are thus accommodated by specific additions or rates which form part of the calculation of the applicable amount for the family. As was the case with SB they are age-related to reflect the increased cost of raising older children. The Income Support scheme also provides for a "family premium" (currently set at £6.15 per week) to be added to the applicable amount where there is at least one child or young person in the claimant's family.

Family Credit is also payable to a person whose income does not exceed an applicable amount.[32] Where his income does exceed the specified amount he is entitled to a partial credit in accordance with a prescribed statutory formula. Like its predecessor FIS, Family Credit is a benefit for low-income families in which at least one member of the couple is in full-time work. There must be at least one child in the household for whom either the claimant or his partner is "responsible." In determining the appropriate maximum family credit the number and ages of children or young people in the household are taken into account. It should also be noted that the presence of children in the family is a component in the calculation of entitlement to housing benefit.

The effect of aggregation in cases of marriage breakdown or parental separation is of fundamental importance. While parents are living together with the child they have no independent claims to either Income Support or Family Credit.[33] Where they are permanently living apart their independent claims revive. The implications of this may be seen where F. leaves M. with the children and sets up a second household with C. and her children. M. will now be entitled to claim state benefits for herself and the children. But, the second family will, by virtue of the aggregation principle, be entirely dependent on F. for support. This is something which clearly ought to be relevant when assessing the relative claims of the first and second families on F.'s income. The aggregation principle casts serious doubt on the view, sometimes expressed by the judges, that the claims of the first family should be accorded priority.[34] The short point is that payments from F.

---

[32] s.20(5) of the Social Security Act 1986.

[33] s.20(9) and (11) of the Social Security Act 1986.

[34] See, for example, the remarks of Ormrod L.J. in *Tovey* v. *Tovey* (1978) 8 *Family Law* 80.

may be of no direct financial benefit to them whatsoever, whereas the same money will be vital to the daily needs of the reconstituted family.

The Social Security system does not provide specifically for family breakdown as a contingency which should give rise to entitlement to state benefits. The Finer Committee's[35] proposal in 1974 for a "Guaranteed Maintenance Allowance" (G.M.A.) for single parents has not been taken up, largely for reasons of cost. Instead certain more limited assistance to single parents is provided by way of a number of ad hoc expedients.

One parent benefit is payable as an addition to child benefit at the current rate of £4.90 per week, but only in relation to the first child. It should be remembered that it will not profit those single parents who are already dependent on Income Support since, like child benefit itself, it counts as income for the purposes of computing entitlement to benefit. The new Income Support scheme also incorporates a "lone parent premium" (currently £3.70 per week) payable where the claimant is a member of a family but has no partner.

4. The Interrelationship of Private and Public Support

Given that private maintenance payments will often not enure to the benefit of the recipients (where they are dependent entirely on state support), it has been contended that the availability of state support should be a factor which the courts should consider in fixing the quantum of maintenance awards. Indeed it might be argued that the private obligation should be extinguished altogether. This latter proposition has been unequivocally rejected by the courts which have held that it is wrong in principle for a man to off-load all his responsibilities towards his first family onto the state. At the same time they have adopted a second principle that any order made against him should not be such as to depress his income below subsistence level.[36] Subsistence level for these purposes is the notional entitlement of a man (M.) and his second family to state benefits including any additional and housing requirements of that family unit. This approach can result in a

---

[35] Report of the Committee on One-Parent Families (1974) Cmnd. 5629.
[36] See, for example, *Ashley* v. *Ashley* [1968] p. 582. and *Barnes* v. *Barnes* [1972] 3 All E.R. 872.

reduction in the standard of living of M. and his family to the level of the official poverty line. Any resources over and above that are regarded as available for the first family. Indeed in *Tovey* v. *Tovey*[37] the effect of the court's order was to leave M. with an income *below* the hypothetical S.B. entitlement of his reconstituted family. This case is however exceptional and represents the high water mark of the private obligation ideology.

In contrast to the courts, the Department of Health and Social Security have, in enforcing the public law obligation, allowed M. a margin of income above subsistence level. This approach is referred to as the "liable relative formula" and is partly designed to provide him with an incentive to continue working.[38] When negotiating with M., the D.H.S.S. is likely to regard as reasonable an offer by him which will leave him with £5 or one-quarter of his net earnings (whichever is the higher) above subsistence level. After a brief flirtation with this approach in *Smethurst* v. *Smethurst*,[39] the courts firmly rejected it in *Shallow* v. *Shallow*.[40] Here the Court of Appeal held that the formula was "nothing more than a negotiating figure" used by the Department which was more likely to be paid regularly than a higher sum imposed on the liable relative. Where the matter went to court, however, the Department was entitled to seek to enforce liability to the full extent. The court's objective appears to have been to achieve broad economic equality between the former spouses at or about subsistence level. It was considered inequitable for the husband to be allowed a margin of resources above this while the wife and children would remain at this level. Hence the husband was considered to be in a financial position where he could afford to pay more than the figure which the "liable relative" formula would have produced.

The court's approach may be criticised for its artificiality. It assumes that the issue was what was a fair apportionment of the husband's income (as if this was the only resource) between the two households. But the real issue, given the availability of state benefits, was what the husband could properly be expected to contribute to the state. It was clear here that whether the one-third formula or the liable relative was applied the wife and children

---

[37] n. 34.
[38] Described in the Finer Report, para. 4.188.
[39] [1978] Fam. 52.
[40] [1979] Fam. 1.

were going to remain at or about subsistence level. It is not self-evident that the proper contribution to state funds which may be expected of former husbands is such as would reduce them to subsistence level, particularly where this would be of no direct financial benefit to their dependants. There are good reasons for thinking otherwise, not least the need to preserve employment incentives.

In the light of these considerations and the major difficulties presented by the enforcement of maintenance orders,[41] it is both surprising and regrettable that the courts have, for the most part, decided to adhere to the harsher and more unrealistic subsistence level approach. In recent years, however, there have been signs that they are beginning to moderate their attitudes. In particular they may now accept that the availability of state benefits for W. and the children *is* relevant to the quantum of the maintenance order. Thus, in *Peacock* v. *Peacock*[42] Booth J. took the view that the fact that W. was receiving state benefits, although not justifying a complete discharge of M.'s liability, was a relevant factor in assessing maintenance alongside M.'s ability to pay and the other factors specified in section 25 of the Matrimonial Causes Act 1973. The question which remains unanswered is precisely how much latitude the courts may be prepared to allow M. over and above his national subsistence level. It is at present far from clear that there is general acceptance that *any* allowance should be made.[43] Nonetheless, there are signs that the courts are moving towards the D.H.S.S. approach of allowing M. some margin of resources, though not as yet in accordance with the liable relative formula or any other recognisable formula.

In *Allen* v. *Allen*[44] it was accepted that W.'s total dependency on state benefits meant that her income would be unaffected by any order against M. M.'s gross earnings were £120 per week and he paid £20 per week to his mother for his keep. He then acquired his own home on mortgage with a weekly payment together with rates of £36. The registrar ordered him to pay £5 per week for W. and £5 for each of the two children. The effect of the order would have

---

[41] Discussed in Colin Gibson in "Maintenance in the Magistrates' Courts in the 1980's" (1982) 12 Fam. Law 138.

[42] [1984] 1 All E.R. 1069.

[43] In *Foot* v. *Foot* (1987) 17 Fam. Law 13, for example, Hollis J. seemed to return to the orthodox view that the receipt of S.B. by the wife was irrelevant to the quantum of maintenance. See also *Day* v. *Day* (1988) 1 F.L.R. 278.

[44] [1986] 2 F.L.R. 265.

been to leave M. with a modest £5.71 per week in excess of his long-term S.B. requirements. On appeal the recorder had raised the order to a total of £35 per week, thereby depressing M. almost to his notional subsistence level. He took the view that M. should be prepared to make some sacrifices. The Court of Appeal restored the registrar's order. The margin of resources which he had allowed was not excessive bearing in mind the public responsibility of the D.H.S.S. to pay W. £60 per week.

The decision is evidence of a greater awareness of the relationship between maintenance and state benefits and the realities of the parties' respective financial positions. The margin allowed would seem to lie somewhere between subsistence level and the result which the liable relative formula would have yielded.

A number of criticisms may be made of the courts' approach in this area. First, it is unfortunate that they should adopt a stance which is inconsistent with that of the D.H.S.S. The real issue is the extent of a man's responsibility, not to his dependents but to the state, and the courts should be more willing to accept the departmental view of what is reasonable. Their failure to do so simply exacerbates enforcement difficulties and leads to the accumulation of massive arrears.[45] Secondly, while a departure from the inflexible subsistence level formula is to be welcomed, it is important that it should be replaced by an alternative approach which is coherent and applied consistently. This cannot be said to be the case at present. Thirdly, the courts' attitude where a man has acquired a second family is open to question. While it is important that his financial obligation to the children of his first family should continue to be recognised it is not sensible, given the effect of the aggregation rule, to regard this as his *primary* obligation. His first commitment must surely be to his second family since, unlike the first family, they will have no independent entitlement to support from the state. They are wholly dependent on the man's support. In providing this he is relieving the state of the burden of providing for them which might exist were it not for their presence in his household. The courts have, for the most part, exhibited an unwillingness to recognise these practicalities of the social security system.

[45] See Gibson, *op. cit.* n. 41.

5. Proposals for Reform

(A) GENERAL

In many cases of family breakdown the custodial parent will, to a greater or lesser extent, be dependent on the state for the maintenance of a minimum standard of living.[46] The non-custodial parent's income will usually be insufficient to maintain his former family at subsistence level let alone above this. This will be especially so where he has responsibilities to newly acquired dependants. We may therefore agree with Eekelaar and McClean that it is "difficult to resist the conclusion that the child whose family is broken should have prima facie recourse against the community to supply the standard of living which that community owes to its children." Yet, as they point out, on the contrary "Western countries have been tenacious in retaining the ideology that a child should look first to its parents for the retaining of its living standards even after the collapse of the family unit."[47]

As a matter of practical enforcement however the existence of the so-called "Diversion Procedure"[48] testifies to the primacy of the state's role. Under this procedure the benefit of any maintenance order in favour of W. or the children is assigned to the D.H.S.S. which will recover any payments made under the order from the clerk to the Magistrates' Court in which it is registered. Meanwhile W. will receive her full entitlement to state benefits from the D.H.S.S. calculated on the basis that there is no maintenance order. The procedure recognises the importance to W. and the children of a regular income which can only be guaranteed by the state. It also acknowledges that maintenance is in effect a contribution to public funds rather than to the family.

It is perhaps appropriate to view the post-breakdown situation as giving rise to a continuation of the partnership between parents and the state in providing for children. Attention may then be focussed on the appropriate overall level of support and how this may fairly be apportioned between the custodial parent, the non-custodial parent and the state. Any newly acquired commitments or resources arising from the reconstitution of the respective

---

[46] In Eekelaar and McClean's survey 57 per cent. of the single parents observed derived no financial benefit at all from maintenance orders because of their dependency on state benefits. *Op. cit.* n. 2, p. 94.

[47] *Ibid.* p. 109.

[48] Described in the Finer Report, para. 4.207.

families of the two parents would be relevant in this exercise. While it must remain the case that the state acts as the primary provider of a *minimum* standard of living it is also true that to maintain anywhere near an *acceptable* standard of living, the resources of the state must be supplemented by the contributions of relatives. To place the entire burden on the state would be to accept that families in general should live at subsistence level. Apart from these considerations of cost, it is suggested that there are good policy reasons why the private obligation towards children should be preserved.

The traditional argument in favour of child support obligations concentrates on the parent's moral responsibility which may be thought to arise from his voluntary assumption of the costs of child-care implicit in his decision to have children. Although there is a community interest in the well-being of children, it is argued that those with children should absorb a proportionately higher element of the cost than should childless persons. But, it is felt, this argument may be presented in a more positive way. If society is serious about parenthood being a status which survives family breakdown, it is important that the major responsibilities which are an integral part of that status should be preserved. If parents are to share in the *benefits* of child-rearing it is a necessary concomitant that they should also share the *burdens*. It will be recalled that the feminist objection to the English style of joint custody is founded on this benefit/burden dichotomy and the allegation that it allows men to exert control over women and children without accepting responsibilities.

It might be objected that since maintenance payments often do not pass directly into the hands of the care-giver, but are recouped by the state, they lack impact as a discharge of responsibility towards the family. There is some force in this argument. Similar objections might be founded on the high level of default in maintenance obligations and the difficulties encountered by women in uprating and enforcing maintenance awards. One solution to the first objection would be to introduce a partial disregard of maintenance payments in calculating entitlement to state benefits. But, it is in the meantime suggested that a financial contribution (albeit indirect) constitutes a significant recognition of the existence of a parental tie. Moreover, in many cases, it may represent the sole remaining tie between the child and the absent parent. We should therefore be slow to remove this at a time when the objective is to increase rather than decrease involvement

205

between children and parents in the post-breakdown situation. Commonsense suggests that at least some caregiving parents will be more inclined to cooperate over contact arrangements, whether defined as access or time-sharing, where the non-caregiving parent is willing to contribute financially to the cost of raising the child. Equally, it suggests that some parents who are making a financial contribution will be more likely to show an interest in preserving physical contact with their children.

We now turn to consider the appropriate level of support and the apportionment of responsibility between parents and the state.

(B) THE LEVEL OF CHILD SUPPORT

Criticism of state benefits for families with children concentrates on the level of support which is widely regarded as inadequate and insufficiently related to the actual cost of raising children.[49] Proposals for reform have advocated a substantial increase in the level of public support, particularly in the case of single-parent families.

One of the principal features of the G.M.A. proposed by the Finer Committee was that it would have been pitched at a level sufficient to take single parents off state benefits even where they were not earning. Other features of the proposed benefit were that it would have been means-tested, but the taper to take account of increased earnings would have been less drastic than that applying to S.B. and the child benefit element would have been unaffected by increases in income. It was envisaged that the adult element would have been extinguished by the time income reached the average level of male earnings. The projected level of support would therefore have been somewhere between subsistence level and average family earnings. The benefit would have been non-contributory and payable to *all* one-parent families irrespective of the contingency which resulted in single parenthood. The intention was to combat the effects of the "poverty-trap"[50] and to offer single parents "a real choice between working and staying at home

---

[49] For an excellent discussion of the role of child benefit see "Mother's Lifeline," *op. cit.* n. 25.

[50] The phenomenon associated with means-tested benefits whereby a family may lose more in terms of extra taxes paid and reduced benefits than it gains from the increase in gross income which brought them about. For an informative discussion see David W. Williams, "Poverty and Unemployment Traps and Trappings" [1986] J.S.W.L. 96.

to look after the children." Primary recourse would have been to the state which would have had the right to seek a contribution from the liable relative. These proposals were rejected on account of cost.

A similar system has however been introduced in New Zealand where a "Domestic Purposes Benefit" is payable to all single parents with the care of children.[51] The rate is determined by the level of widows' benefits. This contrasts with the position in England where preferential treatment is shown to widowed mothers.[52] The contribution of a liable relative is calculated in accordance with statutory formulae.

It would be possible to pursue the analogy with widows' benefits in England and to introduce an insurance based benefit which could provide, in the event of divorce or separation, similar cover to that offered on death. Such a scheme known as CHAID was presented to the Finer Committee by the National Council for the Unmarried Mother and her Child (now the National Council for One-Parent Families).[53] One advantage of this form of provision would be the avoidance of the effects of the poverty-trap so that single parents would be under no disincentive to seek employment.

The above proposals were concerned with the special case of children in one-parent families. More generally there is widespread support for a substantial increase in the level of child benefit as the most effective mechanism for combating child poverty. The Child Poverty Action Group have, for example, argued that it should be raised to a level sufficient to subsume the allowances for children under the then S.B. (now Income Support) and National Insurance Schemes.[54] The effect would be that *all* children would receive the same amount of benefit, which could be age-related. This would apply to children whose parents were in work or out of work. It would apply equally to one and two parent families. Child benefit would then no longer be regarded as a resource for the purposes of the Income Support Scheme and

[51] See W. R. Atkin, "The New Zealand Liable Parent Scheme" (1986) 16 Fam. Law 371.

[52] The widowed mother's allowance is a contributory benefit under the National Insurance Scheme. Since it is not means-tested it is not affected by earnings or any other income which the mother may have.

[53] Discussed in the Finer Report, paras. 5.81–5.86. See also the discussion in Hoggett and Pearl, "The Family, Law and Society" 2nd Ed. (1987) pp. 122–124.

[54] "Mother's Lifeline," *op. cit.* n. 25, Part III.

this would overcome the problem that any increase in child benefit is at present of no financial benefit to families on Income Support. As a universal benefit it would not be susceptible to the adverse effects of the poverty-trap. As to financing the increase, it has been suggested that the most appropriate means of doing so would be to abolish the Married Man's Tax Allowance since the effect would be to transfer resources from families without children to families with them.

This approach does not of itself embrace any special support for single-parent families and would therefore need to be accompanied by an improvement in the level of the adult element of support in order to raise the standard of living in those cases. Since, as we have seen, child support and adult support together form a common purse, in order to achieve a genuine improvement in the standard of living for the familiy unit it is necessary to protect *both* elements against the effects of the poverty-trap. There is little point in protecting the child element against the effects of wage increases if the adult element is not also protected since, as a matter of practice, it will not matter to the family whether the global level of support is reduced by losing entitlement to child support or to adult support. It is therefore essential that any "premium" allowed for single parenthood should also be non means-tested or at least that a very generous means-test should be applied.

As we have seen, the Government has decided instead to continue with the general principle of means-tested support for families with children believing that this is a more effective mechanism for targeting support on families in need. This was the rationale for the introduction of "premiums" for the special client groups including families with children and single parents. Critics point out that any benefits to be derived from these additions will be offset by the loss of other benefits which existed under the S.B. Scheme. Thus, the family premium disguises the loss of the former S.B. allowances for "additional requirements" and "single payments" to meet exceptional needs. In each case the old regulations had prescribed certain circumstances in which extra payments were allowable to provide for the special needs of children. The loss of single payments and their replacement by a system of loans from the newly created "social fund" is widely thought to be likely to cause hardship to families who relied on single payments to purchase essential items for themselves and their children. Similarly, the lone parent premium will be offset by the abolition of the higher long-term rate of benefit which favoured single parents under the S.B. scheme.

Family Credit uses the method of calculation for income support, *i.e.* based on net rather than gross income, and is intended to be more generous than F.I.S. But, again, the increase will be offset by loss of other benefits such as free school meals, dental and optical treatment and other so-called "passport benefits." Moreover, since it counts as a resource for housing benefit purposes, many families will be likely to find that gains made in family credit will be counteracted by loss of entitlement to housing benefit.

The changes in the 1986 Act may be criticised for attaching priority to means-testing in favour of maintaining the value of child benefit in real terms.[55] The reforms do not represent a genuine increase or even a diversion of resources towards families with children.

(c) APPORTIONMENT OF FINANCIAL RESPONSIBILITY BETWEEN PARENTS

The traditional approach to the question of financial responsibility for children in the post-divorce situation is based on the stereotype of a custodial non-paying parent and a non-custodial paying parent. This idea of paying and non-paying parents may not be appropriate where there is a joint custodial arrangement which embraces significant time-sharing. Here it is more realistic to focus on the proper apportionment of financial responsibility between the two parents in whose respective households the child is spending his time.

The English approach to the fixing of the quantum of private support for children seems haphazard and productive of uncertainty and inequality. In so far as systematic calculations have been employed at all by the courts they have been confined to the assessment of *spousal* maintenance. As a flexible starting point they have for many years adopted the "one-third rule" whereby the wife is awarded one-third of the parties' joint income.[56] Child maintenance has then usually been tacked on as a subsidiary award out of what income remains. Such awards have frequently been small and wholly unrelated to the actual cost of raising children. It

[55] For a critical assessment of the 1986 Act see "Of Little Benefit", *op. cit.* n. 25.
[56] *Wachtel* v. *Wachtel* [1973] Fam. 72.

has therefore been suggested that clearer criteria for assessing the quantum of child maintenance should be formulated and that these might be based on standard fostering allowances recommended by the National Foster Care Association.[57] As to the apportionment of responsibility between the two parents cost-sharing and income-sharing formulae have been put forward as mechanisms for injecting greater certainty and uniformity into this process.[58]

Cost-sharing entails the computation of the cost of raising a child and the apportionment of this cost between the custodial and non-custodial parents. Both incomes are considered relevant and parents are required to contribute proportionately in accordance with their relative resources. Appying this formula, if the non-custodial parent's income is three times as much as the custodial parent's income, the former would contribute three-quarters and the latter one-quarter of the cost. Under some versions of this formula an allowance is made to take account of days spent with parents. This is because, during that period, the parent will incur expenses in relation to the child, *e.g.* for food and clothing. Some adjustments may also be made for extraordinary expenses such as school fees and insurance premiums. Versions of the formula have been adopted by certain courts in the United States.[59] The cost-sharing approach has been criticised in that the variables used in the formula are not capable of precise definition. Thus, the cost of raising a child cannot be considered in isolation from the economic status and standards of living of the parents, and must ultimately reflect "social judgments about what a typical family spends on a child."[60] This judgment is shared by Eekelaar and McClean who observe that it is not clear whether the appropriate standard of living should be that of the caregiver, that of the absent parent or some amalgam of the two.[61]

---

[57] See Jenny Levin, "After Divorce . . . " (1982) 1 *Childright* 15. For an alternative approach to the calculation of child maintenance see Richard Sax, Felicity Crowther and Jane Marcus, "Child Maintenance—A Fresh Look" (1987) 17 Fam. Law 275.

[58] For a general discussion of the different variations of formula which might be utilised see Andrea Giampetro, "Mathematical Approaches to Calculating Child Support Payments: Stated Objectives, Practical Results and Hidden Policies" 20 Fam.L.Q. 373 (1986).

[59] *Smith* v. *Smith*, 290 Or. 675, 626 P. 2d 342 (1981) and *Melzer* v. *Witsberger*, 299 P.A. Super 153, 480 A.2d 991, 994 (1984). These cases are discussed by Giampetro *ibid.* pp. 384–386.

[60] Giampetro, *ibid.* p. 380.

[61] *Op. cit.* n. 2, p. 117.

Under the income-sharing approach the cost of raising a child is ignored and the concentration is rather on the aggregate amount of the parents' income. This then forms a common fund which is theoretically available for child support. The total income is then divided between family members and the child support payment is equal to the non-custodial parent's income minus his share in the common fund. This approach also suffers from difficulties in defining the variables. Is parental income, for example, to be limited to taxable income, or could it include savings and property assets and should potential income be taken into account?[62] Nevertheless it provides the basis for achieving an equivalence in the standard of living between the households of the two parents. Eekelaar and McClean advocate a mathematical resource sharing approach using equivalence tables.[63] This enables equalisation of the income of households of disparate membership. For example, it is possible to make a direct comparison between the financial position of a non-custodial parent living alone with that of a custodial parent who has two or three children in her household. It also enables it to be made where the children are split up between the parents' respective households and where either or both of them has acquired a new partner with or without further children.

The use of such formulae would, under these proposals, be qualified by upper and lower limits. The upper limit to child support obligations would be set at a standard referred to as the "normative standard." This would reflect the average income for households of a similar composition and would be higher than the standard implicit in the concept of relative poverty, *i.e.* support at a level sufficient to create a sense of participation in the community.[64] This standard, it is suggested, could be discovered by ascertaining the modal or median level of earnings. Where the payer's resources do not admit of maintenance at this level, the drop in living standards would be borne equally by the two families. At the lower end of the scale the authors advocate abandonment of the equalisation formula largely to achieve equity

---

[62] Potential earning capacity is one of the factors which must be considered in divorce proceedings under the amended s.25 of the Matrimonial Causes Act 1973.

[63] *Op. cit.* n. 2 pp. 117–134. See also Eekelaar and McClean, "Maintenance for Children—More Facts behind the Figures" (1986) 136 N.L.J. 838 and Rosalind Oswald, "Maintenance for Children—Facts and Figures" (1986) 136 N.L.J. 533.

[64] *Op. cit.* pp. 121–122. On the concept of relative poverty see Peter Townsend, "Poverty in the United Kingdom" (1979) Chap. 1.

between payers.[65] It would thus be wrong to allow the formula to produce a result whereby the payer's level of income was depressed below the marginal allowance made by the D.H.S.S. Finally, they suggest that a disregard should be allowed where the effect of the maintenance payment would not be to take the recipients off state benefits.[66] This should be fixed at a level equivalent to the margin of resources above subsistence level which is allowed to the payer under the liable relative formula in order to equalise the state's contribution to broken families.

6. Conclusions

A central issue is whether mathematical approaches to child support are preferable to the system of judicial discretion which we have at the moment.[67] This question has received an affirmative response in the United States where federal laws required all states to develop guidelines for determining the amount of child support orders by October 1987.[68] Significantly, the implementing regulations specified that the term "guidelines" did not mean criteria but rather quantitative standards for setting child support or formulae.[69] The federal initiative was designed to overcome three perceived deficiencies in the case-by-case method of settling disputes over child support. These were:

(1) the inadequacy of orders when compared with the true costs of rearing children;

(2) the inconsistency of orders causing inequitable treatment of persons in similarly situated cases and

(3) the inefficient adjudication of child support amounts in the absence of uniform standards.[70]

---

[65] *Ibid.* pp. 124–125.

[66] *Ibid.* pp. 128–129.

[67] Judicial discretion is not completely unstructured since it must be exercised in accordance with the factors specified in s.25 of the M.C.A. 1973 as amended. But the courts have not as yet adopted mathematical approaches to the calculation of child maintenance.

[68] For a discussion of the federal requirements and of the different guidelines adopted by individual states see Robert G. Williams, "Guidelines for Setting Levels of Child Support Orders" 21 F.L.Q. 281. (1987). See also Sally F. Goldfarb, "Child Support Guidelines: A Model for Fair Allocation of Child Care, Medical and Educational Expenses" 21 F.L.Q. 325. (1987).

[69] *Ibid.*

[70] *Ibid.* p. 282.

Eekelaar and McClean see the standardisation of maintenance
awards as a powerful practical argument in their favour. They feel
that a clearly defined standard could provide a better basis for out-of-
court negotiations and could reduce the scope for the variations inherent in subjective judicial determinations.[71] This view is not shared
by Giampetro who takes the position that mathematical formulae,
whether of the cost-sharing or income-sharing species, can be
selected and used by judges to disguise their policy preferences as to
which party should bear what proportion of the cost of divorce.[72] She
reaches this conclusion because she says: "the variables in the mathematical formulas can be defined according to the judge's whim."

The outcome can also, in her view, be affected by the choice of one
formula over another:

> "If the judge believes that the custodial parent should have the
> opportunity to provide child care full-time and not take paid
> work, she will adopt an income-sharing formula. If alterna-
> tively she thinks women should be required to take paid work,
> she will adopt a cost-sharing formula."[73]

It may be that the answer to Giampetro's last objection would be the
adoption of standard statutory formulae. The arguments seem to
favour an income-sharing rather than cost-sharing model. But there
remains considerable scope for disagreement as to how precisely the
variables should be computed and, more fundamentally, what
should be established as the normative level of support.

As to the correct apportionment of private and public responsibility, there is a strong case for endeavouring to inject some consistency
in an effort to achieve broad equality in the liabilities of parents. At
the very least the respective approaches of the courts and the
D.H.S.S. should be aligned. A more radical solution would be to
remove the issue from the courts altogether, which is substantially
the position in New Zealand. In 1981 the Liable Parent Contribution
Scheme (L.P.C.) was established there. Under this, in cases where a
single parent is receiving the domestic purposes benefit, maintenance is replaced by a contribution assessed by the relevant state
department rather than by the courts. The assessment is in accordance with formulae laid down in legislation. The court's involvement
is then limited to adjudicating on disputed assessments.[74]

[71] *Op. cit.* p. 123.
[72] *Op. cit.* p. 388.
[73] *Ibid.*
[74] See Atkin, *op. cit.* n. 51, p. 372.

213

9. Conclusions

1. Promoting the Interests of Children—
The Limitations of the Welfare Principle

As we have seen, the dominant principle in the law affecting children is the welfare principle or best interests doctrine. In Chapter 1 it was suggested that the promotion of children's welfare is not necessarily as satisfactory as the protection of their "rights".

An examination of the operation of the welfare principle reveals that it is subject to a number of significant limitations.

First, it can only be applied realistically in the context of litigation. For example, we have seen that one interpretation of *Gillick* is that the powers of parents are constrained by a legal requirement that they be exercised so as to promote the welfare of their children.[1] But this welfare limitation is a meaningless restraint on parents' powers unless and until litigation takes place. To say that parents' actions are circumscribed by what is an inherently vague and abstract notion of welfare is on the whole unhelpful, especially since practically all parents would argue that their dealings with their children are intended to further their interests. It cannot crystallise into anything more substantial until the child's best interests are defined by a court or possibly (following *Gillick*) some other decision-maker. If, therefore, respect for children's rights dictates that there should be *automatic* restraints on parents, these will need to be specifically spelled out in legislation if they are to have general application.

Secondly, even where litigation does take place, the interests of children are accorded different weight depending on the precise legal context. Housing accommodation for the children following marital breakdown provides a good illustration. In determining which parent is to have the option of remaining in the matrimonial

---

[1] *Ante*, Chap. 3

home following divorce the decisive factor is likely to be which of them has the physical care of the children. The custody question itself is governed by the welfare principle proper whereby the interests of the children are the "first and paramount" consideration.[2] But in deciding how to exercise its adjustive powers in relation to the home the court will have regard to their welfare as the "first" but not the paramount consideration, thus implying that other factors are also relevant.[3] Further, if one spouse is seeking to evict the other from the home under the domestic violence legislation the interests of the children rank alongside a number of other specified factors, but are neither the first nor the paramount consideration.[4] It is not surprising that these nuances are not always appreciated.[5]

Whether the welfare principle applies in its undiluted form or in one of its watered down manifestations it may be criticised as an essentially indeterminate notion.[6] Mnookin has argued convincingly that the application of the best interests standard results in the value judgments of the individual decision-maker prevailing and diverts attention from the more critical question of who is the appropriate person to take the decision in question. The choice of decision-maker, in his view, assumes overriding importance given that there is no clear consensus in society on what are good child-rearing practices or what can be regarded as the good life for children.[7] In particular it begs the question whether the judiciary are best qualified to determine these matters.

But perhaps the most striking deficiency in the operation of the principle is that it cannot provide an adequate basis for establishing and protecting the interests of children as a class. Individualistic adjudications of what is best for particular children provide no answer to the complex issues of public policy which are raised by practices such as the sterilisation of mentally handicapped minors. Yet, as we have seen, disputes concerning this are

---

[2] Guardianship of Minors Act 1971, s.1.
[3] Matrimonial Causes Act 1973, s.25(1).
[4] *Richards* v. *Richards* [1984] A.C. 174. It seems however that the child's interests may be paramount where, following decree absolute, the court exercises its inherent jurisdiction to grant an injunction for the protection of children. See *Wilde* v. *Wilde* (1987) *The Times*, December 8.
[5] See, for example, *W.* v. *P.* (1987) *The Times*, October 26.
[6] See Robert H. Mnookin, "Child Custody Adjudication: Judicial Functions in the Face of Indeterminacy" (1975) 39 *Law and Contemporary Problems* 226.
[7] Robert H. Mnookin, "Thinking about Children's Rights—Beyond Kiddie Libbers and Child Savers" (1981) 16 *Stanford Lawyer* 24.

presently resolved on an individual case by case basis. Indeed, the former Lord Chancellor has denied that issues of public policy are at stake in these cases.[8] A similar approach may be observed in relation to the practice of surrogate motherhood. Here the courts have studiously avoided the difficult policy issues concerning the enforceability of private surrogacy contracts and the distribution of parental rights under them. Instead they have confined themselves to determining what they consider to be the right custodial disposition following the birth of a child pursuant to such an arrangement.[9] Moreover in *Adoption Application (Payment for Adoption)*[10] they allowed the adoption process to be used as a means of giving indirect effect to a private surrogacy arrangement, thereby avoiding the thorny issue of its validity. The day after this case was decided, in *Re P. (Minors) (Wardship: Surrogacy)*[11] a surrogate mother was allowed to retain the care of twins in the face of a demand by the commissioning parents. There is surely no better illustration of the inadequacy of individualised justice in formulating standards or principles to govern controversial practices. Clearly the state has a role in this area by enacting statutory guidelines.

Just as it is important that general principles should be established to govern sensitive issues affecting children, it is necessary that legal remedies should be available to children as a class. It may be that public law remedies will be used more frequently in future for this purpose. We saw earlier that judicial review has been successfully invoked to challenge certain decisions of local authorities relating to children in their care.[12] But if this procedure is to have any impact in vindicating the group interests of children, some relaxation in the rules of *locus standi* will be necessary in order that representative organisations may present arguments on behalf of *all* children potentially affected by the outcome of a legal dispute.[13]

2. Accommodating the Interests of Parents

In considering how the interests of parents may be accommodated and balanced within the legal system, the welfare principle

---

[8] Lord Hailsham in *Re B. (A minor)* [1987] 2 W.L.R. 1213, *ante*, Chap. 6.
[9] See *A.* v. *C.* [1985] F.L.R. 445; *cf. Re C. (A minor) (Wardship)* [1985] F.L.R. 846.
[10] [1987] Fam. 81.
[11] (1987) 2 F.L.R. 421.
[12] *Ante*, Chaps. 4 and 5.
[13] Discussed by J. Levin, "Interested Parties" [1985] October, *Legal Action*, 10.

again presents us with a dilemma. For, if the interests of children are the "paramount" or sole consideration in legal disputes, the respective claims of the opposing parents are ostensibly irrelevant. The reality, of course, is very different. The law must and does take account of competing parental interests and choices habitually have to be made between the respective claims of two divorcing parents and those of local authorities and parents or third parties with an interest in the children concerned. These preferences are manifested in the reallocation of parental powers and responsibilities.

We have seen that a major policy issue in the post-divorce context is whether it is possible to share out these powers and responsibilities in a way which allows both parents to participate in the future life of the child. The alternative is to place one parent with physical care in total control.[14] It must be conceded that, in the final analysis, the answer to this question should depend on the courts' assessments of the needs of individual children taking into account the wishes of the parents and the children themselves. Nevertheless, it is suggested that these decisions should be taken in the light of broad policy directives laid down by Parliament. The view taken here is that this policy orientation should favour joint responsibility with shared decision-making and shared physical care to the fullest extent which is practicable in individual cases.

The practical objections which might be raised to such an arrangement are not as formidable as might appear at first sight. If we draw an analogy with the public sphere, the concept of voluntary care is dependent on co-operation between local authorities (who have the physical care of the child) and absent natural parents over important issues affecting the child. We saw that this partnership ideal will be given greater impetus by the implementation of the recommendations in the Review of Child Care Law and the White Paper on the Law on Child Care and Family Services.[15] How far it is permissible to juxtapose in this way the principles of the public and private law affecting children is an interesting question. It might be argued, for instance, that if the principal criterion governing the physical removal of a child from a parent in care proceedings is to be the risk of harm to the child, a similar principle should govern the redistribution of parental powers and responsibilities following divorce. This might support a legal presumption in favour of continued physical care and decision-

[14] *Ante*, Chap. 2.
[15] *Ante*, Chap. 4.

making by *both* parents except where it could be demonstrated that this would entail a risk of positive harm to the child.

This juxtaposition was recently presented to the House of Lords in *Re K.D. (A minor) (Ward: Termination of Access)*[16] in the context of a mother's access to her child who was in the care of a local authority. She argued that she had a legal right to access which was supported in English statutes and other authorities. She alleged that it was also recognised by the European Court of Human Rights in *R. v. United Kingdom*[17] as a fundamental element of family life protected by the European Convention on Human Rights. Accordingly she argued that her legal right to access, although it could be overborne by considerations of the welfare of the child, must prevail and be given effect to where there was no positive evidence that access would be damaging to the child. She invited the House to reconsider its approach in *J. v. C.*[18]

Her argument failed, but an interesting feature of this case was the attempt to import the private law principles on access into the sphere of public law where the contest was not between two parents but between one parent and the state. The House of Lords apparently raised no objection to this and based their decision on the ground that there was no conflict between the approach in *J. v. C.* and the European Court's decision. According to Lord Oliver, both expressed the single common concept that the natural bond and relationship between parent and child gave rise to universally recognised norms which ought not to be gratuitously interfered with and, if interfered with at all, only where the welfare of the child dictated it.

Turning to the relationship between the respective interests of children and adults the primary difficulty is how to determine when they coincide and when they are in conflict. The most important contribution which the *Gillick* decision has made is its rejection of the theory that the interests of children and parents *necessarily* coincide. Considerable progress has been made in certain areas of the law in recognising conflicts of interest and safeguarding the independent claims of children. Thus, in care proceedings the court may make a separation order prohibiting parents from representing the child.[19] We have also seen that in

[16] [1988] 1 All E.R. 577.
[17] 6/1986/104/52. (1987) *The Times*, July 9, 1987.
[18] [1970] A.C. 668.
[19] Children and Young Persons Act 1969, s.32A.

the medical context parental wishes may be overridden to safeguard the health of their child.[20] In the educational sphere however there is still a strong tendency to equate the interests of children and parents.[21]

It should not be thought however that their respective interests necessarily conflict any more than that they necessarily coincide. In some instances there appears to be an inclination to manufacture a separation of interests which are in fact coincidental. The interests of unmarried fathers are, for example, assumed to be sufficiently distinct from those of their children that the denial of automatic parental rights may be presented as a matter affecting only the fathers. It has been argued that this is an inaccurate representation of the function of parental rights which is to define in law the *mutual* relationship between parents and children.[22] The interests of fathers and children are intimately connected, not least because the creation of automatic paternal rights would enable a true abolition of the legal concept of illegitimacy. Similarly, it is arguable that it is wrong to regard the maintenance claims of parents and children as separate since in reality they are interdependent.[23] The important point is that the *potential* for conflict between parent and child should be recognised without assuming its existence. It is equally important that specific recognition should be given to independent parental claims. Fundamentally, it is not necessary to go so far as to deny the existence of parental rights in order to foster the rights of children. A more realistic position is to accept that *both* have rights which may or may not come into conflict.

3. Defining the State's Interest

It has been seen that the state's interest in children is principally a protective or paternalistic one and that local authorities and the courts may be seen as two agencies of the state performing complementary roles.[24] But the state's interest is also reflected in the large body of legislation affecting children and young people. It is through this that policies affecting children at large may be

[20] *Ante*, Chap. 6.
[21] *Ante*, Chap. 7.
[22] *Ante*, Chap. 2.
[23] *Ante*, Chap. 8.
[24] *Ante*, Chaps. 4 and 5.

established. It is also through legislation that the jurisdiction of the courts is defined. One of the criticisms of wardship in particular is that it is largely unrestricted by statutory limitations. While this allows considerable flexibility it can lead to inequality of treatment in important areas affecting the welfare of children. It is therefore suggested that it is the state's role, through legislation, to set limits to the powers of the courts over children and to establish guidelines for the resolution of disputes. The proposals of the Law Commission for a statutory "check list" of factors in custody cases would be a welcome innovation in the process of structuring judicial discretion.[25] The adoption of mathematical formulae in maintenance disputes would also be a desirable reform.

Establishing legislative standards is important where activities may be considered to touch on the fundamental human rights of children and young people. There are some areas in which the right course is to universalise treatment of children. This principle of universality is widely accepted in relation to compulsory education and restrictions on child labour. Issues such as sterilisation and surrogacy also affect basic human rights and are appropriate for statutory control. One option would be to prohibit them completely, thereby producing theoretical equality of treatment for children at a stroke. If it is thought desirable that they be allowed, they should be properly regulated by statute and not left to the personal predilections of the judges.

Conversely, it is equally important that legislation should itself be subject to judicial review. We have seen that the actions of local authorities may be questioned by this means. But more significantly legislation affecting children needs to be tested to ensure its conformity with their basic human rights. In England this is difficult because of the absence of a written constitution and Bill of Rights. The position here may be contrasted with that in the United States, where the courts have power to review the constitutionality of legislation. The starting point there is that children have the status of persons under the constitution and consequently enjoy the protection of the Bill of Rights.[26] So obviously do parents. Both therefore have fundamental rights which may coincide or conflict as we noted in relation to medical issues.[27]

[25] Law Com. No. 96, para. 6.38.
[26] In *Re Gault* 387 U.S. 1, 13 (1967) Forbes J. said that "neither the Fourteenth Amendment nor the Bill of Rights is for adults alone."
[27] *Ante*, Chap. 6.

Federal and state authorities in the United States are obliged to ensure that legislation passed by them does not infringe these constitutional fundamentals. The basic effect of recognising that children are persons under the constitution is that the liberties enjoyed by adults are in principle equally applicable to them. Significantly, these basic rights (as interpreted) include personal decision-making. The result, it is submitted, is to create a presumption in favour of allowing children the right of self-determination. Statutory restrictions on this must be legally justifiable as furthering a "significant state interest." In this way it may be thought that American law is more receptive (at least in theory) to the objective of striking a balance between autonomy and protectionism. Importantly, judicial control of legislation also enables an evaluation of the laws affecting *all* children. This ensures a measure of egalitarianism which should be an important element in the furtherance of children's rights. Thus, it has been said that "a necessary feature of children's rights is that they be genuinely universal, appropriate for children everywhere."[28] The constitutional litigation in the United States has involved the courts in a close consideration of the fundamental interests of children, parents and the state. These issues are not confronted as directly in England since they are obscured by excessive concentration on the process of ascertaining the best interests of individual children.

For these reasons a Bill of Rights would be calculated to assist the children's rights movement in England and sharpen awareness of the various interests at stake in disputes concerning children. The general arguments in favour of a Bill of Rights have been rehearsed elsewhere.[29] Present indications are that it is unlikely that such a development will occur in the foreseeable future. The best hope would seem to be incorporation of the European Convention on Human Rights into English domestic law. As matters stand, a ruling by the European Court requires implementation in domestic legislation and states are left with considerable discretion as to how this is to be achieved. Nevertheless such a ruling may be instrumental in hastening changes in the law. It is to be hoped that the ruling of the court in *R. v. United Kingdom*[30]

[28] V. Worsfold, "A Philosophical Justification for Children's Rights" *Harvard Educational Review*, 44 (1974) 142, 149.
[29] See particularly M. Zander, "A Bill of Rights?" 3rd Ed. (1985). For a discussion of the value of the European Convention for children's rights see "European Convention on Human Rights" (1987) 39 *Childright* 11.
[30] n. 17.

221

will serve to expedite the reforms to the child care legislation. In this case the Court held that procedures and remedies relating to the restriction or termination of access to children in care were in violation of the Convention. The Convention is utilised by individuals by way of application to the European Commission and, if the complaint is declared admissible by it, thereafter to the Court. Most applications have alleged infringement of *parents'* rather than children's rights under the Convention. It is to be hoped that the coming years will see the Convention used more frequently to assert the independent rights of children.

Index

231

236